From Azaleas to Zydeco

From Azaleas to Zydeco

My 4,600-Mile Journey through the South

Mark W. Nichols

BUTLER
CENTER
BOOKS

The Butler Center for Arkansas Studies
Central Arkansas Library System
100 Rock Street
Little Rock, Arkansas 72201
www.butlercenter.org

Second edition: January 2014

ISBN 978-1-935106-65-4
e-ISBN 978-1-935106-66-1

Project manager: Rod Lorenzen
Copyeditor: Ali Welky
Editors: Sally and Huey Crisp
Book and cover design: H. K. Stewart

      Library of Congress Cataloging-in-Publication Data
Nichols, Mark W.
 From azaleas to zydeco : my 4,600-mile journey through the South / Mark W.
Nichols. -- First Edition.
      pages cm
 Includes bibliographical references and index.
 ISBN 978-1-935106-65-4 (pbk. : alk. paper)
 1. Nichols, Mark W.--Travel--Southern States. 2. Southern States--
Description and travel. 3. Southern States--Social life and customs. 4.
Popular culture--Southern States. I. Title.

 F209.N54 2013
 917.504--dc23

                              2013032180

Printed in the United States of America
This book is printed on archival-quality paper that meets requirements of the
American National Standard for Information Sciences, Permanence of Paper,
Printed Library Materials, ANSI Z39.48-1984.

The publishing division of the Butler Center for Arkansas Studies
was made possible by the generosity of Dora Johnson Ragsdale and
John G. Ragsdale Jr.

To all of those
Nicholses, Carters, Lemons, Murphys,
Harkinses, Hollands, and Ellerds
who preceded me

Table of Contents

Acknowledgments

I have refrained from following the advice of Clay Travis about acknowledgments in his hilarious book about SEC football, *Dixieland Delight: A Football Season on the Road in the Southeastern Conference*. He says to mention as many people as you can because it will aid in book sales. But I'm keeping my acknowledgments brief.

First, my wife, Cheri. As one female cousin said to me after I explained to her that I was traveling the South one week at a time: "Your wife sure is nice. I'd never let my husband go gallivanting around the South like that." I agreed, but I'm not sure that Cheri knows how much I appreciate the inconveniences she endured in letting me do what I wanted to do. Maybe this is a good way to tell her.

Next, my son, Will. I didn't realize that with a little bit of planning, Knoxville could be such a crossroads of the South. It was fun to pass through and see him happy in the place where my father went to college.

I must thank my sisters, Gail and Anita, and their husbands, Ron and Buddy, for their gracious hospitality in Georgia and Florida throughout my travels. I think the only gift I ever brought them on my many visits was some hand-rolled cigars from the Columbia Restaurant in Tampa (which, now that I think about it, neither sister probably appreciated).

As I traveled, I visited my cousin Linda Hasty, niece Allison Barger, and second cousin Nanette Fields on their home turfs as I passed through. Even though he's technically not family, my friend Daniel Carey got me a good rate at a good hotel in Savannah and, in less than two drinks at a local water hole, told me more things about Savannah than I could ever use. Likewise, ex-Arkie John Pagan's help in navigating Richmond was invaluable. In the same vein, I'd like to acknowledge Blake Eddins, Bob Denman, Brian Nolen, Dabbs Cavin, and my cousin Alan Holman. Their help made my understanding of Montgomery, NASCAR, South Carolina, and the Civil War much better. Early in the process, my friends Ted Parkhurst, Rex Nelson, and Jay Edwards gave me invaluable assistance, and my old college friends Scott McKibbin and Roger Shinness provided great insights and feedback, especially in the early part of my travels. And I can't forget Laura Hudgins, the former proprietress of the New Harmony Coffee House. Because of her hospitality, I stumbled across Mr. Daniels' book.

I'd also like to thank Bobby Roberts of the Central Arkansas Library System for recommending that I meet Rod Lorenzen. It was Rod's recommendations that really got this thing done. He first suggested that I take the manuscript to Sally and Huey Crisp to see if they would edit it. Sally is the director of the Little Rock Writing Project and a faculty member in the Department of Rhetoric and Writing at the University of Arkansas at Little Rock. Huey recently retired as director of composition and instructor in rhetoric and writing at UALR. Not only are they great at what they do, they are fun to work with. Besides being marvelous editors, Sally and Huey found Sarah Fleming, who created the map of the Journey.

Rod also recommended H. K. Stewart, and through his wonderful work, pictures got integrated into a manuscript, a cover took shape, and an actual book got printed. Rod also got Ali Welky to undertake the thankless job of copyeditor. I can't thank him and her enough. As we begin the modern process of marketing and I transition to a new role of itinerant bookseller, I'm relying on my young friend Sandra McGrew to guide me through these newfangled social media.

Finally I'd like to acknowledge my mother, Carol Harkins Nichols. She was very interested in talking about my Journey through the Southland, but I think she was a little uncertain about why I was doing what I was doing. Once, she smiled and said, "At least you'll be more interesting to talk with at cocktail parties." We had a lot of laughs and a few arguments about the South. She died in September 2011 and never got to see the final product. I hope she'd be pleased.

Introduction

A few years ago, I visited a coffee shop in a small midwestern town. The shop's owner leased space to a local entrepreneur who sold used books. The books sat on crude wooden shelves in no particular order. On one shelf I saw an old frayed volume, its tan cover bordered in faded green. The spine bore a title that intrigued me, *A Southerner Discovers the South*. The author, Jonathan Daniels, was unknown to me. Later I learned that Mr. Daniels was publisher of the *Raleigh News and Observer* but had left his North Carolina home in the spring of 1937 to tour the South and record his experiences and observations of the region during the Great Depression.

Browsing the book, I discovered across from page 12 a not-to-scale map captioned "Route of the Journey." I found the map intriguing. It showed the path of his tour with some seventy-five places noted on it. I calculated that Mr. Daniels traveled 4,600 miles over the course of his Journey, quite a distance on Depression-era southern roads. The route included the South's largest cities—Atlanta, Chattanooga, Memphis, New Orleans, Birmingham, and Charleston—along with nine southern state capitals. It also passed through little-known towns such as Scottsboro, Marked Tree, Union Church, Opelousas, and Thomasville. The map revealed obscure southern places like Caesar's Head, Copperhill, Friars Point, and Lumpkin.

To be truthful, I was ambivalent about buying the book. At $22.50, it seemed a bit pricey for a used book (which originally retailed in 1937 for $3.00). But the map kept calling me, especially the dot that denoted the town of Florence in northwest Alabama. My mom had lived in Florence during her high school and college years when her father worked for the Tennessee Valley Authority, bringing electrical power to the South. I figured that even if the book didn't prove especially interesting, Mom would enjoy it because of the reference to Florence.

Long story short, I bought the book and read it. The writing style was dated, and Mr. Daniels referenced people, places, and events I'd never heard of. But the book was intriguing. He wrote of conversations with hitchhikers and governors. He saw the country's first ecological disaster in the Tennessee hills. He visited the places where labor unions had been broken and where the South's most infamous trial took place. And that was just his first week of traveling.

When I had finished the book, I found I was still wondering about those places on the map. For example, Mr. Daniels toured the country's largest cotton plantation at Scott, Mississippi. Five thousand sharecroppers lived and worked the land there during the thirties. I wondered, since cotton production has become so mechanized, what had become of Scott, Mississippi. Ducktown and Copperhill, Tennessee, the site of a Tennessee copper-smelting industry—what's there now? And St. Martinsville, Louisiana, the heart of Cajun country, where most of the residents didn't speak English: What's St. Martinsville like today?

I'd never heard of the Cone brothers of Greensboro, North Carolina, their pine trees, or their mill village called Proximity. Greensboro, a major metropolitan area, is famous as the site of America's first sit-in during the civil rights movement. I wanted to see Greensboro and check out the Cone pines. Though the mill at Proximity is long gone, modern-day entrepreneurs have taken the name and developed this country's first LEED-certified platinum hotel in Greensboro. (More on the Proximity Hotel later.) Soon I decided to recreate Daniels' entire Journey. I'd visit all the dots on his map. And so I did. By the time I finished my Journey, I had visited all 75 places listed on the map and added a few dots of my own. Now the map has 82 dots, each one representing a note in the song of the modern South.

During the seventy-five years since Mr. Daniels toured it, the South has changed mightily. No longer is it America's backward, third-world region. Much of the change has been economic. Two generations ago, the textile industry began abandoning the southeast in search of lower-wage workers in third-world countries. Today, southern textile mills are being destroyed or adaptively reused throughout Virginia, the Carolinas, and Georgia, oftentimes being turned into upscale housing for the progeny of "lint heads." Automobile manufacturers, both foreign and domestic, are locating new plants in the right-to-work states of the old Confederacy. The southern coastline is no longer barren wasteland; it is now overrun with retirees and vacationers.

But the changes are not all economic. Since Mr. Daniels came through here, the movement to grant full civil rights to African Americans began. While it may not be finished quite yet, the early days of the movement are now the stuff of heritage tourism. Dismantling *de jure* segregation has allowed all southerners a shot at a middle-class existence, and the rise of the middle class has changed the South profoundly. There's been a lot of change since Mr. Daniels drove through here, but the southern states still make up a most distinctive region.

I didn't want to be a tourist. I wanted to feel more like an out-of-town friend or relative coming to visit. I decided to break up the Journey into week-long segments and see what there was to see. Before every trip, I researched to find someone interesting to interview or something interesting to see. Friends and family provided valuable contacts in these places. One of my sisters knew people in Nashville's entertainment business and, more importantly, told me about Birmingham-made Milo's Famous Sweet Tea. A brother-in-law gave me some great out-of-the-way places in Florida and on the Gulf Coast. Sometimes I just went to the place and hung out, seeing what there was to see. I often handed people a copy of Mr. Daniels' map. Seeing the map provided most people an answer to the question, "What brings you here?"

After each foray, I returned to Little Rock to write an initial draft of the week's experience. Once I had the draft down, I would begin researching the next set of dots on Mr. Daniels' map. It took him less than forty days in 1937 for his Journey, but mine took the better part of two years.

My Journey became a family affair. I took the opportunity during my travels to become reacquainted with my extended family. I imposed on siblings, cousins, nieces, and in-laws in eight of the ten southern states. Most of these family members seemed normal, and all were gracious. Only Louisiana and Mississippi contained no family relations close enough for me to impose upon.

With so much time on the road, music became a big part of the Journey. I found it was better to play the music I'd learned about in the previous segment of the Journey. So I listened to the honky soul of Alabama Shoals while traveling through Mississippi and the Louisiana Cajun country. When I got back to Alabama, I played Delta blues, zydeco, swamp rock, and the Cajun music I'd heard a few months before. I listened to Hank Williams at his Montgomery, Alabama, cemetery plot. In Georgia, I prepared to check out southern hip-hop; sadly, I never found a tour guide. So I sampled Goodie Mob, Big Boi, Ludacris, and Lil Wayne, among others, while exploring Florida and the low country. I haven't even mentioned listening to Nashville's best: a great CD chronicling "Linthead stomp" or the Drive-By Truckers. I can't believe the Drive-By Truckers aren't huge. They've written such great songs about the South. Music is beyond the scope of the book, but check out "Songs from the Journey" at the end of the book for a playlist of the best songs from my travels. It's a true sampling of great southern music.

I discovered a lot of food. As a child, I was such a picky eater that I often just ate bread. So I'm no foodie, but I'll tell you, the food was good. Most of the meals I had were just delightful, from a truly amazing society luncheon in Natchez to the cornbread served as an appetizer at the Olde Pink House in Savannah. I mentioned to my mother that the cornbread in Savannah was so good I asked the waiter for their secret. When I told her his answer—"The kitchen adds lots of sugar"—she replied authoritatively and categorically, "Only Yankees put sugar in cornbread." Thus began the great cornbread controversy. I tried to tie down the story of Yankees, sugar, and cornbread during the Journey, but the whole thing became so complicated that any further discussion of it is also beyond the scope of this book.

I sampled as much local food as I could, from Delta tamales, Cajun boudin, fried okra (no boiled okra!), to barbecue with its many variations. Some of the food was not so common, like the delicious dandelion salad created by Chef Jay of Lucky 32 Southern Kitchen in Greensboro, North Carolina, and the shrimp at Soileau's Dinner Club in Opelousas, Louisiana. I sampled Cheerwine soda in North Carolina, Blenheim's ginger ale in South Carolina, and white lightning (clear corn whiskey) in Virginia. I consumed far too many Moon Pies, Goo Goo Clusters, and boiled peanuts as I headed from town to town. I made a point of eating crawfish, shrimp, and Karo pecan pie whenever available. I don't think I ate *any* franchised fast food.

And the people: It's easy to say that getting to meet so many interesting and wonderful people was the best part of the Journey—because it's so true. Except for one or two notable exceptions, the people on the Journey were kind, friendly, and helpful. I know there are friendly people everywhere, but southern friendliness is different. I believe part of it is the natural kindness found throughout rural America, and, remember, most of the South is still rural. The other part is that southerners still teach youngsters to look others, even strangers, in the eye and acknowledge their existence. So I often wandered around and looked people in the eye, and after they'd seen the map of the Journey, another adventure would begin. I encountered one very rude "cracker" in the hills of Tennessee. He stands conspicuous in my memory in stark contrast to the many interesting and wonderful people I met.

I met bee keepers, cheese makers, crawfish "bawlers," duck callers, and one licensed alligator hunter. I met a few politicians: two governors, one current and one former, a state attorney general, and a bunch of mayors. I chatted with a fashion mogul, struggling musicians, and even one MacArthur Foundation genius grant winner. Southerners like sports, and I'm no exception. I attended a polo match, a lacrosse game, a college baseball game, a minor league baseball game, and an SEC football game (but, sadly, no ACC basketball game).

I crossed the majestic Mississippi River six times by bridge and once by ferryboat. Since I was heading farther south at each crossing, the mighty river grew wider and wider. Besides the Mississippi, I saw other rivers up close—the workhorse Catawba River in the Carolinas, the rock-strewn Ocoee River near the Georgia-Tennessee state line, the sultry Bayou Teche of Cajun country, and the Cooper (pronounced "Coupa") and Ashley Rivers at Charleston, South Carolina.

Three final notes on my Journey: First, I didn't have any rules, meaning I didn't do things the same way very often. As a result, I took pictures of some people but not others. So don't read anything into the lack of a picture. I also had no rules for including or excluding a topic. (Well, I did have one rule: my Journey would not include a visit to a Mississippi brothel as Mr. Daniels' Journey had!) Second, though it might have made sense to recreate the Journey in Daniels' sequence, I didn't. I skipped around. So you'll see that the seasons are out of order. It may be winter in the mountains of western North Carolina, but early autumn in the Tennessee hills a few miles up the road. Finally, though I traveled from 2008 to 2010, I call my effort a late twentieth-century review of the South. I say this because I used the Internet, but no smart phone, Twitter, or Facebook. The only twenty-first-century encroachment was the occasional reliance on a GPS device that my son bought me after I got lost trying to get around Mobile, Alabama.

Now that the Journey is done, I hope what follows does some justice to the wonderful people and places I've seen. The map of all my stops is on the next page.

The Third Battle of Manassas

Jonathan Daniels began his 4,600-mile Journey crossing the Potomac River from the District of Columbia into Virginia on what was then a new bridge. He stopped to talk with a retiree fishing off the bridge before going on to the Custis-Lee House at Arlington National Cemetery. He writes:

> You turn into the long Memorial Bridge. Look up, then, and see it on the hill. Arlington by any seeing must be the façade of the South. Grandly and sweetly and green the hill runs up to the great house from the river.

The ornate, early twentieth-century bridge still carries traffic across the Potomac River into Virginia. The bridge was designed as a symbolic reunification of the North and the South after the War for Southern Independence by connecting the Lincoln Memorial with Robert E. Lee's house. Congress delayed funding the bridge for a couple of decades until President Harding got caught in a three-hour traffic jam on the way to dedicate the Tomb of the Unknown Soldier. After that incident, Congress moved quickly to get the construction started, and the new bridge opened in 1932.

I wanted to recreate the Journey's beginning in a similar fashion—a leisurely drive over the Potomac River on the wide bridge into Virginia. I planned to drive past the Lincoln Memorial, locate a parking place somewhere near the bridge, and walk onto the Memorial Bridge. Once on the bridge I would ask a pedestrian to take my picture with the Custis-Lee House and northern Virginia in the background. I figured it would take about an hour and I could be on my way to Manassas.

Bad idea. The Washington metropolitan area has 5.5 million people now with northern Virginia, "NoVa," being its most populated part. And that doesn't count tourists. Forget about finding a parking place near the bridge; the tourists have them all. Traffic signs announced road construction projects and the resulting detours. Under the best of circumstances, Washington traffic for a southern boy from a small city was intimidating. With construction detours, lane closures, and lost tourists, it was a mess. Cars to the left of me, detour signs to right.

Once on the bridge, the traffic wasn't too bad. Unfortunately, though, there is no sweet or green view of the great house, only of high-rise office buildings. I thought, *This is not really the South; this is Anywhere, America.* I was 500 miles due east of Cincinnati and 1,000 miles east of Kansas City. Two great cities—but no one would ever accuse them of being southern. I decided to head toward Manassas, leaving the ghost of Warren Harding and his three-hour traffic jam in my rearview mirror.

Staying just ahead of the commuting hordes through thirty miles of urban and suburban landscape, I turned off Interstate 66 at Exit 47. The entrance to the Manassas National Battlefield lies less than a mile from this exit. The battlefield is an undeveloped oasis in the middle of the Washington metropolitan area, a metropolitan area which extends miles west all the way to West Virginia.

Manassas is perhaps the most famous battlefield in the South. Two separate and important battles were fought here. Remember, Yankees named Civil War battlefields after nearby rivers, creeks, or other natural reference points. Rebels named the same conflict after man-made reference points like the nearest town or significant building. They called the first pitched battle of the conflict First Manassas, after the nearby town. Unionists called that same battle Bull Run, for nearby Bull Run Creek. A year later, the Second Battle of Bull Run, or Second Manassas, as it's called in the South, occurred here.

Both battles were significant conflicts. First Manassas was a resounding Confederate victory in which the Union army left the battlefield in complete disorder. The retreating army had to dodge civilians from Washington DC who'd come to picnic and watch what had been advertised as an easy Union victory over the outgunned Rebels. First Manassas let the Yankees know that forced Unionification would be no easy task. Second Manassas, also a Confederate victory, was a much bigger battle in which 10,000 Union troops were killed or wounded. From the Confederate perspective, Second Manassas could be considered the high-water mark of the war since General Lee took his troops from this field into Union territory and fought the battle of Antietam Creek (or the battle of Sharpsburg as it's known in the South), the bloodiest day in the war. But for the Rebels, the war was all downhill from there.

After the war, Manassas reverted to its quiet rural setting again. It remained that way until the late twentieth century. As metropolitan Washington encroached, Manassas once again became a battleground. This time the battle was between competing land uses.

Today, 5,000 acres of grassy battlefield contrasts sharply with the concreted, developed, and overbuilt suburbia that surrounds it. These contrasting land uses have created a third battle of Manassas which has been fought and refought during the past generation.

Shoppers came first. In 1988, developers proposed building a shopping mall right next to the battlefield. Locals formed a group they called Save the Battlefield to oppose the development. Litigation ensued. The dispute was resolved when the federal government took the mall land as a buffer for the park. The local papers called the mall battle "the third battle of Manassas."

A few years later, in 1993, the Disney Company proposed to build Disney America on 3,000 acres of land about four miles away from the battlefield. Disney's plan envisioned more than 2,200 housing units, almost two million square feet of commercial space, 1,300 hotel rooms, two golf courses, a 280-acre campground, and a thirty-seven-acre water park. With more than 30,000 people visiting DC every day, Disney saw an opportunity to enhance the capital-visiting experience. In the District of Columbia, tourists could visit actual historic sites: the White House, Capitol Building, and the memorials to Washington, Jefferson, and Lincoln. In suburban Virginia, Disney proposed a Lewis and Clark whitewater raft ride and a roller coaster through the Industrial Revolution to give the tourists history-flavored entertainment. Soon after Disney announced its plans, Virginia governor George Allen announced, "Virginia is open for business," adding that state subsidy of the park would be a "darn good deal" for Virginia.

Governor Allen's sentiments were not shared by all. The Piedmont Environmental Council, with members named du Pont, Mellon, Harriman, and Duke, came out against the project and started a media campaign showing Mickey Mouse with his hand out, asking the question, "Brother, can you spare $158 million?"—the amount Disney had requested in public aid for bringing jobs and an increased tax base to the area.

The National Trust for Historic Preservation joined the fight with an open letter in the *Washington Post* to Disney chief Michael Eisner, asking Disney to reconsider the location of the park. In the face of well-funded opposition promising lawsuits and environmental reviews, Disney abandoned the project. It claimed that the increased costs, negative publicity, and the burden on management's time and attention caused this reconsideration. This time the *national* press called the battle over Disney America "Third Manassas." (Others may have referred to it as the Third Battle of Bull Run, but they would have been Yankees.)

Even without the Mouse, more people came to the area. Ultimately the Disney America land was developed, mainly into housing tracts. The new housing simply increased the pressure on local infrastructure, particularly the roads.

Around Manassas Battlefield, traffic is terrible, as the NoVa refrain goes. Battlefield Park is intersected into quadrants by the Lee Highway and Virginia Highway 247, four- or five-lane highways which carry 30,000 vehicles every business day. These two highways are reduced to two-lane roads through the park. During rush hour, gridlock starts early. It makes crossing the Memorial Bridge from DC look like child's play.

To widen the roads, add turn lanes, and create bigger shoulders within the park would require taking additional park land. Recently, a Battlefield Bypass Study reviewed the feasibility of relocating Lee Highway and Route 234 from the park and creating a route around it. The bypass proposal anticipates closing the roads through the park, which would be good for parts of the park. But new, bigger roads would be built near other parts of the park, creating development pressure there. Another controversy, another battle over Manassas—or if you prefer, Bull Run.

Polo Place

It's hard to know precisely when you leave NoVa. Uncut grass lots and buildings needing a paint job dot the sides of the highway. Hand-painted signs nailed to trees advertise local tradesmen. There's still a lot of traffic, but no longer urban. Things are beginning to look southern.

South from Manassas, the roads have great names: the James Madison Highway, Zachary Taylor Highway, Old Plank Road. Localities now develop brand highways for marketing purposes. Virginia Highway 20 has been renamed Constitution Highway. I assumed the highway leads to mansions owned by the major figures in our Constitution's creation: Montpelier, James Madison's home; Monticello, Thomas Jefferson's home; and just past Monticello, James Monroe's home, Ash Lawn. It doesn't, and I never discovered why they named it Constitution Highway.

I left Constitution Highway at Orange, Virginia, and the surroundings soon changed once again. No deteriorating buildings or hand-painted signs. The land was neatly mowed and well-fenced. From the road, a traveler sees rolling hills and big, well-kept houses perched on ridges overlooking lush green valleys. All these houses have spectacular views of this pretty country. Obviously, these people are doing well. I'm headed to what has been called the best place in America to live— Charlottesville, Virginia.

I'll confess now that I was concerned I wouldn't like Charlottesville. Members of my family sing its praises, but when pressed they can't provide many details that distinguish Charlottesville from a number of other fine southern towns. Charlottesville has all the *indicia* of one of those southern places you should mistrust. It's a pretty place that wins a lot of awards. But it can't be as nice as people contend. It may be home to a fine state university and a World Heritage Site, one of only a handful in the eastern half of the United States. But those attractions were developed by the third president of the United States, Thomas Jefferson. Outside of Thomas Jefferson's contributions—locals still refer to him as "Mr. Jefferson"—what has Charlottesville ever done?

Also, the biggest band from Charlottesville is the Dave Matthews Band. I have lots of friends who really like the Dave Matthews Band. But I've never gotten them. I mean they're fine musicians, probably nice people, but their music doesn't set my toe to tapping. They may be the biggest band to come from the area, but I'm afraid they represent the vibe in Charlottesville, and I'll be out of step with it.

Charlottesville is a university town, home to the University of Virginia. One of the things you quickly learn about Charlottesville is that they are proud of their university. In fact, students must take a one-hour history course called "Mr. Jefferson's University."

A college town is a good thing pretty much anywhere. The optimism of 14,000 young people with backpacks and new ideas, waiting for the weekend to begin on Wednesday or Thursday, is infectious. But the same thing occurs on campuses all over America. So can Charlottesville really be one of the best places in America?

Don't get me wrong. It's a nice place—a university town big enough that kids can live off campus, but small enough that they still can walk to class. Excuse me: Don't call it "campus." In Charlottesville they have a different vocabulary. The campus is called "the Grounds." UVA doesn't have a quad; it has "The Lawn." My niece wasn't a senior there; she was a "fourth year." At the end of that year, she took part in "final exercises"—not graduation ceremonies. I met her at a great restaurant, the Virginian, located at "the Corner," a commercial area next to campus which at other places is usually called "the Strip."

With one exception, these terms strike me as a tad pretentious. That exception is The Lawn, the beautiful Thomas Jefferson–designed quadrangle. At one end of The Lawn is the Rotunda. Inspired by the Parthenon, the Rotunda originally housed the library. The Rotunda faces Old Cabell Hall on the other end with ten buildings, or pavilions, in between. Behind these pavilions are beautiful gardens. While the Corner is really just like any other college strip, The Lawn is wonderful, and calling it a quad doesn't give proper credit to our third president who designed it. The Lawn is part of the Jefferson World Heritage Site, one of only twenty such sites in the country.

One of Charlottesville's charms is its small-town atmosphere. A few decades ago, the city gave up the right to annex the surrounding Albemarle County land in order to induce the County to enter into a revenue-sharing agreement. As a result of the agreement, Charlottesville cannot expand its geographic boundaries. Its density has increased: Charlottesville is now a town of about 45,000 residents. Still, most of the area's growth has been out in the county, which now has more than twice as many residents as Charlottesville.

Besides outgrowing Charlottesville, Albemarle County has become gentrified. Driving around, I saw no working farms and no tractors, combines, or overloaded pickup trucks slowing traffic on these farm roads. A lot of high-end SUVs and sports cars zip down these twisting roadways—through well-manicured and beautifully fenced rolling farm land. No money crops like cotton or soybeans grow around here; this land produces primarily alfalfa or other hay crops. And grapes: The area boasts a local wine trail with twenty-four stops.

I visited one of these wineries, but I wasn't there for the wine. I was there to see the ponies—polo ponies. All summer long, the King Family Vineyards hosts the local Roseland Polo team against other area polo teams. My part of the South doesn't have polo, and so I thought this would be a great time to take in a new sport.

A few hundred people had backed their vehicles up to the side of the polo field, spread out blankets or pop-up tents between the car and the field, and popped open wine bottles in anticipation of the impending action. Not surprisingly, the crowd appeared to be affluent white people. The only real exception was the group next to my car composed mostly of engineering students and their dates.

Luckily, our hosts, the King family, are familiar with polo-ignorant people. Before the game, they sent a nice young man in a golf cart down the side lines selling bottles of wine and handing out papers summarizing the rules of engagement. He also sold t-shirts and baseball caps in various pastel colors.

The polo crowd looked surprisingly like tailgaters at a high school or junior high school football game, except that there was almost no interaction between the spectator groups. During football tailgates, the crowd arrives in small groups, but soon there's a lot of interaction among tailgating groups, and it becomes a larger social event. Not so with these polo fans. Each polo group operated like a self-contained unit spread out on blankets. Evidently they had come to support one player or horse or to drink wine in a spectacular setting. Kibitzing with others didn't seem to be part of the deal. There wasn't much interaction between the crowd and the players either. The polo players and their horses stayed at one end of the field, fully preoccupied with getting ready. The spectators sat quietly on the sidelines talking only within their own small group.

I knew polo was a war game invented in the Middle East and Asia to prepare both horses and riders for battle—the extent of my knowledge. I learned that polo is a game played by two teams of four horsemen in an area the size of three football fields. It's a lot like hockey on horseback, with the object of the game being to strike a ball with a mallet through a goal. Actually the mallet doesn't have to cause the ball to go into the goal; it counts even if the horse knocks it through.

There are two halves of twenty-one minutes of play. The halves are divided into three separate seven-minute periods called "chukkers." Long breaks between chukkers are necessary to allow the ponies to be rested and switched out.

The "ponies," as they are called, are full-size horses bred for sprinting, endurance, and agility. Polo ponies have to become acclimated to having a mallet swung past their head and to getting hit by the ball. One horse got hit with the ball early in the match and hobbled for a few strides, running off the effects of the blow, just like Little League players are advised to do by their coaches.

Polo near Charlottesville

At half time, the crowd is invited onto the field to repair the damage by "stomping divots." Little kids get to let off some steam, and adults get to work off the effects of the wine they've consumed during the first half on a bright ninety-degree Virginia Sunday afternoon. Again the crowd, except for a few children, operated in self-contained groups, repairing the field independently from other groups.

The match kept my interest for the first two chukkers, but my attention waned after that. I'll chalk it up to having no one to explain what was taking place on the field. Soon the match consisted of eight horses and riders chasing one another up and down the field. I turned my back on the field to appreciate the beauty of the land. It's really spectacular. Green rolling hills contrasting with white clouds floating above them.

Three chukkers, twenty-one minutes of polo, may not seem like a lot, but it was plenty for the uninitiated. I had thought about going to the Farmington Hunt Club to learn about fox hunting. In Virginia, these hunt clubs have property to house hounds so the members can hunt fox in the surrounding area. It's a tradition-laden activity brought to the Virginia Colony by the English. The Farmington Hunt Club has been around since 1929. It and the eighteen other clubs in Virginia are members of the Master of Foxhounds Association of America. The association was formed to provide oversight of hunting clubs and a way of registering hunting lands. Once registered, the club claims territory, and no other member club may hunt in that territory without permission from the club. With urban sprawl, hunting territory and wild game populations are under tremendous pressure, and registration of hunting territory is one way to prevent overhunting. Registering hunting land is a pretty interesting concept, and I wanted to visit the hounds—never called dogs—but the national pastime called. The NCAA super-regional baseball tournament was being played—the Oklahoma Sooners against the Virginia Cavaliers. This is America, and baseball took precedence over the fox hunt.

So there you have it, Charlottesville, a place where you can watch polo, fox hunting, and baseball, all on the same day, surrounded with spectacular scenery. Nearby, tourists wandered around Monticello, Thomas Jefferson's house, and I'm sure a few young people studied. I'm not sure that I'm ready to say this is the best place in the nation, but as they say in the swampland of Louisiana, "they do auwlriiight."

Travel Notes:
What's a Cavalier?

When the United States first became populated with white people, most of them came from Great Britain. Puritans went north to New England. The South, which at that time consisted only of Virginia, got Cavaliers. I'm not sure why these Englishmen migrated to different places, but it may have to do with the fact that they didn't get along too well back in the motherland.

Now I'm not great on my English history, but the Cavaliers were supporters of King Charles I, while the Puritans were not. I think that the Cavaliers didn't mind making life miserable for the Puritans during the time his majesty had his head. In 1649, however, things changed when his majesty was beheaded and Oliver Cromwell took over the government. After the loss of their king, a bunch of Cavaliers came to Virginia. For reasons I don't entirely understand, many Cavaliers received large land grants. Soon these Englishmen formed a class-based society like they had in England, with the Cavaliers as the landed aristocracy. Virginia's society at that time mirrored England's; there was an official religion, little social mobility, and no free school or press. Sir William Berkeley, the longest-serving royal governor put it this way:

> I thank God, there are no free schools nor printing, and I hope we shall not have these [for a] hundred years, for learning has brought disobedience, and heresy, and sects into the world, and libels against the best government. God keep us from both!

Washington, Randolph, Lee, Skipwith, Madison, Monroe, and Tyler, all Cavaliers, are famous in early American history. Through them, Virginia became known as the cradle of presidents. Not so much anymore. Of the eight presidents who called Virginia home, only one came after the Civil War.

Cavalier survives today as the nickname for the University of Virginia athletic teams. I prefer UVA's unofficial nickname: Wahoo. In Charlottesville, I asked a store employee selling college wear to tell me what a Wahoo was. He didn't know. He didn't know what a Cavalier was either. My niece later said that a Wahoo is a mythical fish that can drink twice its weight. That's better than a Cavalier any day.

Some thirty years ago, a Virginia author named Garrett Epps wrote *The Shad Treatment*, a novel set in Richmond, the capital city of Virginia, introducing his reader to an aristocracy that ruled the city. The aristocracy dominated the rosters of two social clubs, the Country Club of Virginia and the Commonwealth Club. They owned weekend retreats on the Rappahannock River, their "Rivah houses," which they grandly identify in a southern accent not really known outside the Tidewater area of Virginia.

I am told that Mr. Epps' accounting of Richmond society is largely accurate even today and that, though there have been changes over the years, the aristocrats still control things. I'm told that it would not be inaccurate to compare modern-day Richmond to Barbados, where the political power is held by the black underclass while a small group of white patricians retains the economic power. The only real difference from Barbados: The economic power holders in Richmond have very stilted southern accents.

My source, an immigrant from Arkansas who has lived in Richmond for fifteen years, describes Richmonders:

> Richmonders are insulted when their state capital city is compared with other Southern state capital cities. Richmonders are easterners. They compare their city with Baltimore, Wilmington, or even Philadelphia and Boston. They do not consider Little Rock, Montgomery, or Tallahassee counterparts.

After visiting Richmond, these observations seemed valid to me. Introducing myself as being from Arkansas, I could tell people weren't familiar with my home state and no one mentioned having visited. Richmond isn't as provincial as New York City—where someone once asked me if Arkansas was near Iowa. I replied, "It's close. Take the Lincoln Tunnel, head west, and make a left before Des Moines." Most Richmonders indicated that Alabama, Mississippi, and Arkansas were indistinguishable to them, probably located in some far-off land.

Downtown Richmond, home to Virginia Commonwealth University, was a tattooed, pierced counterpoint to the bow-tied, seer-sucker-wearing lawyers and bureaucrats who scurry around the state capital and nearby courthouses during the daylight hours. I noticed so many bowtie-wearing men that I did a little research to see if the bowtie was invented here. The bow tie, according to Wikipedia, orig-inated among Croatian mercenaries during the Prussian wars of the seventeenth century. For whatever reason, this wartime neckwear has found a home in Richmond. Bowties are downright ubiquitous in Richmond. The local tourist television channel, which played on the hotel room TV, got into the bowtie thing. The Richmond Tourist Association sponsored a hip-hop song called "RVa" about things to do around Richmond. One singer described tubing down the James River, and the other rapped about putting on a bowtie before going clubbing. (This may well be the only reported use of "bowtie" as a lyric in a hip-hop song.)

Immediately west of downtown Richmond is the Fan district. The Fan is so named because it fans out from downtown to The Boulevard. The Fan developed in the late nineteenth and early twentieth century as Richmond's streetcar suburb. Because Richmond was more densely populated at that time than any other place in the South, there aren't many neighborhoods like the Fan in the South. Atlanta, Birmingham, or New Orleans might have similar suburbs, but the Fan resembles the streetcar suburbs of Louisville, Kentucky, or St. Louis, Missouri, more than other southern cities.

The Fan terminates at The Boulevard. As my friend says, only in Richmond is a road named *The* Boulevard. But there at the end of the

Fan and facing The Boulevard, three buildings sit in a row—the Virginia Historical Society, next to the United Daughters of the Confederacy headquarters, then the glitzy new Virginia Museum of Fine Arts.

The Virginia Historical Society started celebrating Virginia's history in 1831. Its first president was John Marshall, the same guy who was chief justice of the United States for over a third of a century. The society lists its past presidents above the entrance to the museum. It appears that all of them are male and, I would be willing to wager, white. Needless to say, the Historical Society represents old Richmond society.

The society's home is called Battle Abbey of the South. The most impressive part of this very impressive building are the murals entitled "The Four Seasons of the Confederacy." The murals were painted by a Frenchman whose work was interrupted by service in World War I. After seeing trench warfare, the artist declared he now knew war, destroyed his pre-war sketches, and repainted a non-idealized version of war.

The other end of this trio of buildings is the Virginia Museum of Fine Arts. This building reflects modern Richmond. Opening during the Great Depression in 1936 with government support, the Virginia Museum of Fine Arts has expanded a number of times over the past eighty years. It now has a 13.5-acre site, 134,000 square feet of collection and exhibition space, and a 600-space parking deck. Its most recent expansion was celebrated with a sand mandala created by Tibetan monks. For those not in the know, a mandala is a ritual in which a complex sand painting is created over several weeks, then ceremonially destroyed. Though both museums are integral parts of the Richmond establishment, no one believes the Historical Society would use a Buddhist ceremony to celebrate one of its events.

Sandwiched between these buildings is the national headquarters of the United Daughters of the Confederacy. The United Daughters of the Confederacy is a women's heritage organization limited "to those women not less than sixteen years old who are blood descendants, lineal or collateral, of men and women who served honorably in the Army, Navy or Civil Service of the Confederate States of America, or gave Material Aid to the Cause." In back of the imposing marble building sits a Civil War-era cannon.

I didn't realize that the United Daughters of the Confederacy was still operating, but it has chapters in thirty-three states. My friend says there is a lot of coming and going from the two museums; however, no one he knows has seen anyone actually enter or leave the UDC building for years. (He told me he's been tempted to use his mother's UDC membership certificate to see if he could be admitted into the building.)

That's not to say the UDC is not still active. One of its objectives is "To collect and preserve the material necessary for a truthful history of the American Civil War and to protect, preserve, and mark the places made historic by Confederate valor." Another is "to assist descendants of worthy Confederates in securing a proper education." To promote these ideals, the Tennessee UDC chapter sued Vanderbilt University over the university's decision to remove *Confederate* from the building named *Confederate Memorial Hall*. Evidently, the UDC chapter had given Peabody College, the previous owner, $50,000 to include dormitory space in a college building. For this contribution, the UDC got the right to send girls to live in the dormitory rent free—and the right to name the building. In a unanimous decision, the Tennessee Court of Appeals over-turned the trial court and declared that the UDC could hold Vanderbilt to the terms of its Depression-era agreement. As a result of the UDC's efforts, the word Confederate still resides on Memorial Hall in Nashville.

As my friend predicted, I saw no activity in or around the building. I thought I would try to gain admission to see what they did in the build-ing or to ask someone about their plans for celebrating the sesquicen-tennial of the American Civil War. But standing at the front of the building, I decided I really didn't care.

All Come to Look for America

In 1780, the state of Virginia moved its capital from Williamsburg to Richmond. For the next century and a half, time passed Williamsburg by and it deteriorated. In February 1924, the rector of the local Williamsburg Episcopal Church attended a Phi Beta Kappa dinner in New York City. The rector met John D. Rockefeller Jr. there. The rector from that small southern town, Reverend W. A. R. Godwin, inquired whether Mr. Rockefeller might be interested in providing funds to build a Phi Beta Kappa Memorial Hall in Williamsburg. (Williamsburg is the home of the College of William and Mary, the site of the society's founding.) From that first pledge through 1966, the Rockefeller interests supported what has become known as Colonial Williamsburg. It's estimated that they contributed $70 million restoring Williamsburg to its glory days in colonial America when, as the capital of Virginia, it was one of the most important cities in North America.

When Mr. Rockefeller first took an interest in Williamsburg, it was a sleepy southern town. Significant buildings, such as the Capitol and the Governor's Place, already had been lost to decay. But almost ninety colonial-era structures remained. Complicating the re-creation was the presence of more recent buildings: houses, gas stations and commercial structures. Other colonial capitals—New York, Philadelphia, or Boston—had become major modern cities and had shed their colonial past. Downtrodden Williamsburg was the only remaining place in America where the colonial days could be authentically recreated.

Undertaking this grand task, the Rockefellers created what has now come to be called heritage conservation in America. Williamsburg cannot be considered "historic preservation" because old buildings were destroyed and reproduction colonial-era structures built. This creative destruction was necessary to meet the larger goal of creating a narrative of this country's founding. Williamsburg is a living museum, a place where modern Americans can see how their ancestors lived.

Visitors line up to tour a building in Colonial Williamsburg.

Williamsburg is fantasy land. Tourists tour buildings as they would have looked during the 1700s. Re-enactors create colonial-era characters such as a chicken thief or a felon held in the colonial gaol. Artisans can be found brick-making, coopering, and shoemaking using methods pre-dating the Industrial Revolution.

Colonial Williamsburg is the center of one of the premier historical attractions in the United States, America's Historic Triangle with

Jamestown and Yorktown. The Colonial Parkway connects these three sites of American history. As it might today, the attention and investment by a prominent family such as the Rockefellers in an altruistic venture attracted the attention and assistance of the federal government. After the Rockefellers got involved in Williamsburg at the height of the Great Depression, Congress funded the Colonial Parkway. The Parkway is twenty-three miles long, starting at the Yorktown Bridge and ending at the James River in Jamestown. The National Park Service describes the Parkway as a national monument linking the three sites into a "single coherent reservation free of modern commercial development." With limited access and a 500-foot right-of-way, the Parkway maintains continuity from one historic site to another.

Colonial Parkway between Williamsburg and Yorktown

The Colonial Parkway provides a wooded, non-commercial introduction to Colonial Williamsburg. The road, canopied by large trees and coupled with the complete lack of development, creates the impression that one has left modern America. Even though a modern interstate is available only a few miles away, locals use the Colonial Parkway when traveling between Williamsburg and Yorktown, especially during rush hour. Many prefer the leisurely forty-five-mile-per-hour speed limit of the three-lane Colonial Parkway with its views of the James River to the bumper-to-bumper traffic on the interstate.

The Rockefellers intended to create an idealized view of the colonial era and this country's founding. Creating jobs was not their motivation. But in recreating Williamsburg, the Rockefellers recast the economy of the Tidewater peninsula between the James and York Rivers, which attracts many tourists. Many immigrants serve these tourists. The fiddler who plays nightly at the Chowning Tavern immigrated some thirty years ago to Williamsburg from the Isle of Argyle. Calling him a fiddler is misleading because he plays any number of stringed instruments—along with playing the bagpipes. His official title is senior tavern entertainer, which sounds too corporate. Fiddler is better. For decades now, he has performed eighteenth-century tavern music, sharing early American music with tourists who come to the tavern to eat.

The hotel night clerk is first generation, but he considers himself a local. He's lived in Williamsburg most of his life, having moved as a young child with his mother from Martinsville, Virginia. Being marched with his classmates like a column of ducks through groups of tourists is one of his earliest grade school memories. He's excited to have an entry-level position with Colonial Williamsburg while going to college. It's how his mother started when she arrived here.

The seating hostess at the Chowning Tavern emigrated recently from Van Buren, Arkansas, a few miles from Indian country (Oklahoma). She told me she left Arkansas with her two children and moved to Williamsburg—even though she didn't know anyone in Williamsburg and hadn't even visited. She came because "there is so much history here." She loves Williamsburg. She works two jobs to make ends meet. Her children attend the local public school. Her son plays in the school orchestra. She noted that this wouldn't have occurred in Arkansas because the public school didn't have an orchestra. She said her daughter was being challenged academically for the first time in her life.

My friend Jane Owen once said of the greatness of America's pioneers:

They came this way to give America their brains, their hearts, and their pocketbooks. They didn't come and say, "What's in it for me?" They came to use their talents to better themselves in this place.

That spirit is alive today in Williamsburg.

Travel Notes:
What's a Tar Heel?

North Carolina has a strange nickname—the Tar Heel State. What, exactly, is a Tar Heel? Medical condition? Maybe, but probably not. Is it one word or two? Generally, two. More importantly, why do these people go by that name?

The derivation of *Tar Heel* is murky. It somehow originates from North Carolina's primary export during the eighteenth and nineteenth centuries—naval stores. From before the American Revolution through the end of the Civil War, North Carolina sent more naval stores to its sister colonies and England than any other place. Pine trees were burned to produce tar and pitch, and pine sap was collected to produce turpentine. All three products were necessary to keep wooden ships seaworthy and productive. All three were very dirty, nasty enterprises.

In his 1941 book *Tar Heels: Portrait of North Carolina*, Jonathan Daniels writes that the English soldiers gave the people of North Carolina the nickname during the Revolutionary War. Supposedly the North Carolina colonists dumped their tar into the Tar River to keep it from falling into British hands. The colonists threw so much tar into the river that when the British soldiers crossed, they got tar on their feet. As the native North Carolinian Daniels says:

> I got North Carolina dirt on my feet, if not tar on my heels that will be there till I die. The North Carolina earth sticks to its sons at least as adhesively as that tar, thrown into a river to keep it out of Lord Cornwallis' hands, which his soldiers got on their heels when they forded the stream. They gave us our queer nickname then. And it has stayed with us longer than the original pine forests from which so much tar and turpentine came.

Modern-day historians dismiss this story as legend. Most now believe that Tar Heel was an insult directed at Rebel soldiers from North Carolina. The term was used by Virginians either to deride the North Carolinians as backwoods hicks or to chide them because North Carolina took so long to secede from the Union. (Only Tennessee took longer.) Modern historians note that the first written reference to Tar Heel comes from a February 1863 entry in a Rebel soldier's diary: "I know now what is meant by the piney woods region of N.C. and the idea occurs to me that it is no wonder we are called Tar Heels."

The term was used later in the war more positively by Confederate general Robert E. Lee, who supposedly said after a battle, "Thank God for the Tar Heel boys." By 1864, it was no longer a term of opprobrium. Late in the war, the governor of North Carolina addressed his troops as "fellow Tar Heels."

Outside the South, the term still maintained a negative connotation. In 1875, an African-American congressman from South Carolina discussing race relations noted that many whites were "noble-hearted, generous-hearted people," but others were "the class of men thrown up by the war, that rude class of men I mean, the 'tar-heels' and the 'sand-hillers,' and the 'dirt eaters' of the South—it is with that class we have all our trouble." The *New York Tribune* noted that not all North Carolinians were worthless, that some "really like to work, which is all but incomprehensible to the true Tar Heel."

By 1893, the term was sufficiently positive for the state university to name the student newspaper *The Tar Heel*. A few years later, the *New York Evening Post* identified Jonathan Daniels' father Josephus Daniels and Thomas J. Pence as two Tar Heels holding important posts in Woodrow Wilson's campaign.

Today it's not only the state's nickname, but it's also the nickname of the University of North Carolina sports teams. Not bad—for a state to take an insult and incorporate it as its nickname. And it's an improvement on the old nickname for the state—the Old North State. Tar Heel is also a better nickname than "sand hillers" or "dirt-eaters," names the Reconstruction congressman might have suggested.

Besides its nickname, North Carolina's early history is noteworthy because it was one of the last colonies to adopt the U.S. Constitution. The first time the North Carolina Constitutional Convention delegates voted, they voted overwhelmingly to neither ratify nor reject the Constitution. The main sticking point, it seems, was that the proposed constitution didn't explicitly restrict the federal government's power on the inalienable rights of freemen. Articulating the rights of freemen was important to North Carolinians because they had passed a Declaration of Rights when they broke from the crown and formed their independent state in 1776. The freemen of North Carolina weren't keen on letting these rights be reduced just to organize a federal government. So in June 1789, largely as an accommodation to the Tar Heels, James Madison submitted a Bill of Rights as an amendment to the proposed constitution. Madison's strategy worked, and in November 1789, the North Carolina Constitutional Convention ratified the Constitution. A few months later, North Carolina was one of the first states to ratify the Bill of Rights.

Dobbies and Pout Houses

Warren County, North Carolina, sits near the Virginia border. Its county seat is Warrenton. Jonathan Daniels stopped here in 1937, supposedly to locate a poker game said to have been going on since the Civil War. Evidently, the city fathers played poker while letting progress pass them by. Downtown Warrenton consists mostly of a quaint little courthouse, an old hardware store which now houses a café, and the Warren County Restoration Center which ironically resides in a tumble-down, unrestored building.

Just off the square, I saw a sign in the window of a hair salon advertising "Relaxer and a Dobbie—$50.00." Turns out a relaxer is a process in which a chemical, lotion, or cream is used to make hair less curly—the opposite of a perm. I had never heard of a dobbie. The shop was closed so I couldn't go in and ask. With my straight hair I don't need a relaxer treatment, but a dobbie could be a good thing for a balding middle-aged guy. Questioning the across-the-street restaurateur and a few of his customers yielded no information about the subject. Since there was no one else downtown this Saturday afternoon, I guess dobbies will remain a mystery to me.

Founded in 1789, Warrenton is about the same size today as it was a couple of hundred years ago—a little less than a thousand people. It has an impressive number of historic structures for such a small town, which indicates that sometime in the last 230 years, Warrenton must have done pretty well. Not now though. Now there are a lot of abandoned buildings—well-built buildings which now have no useful purpose.

In a state which has come to typify the New South, Warrenton missed out. It appears to be one of the many stagnating farm towns you can find in most any state. With little local industry, there are no good jobs nearby. It's too far from Raleigh for its inhabitants to commute to the good jobs there. As I drove around this little town, I wondered whether the twenty-first century will be kinder than the last two have been. Could the Internet change a town like Warrenton from its downward trend? Will people come here for the housing stock and the slower pace of life if they can connect to work by the Internet? I wonder if the schools are any good. Would that make any difference?

Warren County Restoration Center

It's at least twenty-five miles from Warrenton before any newly constructed housing is visible from the highway. It's another twenty to twenty-five miles past that before the urban sprawl of Raleigh comes into view. Raleigh must be growing toward the south or west and not northeast toward Warrenton. I wondered if someone else documenting the South in seventy years will find Warrenton's population remaining about 1,000.

Driving toward Raleigh, I saw a billboard admonishing travelers: "Don't let fancy stores overcharge you." Another advertised a new inventory of "pout houses." Underneath the sign were small buildings which looked like oversized doll houses. Later, in Greensboro, I discovered that pout houses are little sheds, outbuildings, usually unheated and with no running water where the man of the house can pout (that is, smoke) without the woman of the house complaining. It's also used when he is out late and needs to sleep off a night's revelries without bothering the wife. Since I don't smoke, I'm not sure I need a pout house unless I can get a dobbie there.

The Research Triangle

Unlike most southern state capitals, Raleigh doesn't draw its economic vitality from an expanding state government. Raleigh's vibrancy comes from a bold experiment started some fifty-five years ago—the Research Triangle. In the early 1950s, Raleigh was designated one of the vertices in a triangle of research to be formed with Durham and Chapel Hill, specifically, the area's educational institutions. The three universities were North Carolina State University in Raleigh, the University of North Carolina at Chapel Hill, and Duke University in Durham. The state government and business leaders called on these three schools to act, in appropriate circumstances, as a unified academic community. To say the experiment has worked would be an understatement. The whole area has been transformed by the Research Triangle. What started as a three-county endeavor has become an eight-county area with a population of more than 1.7 million people.

The idea for the Research Triangle arose around the midpoint of the twentieth century when North Carolina was not doing well economically. The state had just fallen to third to last in per capita income, ahead of only Arkansas and Mississippi. Things were not good for North Carolina. Largely dependent on agriculture, North Carolina had an agricultural base which consisted mainly of small farms. Small farms were economic dinosaurs, and the average North Carolina farm was the smallest in the Union at just sixty-seven acres. Just as problematic was its industrial base.

Long-term prospects for North Carolina's two major industries, textiles and furniture making, were little better. Even worse for the average worker, both industries relied on low wages to maintain competiveness. All in all, the future wasn't bright in the Tar Heel State during President Dwight Eisenhower's terms.

Most southern states attracted industry during this period by trumpeting a cheap labor force and low property taxes. With the Research Triangle, North Carolina state leaders employed a different tactic: They would attract industry by the three local universities combining resources to assist and encourage area businesses. The state's leaders started by forming a for-profit corporation, owned in large part by residents of New York City, to option and purchase some 4,200 acres of undeveloped land between Raleigh and Durham. This land ultimately became the Research Triangle Park.

The governor and prominent businessmen then approved a subscription drive to raise $1,250,000 to form the Research Park Institute, build a building to house the institute, and acquire the Park from the for-profit group. By 1959, some 850 subscribers pledged a total of $1,425,000 and formed the non-profit Research Foundation of North Carolina which became the owner and developer of the Research Triangle Park. One of the founders of the non-profit foundation stated:

> Indeed, because North Carolina had no special advantage or resource in the area of economic development, it will be the intangible qualities of the State that will determine the course of development over the next fifteen years.

He was wrong. It didn't take fifteen years. It took only four months for the Park to announce its first industrial tenant.

Who saw North Carolina as a center of scientific research in the early 1960s? No one did. An enlightened area in the South might hope to get a paper plant or a pallet factory—if it worked real hard. But recruiting scientists to work in a lab in the mid-twentieth-century South was fantasy. In 1964, an article in the *Winston-Salem Journal-Sentinel* extracted the essence of North Carolina's new approach:

> What is the Research Triangle? ... There is no simple answer because the Research Triangle is many things....It is a place, a geographical

location. It is both an idea and a practical concept. It is a triad of operating institutions, interlaced with both private and public interests and support, and with three great universities as its cornerstones....It is also a physical reality, a center of research in science and technology, something which has become a complex of new landscaped buildings, modern offices and gleaming laboratories.

In 1965, the Park really took off. IBM and the U.S. Department of Health Education and Welfare announced the development of substantial projects there. Since that time, the Park has seen steady and stable growth.

Over 157 organizations reside in the Park now. They employ more than 39,000 people at an average salary nearly forty-five percent higher than regional and national averages. Rick Weedle, president and CEO of the Research Triangle Foundation of North Carolina, estimates that 1,800 companies have started in the Triangle. The Triangle has birthed so many start-ups that an announcement for a new company hardly gets noticed.

The Park, sometimes referred to as RTP, is beginning its second fifty years. During the first fifty years, the main task was to fill it up. By the end of 2007, the Park was home to more than twenty million square feet of developed space within its 7,800 acres. Attracting industry into the Park spurred growth outside the Park where similar industries and office parks located to be near the activity. RTP's neighbors include the country's largest privately held software firm and the world's largest pharmaceutical contract research organization.

There's no doubt that the Triangle has changed the region. As CEO Weedle observed:

The effect of the Park over the last 47 years has worked to transform the region and the state. This impact has resulted in a change in the composition of the region's industries, an upgrading of the capacities at the three flagship universities—as well as through all institutes of education throughout the region and state, and a global brand that has built the reputation of the region and state as one of the leading areas for high-technology innovation.

Former University of North Carolina president William Friday stated it a little more succinctly: "Research Triangle Park is the most significant economic and political manifestation of will in the state in the last century."

Research Triangle Park looks now to the future. Rick Weedle believes that the next fifty years will be characterized by organic growth—self-generating growth arising from the capability presently residing in the Research Triangle. Weedle put it simply:

> Smart people like each other and want to be around one another. Another advantage for smart people is that moving between academia and industry is easy and encouraged within the Triangle. Smart people are confident that they can do research in an academic setting and then go into the private sector to develop practical applications of that research.

There is no denying that many in the Research Triangle are recent immigrants. Many accents are harsh; you don't hear a lot of that sweet North Carolina lilt. Southern drawls are infrequent—so infrequent that I noticed the first one I heard one day. I stopped to get gas. The cashier was a young female obviously of Indian descent. She said "fine" and "rain" with a nice drawl in the midst of a bunch of people who barely moved their jaws as they asked for gas and "kwawfee." As my second cousin, Nannette Fields, a resident of Chapel Hill since the late 1940s, said of the newcomers, "They're all Yankees." Then she quickly added, "Not that there's anything wrong with that."

Imports have brought with them different games. For example, a number of them play lacrosse. I bet if you ask people in Montgomery, Alabama, or Thomasville, Georgia, to name their favorite lacrosse teams, you'd be met with a big ole "Huh?" They may know one lacrosse team, Duke University's team, largely because of the recent news involving the lacrosse team, a lacrosse team party, and a young woman who was not a student. It just so happened that the afternoon I was there, Duke's lacrosse team hosted the Blue Hose of Presbyterian College, a small liberal arts college of 1,300 students from Clinton, South Carolina. They're playing lacrosse in South Carolina, too? Who knew?

Lacrosse is an old Native American game, played with a hard rubber ball. Players carry long metal sticks with netting on the end. The players run, carry, and pass the ball with these sticks. The object of the game is to hurl the ball into the opponent's goal while the opposing team tries to stop them by banging into them as they run or using their sticks to chop at the opponents' sticks. The game reminds the uninitiated of hockey without ice or skates—or maybe even polo without the ponies.

Duke is a stylish place that has the feel of a country club. A private school, it's obviously well-funded with first-rate physical facilities, including its own lacrosse stadium. Tickets to the game were a bargain at $5.00. Parking places were available next to the stadium, and you didn't have to wait in line to get in. The stadium reminded me of a small college football stadium, with a set of metal bleachers on each side of the field extending from about the twenty-yard lines (if this were a football field). There's a handsome building that appeared to be restricted to donors and VIPs.

Blue Devil lacrosse players waiting to sing the national anthem

I was glad I had gotten there early because the music for the pregame warm-up was head-banging metal music. And I was close enough to the players to hear them sing the national anthem. Duke may have great lacrosse players, but I'm guessing singing careers are unlikely when their eligibilities end.

The game started with two players scrapping for the ball at mid-field. Duke won the scrap and, after two quick passes, the Blue Devils scored a goal in the first eleven seconds. It looked like a long night for the Blue Hose, who fell behind 6-1 early in the second period. But the Presbyterians rallied late in the second period and cut the deficit to four at half-time.

During half-time I struck up a conversation with another spectator. In an accent that obviously wasn't native, my new friend explained that local lacrosse clubs have been developing local lacrosse talent for years. He told me the area's girls' lacrosse teams were the best in the country and the boys' teams rivaled those in Denver and California.

I must admit ignorance here. I know California has everything, but Colorado is a hotbed of lacrosse? He explained further that in the past few years, lacrosse had become a big club sport in Florida. So Florida is now a fertile recruiting territory for area college lacrosse teams. In hopes of changing the conversation to football, I joked that the lacrosse coaches could piggyback recruiting trips to Florida with the football coaches. When he didn't bite, I asked if he was native to North Carolina: "Nope, moved here from Jersey ten years ago." No kidding.

The second half began the same way that the first half had—with a quick Blue Devil score. A few minutes later, Duke scored again to go up by six. Since the final outcome was no longer in doubt, I left for Greensboro and the start of the Piedmont, fifty-five miles to the west.

Sustainability in Greensboro

Greensboro is the major city in the area that North Carolinians call the Triad, an area formed by the cities Winston-Salem, High Point, and Greensboro. (Remember, the name "triangle" was taken already.) The Triad has a population of 1.6 million people. The greenest hotel in America is located in Greensboro—but not because of the town's name.

The "green" in Greensboro honors General Nathanael Greene, the Quaker Revolutionary War hero. The Quaker influence in Greensboro doesn't stop with its name. Largely because of its Quaker influence, Greensboro was an important stop on the Underground Railroad. Some believe the whole Underground Railway was founded in Greensboro by a local Quaker, Vestal Coffin. Others think it was simply one stop, an important one, on the routes leading from North Carolina to Indiana. Either way, when a slave ran from a North Carolina plantation in the 1840s or 1850s, Greensboro was likely the first stop for the slave hunters.

Not surprisingly, Greensboro has since had its share of civil rights history, and today Greensboro is an important stop for any civil rights history buff. In fact, the Greensboro Woolworth's was the site on February 1, 1960, where the African-American civil rights movement first used sit-ins as a nonviolent strategy for desegregation in the South. Today that store is a museum.

Greensboro is located in a pretty area called the Piedmont. The Piedmont's rolling foothills connect the coastal flatlands of Virginia,

North Carolina, and South Carolina with the mountainous western parts of those states. The Carolina Piedmont starts at the Virginia-North Carolina border forty miles northeast of Greensboro and runs southwesterly through North Carolina past Greenville, South Carolina, and some say into Georgia. Jonathan Daniels, who grew up some seventy-five miles away in Raleigh, noted that the North Carolina Piedmont is different from his flat part of the state.

The Piedmont sure is pretty hill country. It is the kind of rolling hill terrain where you find yourself standing and staring toward the distant hills.

Nothing in the history of Greensboro foreshadowed the placement of America's first LEED-certified platinum hotel there. A project of local businessmen Dennis Quaintance and Mike Weaver, the hotel opened in 2007. Dennis and Mike named the hotel Proximity, after the Proximity Mill. At one time, the Proximity Mill was the biggest denim manufacturing plant in the United States. The Proximity Mill is no longer standing, torn down in the 1970s, a victim of the deterioration of the textile industry in the later part of the twentieth century. The Proximity was built on pastureland outside of town. The hotel does not even replicate the building style of the mill, only taking the name of the locally famous landmark.

The first step in building the nation's first platinum LEED building began with the search for a building type. The developers began an extensive architectural archeology search throughout the country to see what historical building type they might build.

The textile industry had come to the Piedmont soon after the War (for Southern Independence or against Northern Aggression; take your pick) and became Greensboro's dominant industry throughout most of the twentieth century. Keeping in mind this historical connection, Dennis and Mike limited their search to textile plants. The developers decided that the most sustainable textile building style was the 1939 Cut and Sew Factory. It was a considered decision. By 1939, the textile industry had developed the use of natural light and air currents to make factories productive. After World War II, architects relied on more artificial means to make buildings efficient. Dennis and Mike decided pre-war textile buildings reflected an optimum in sustainable design.

The Proximity Hotel

After settling on the style of the building, they began what they called "a sustainable and adaptive re-use" of a new building. The developers instituted over seventy sustainable practices which led to its certification. The building uses forty percent less energy than a conventional hotel. The roof has 100 solar panels which heat about sixty percent of the water used by the hotel and the restaurant. The morning I visited, the solar panels actually generated more electricity than was needed to heat the water, and the hotel sold the surplus power to the local utility company. The hotel restaurant relies on geothermal energy to cool its refrigerators. It is equipped with a regenerative drive elevator. I don't understand the physics of it, but I understand that a regenerative drive elevator does something with the elevator's counterweights so it captures power from the trip up and reuses it on the way down, consuming less energy overall.

Since Dennis and Mike want to see if these practices are truly sustainable and cost effective, all of the Proximity's systems are monitored by the local university to document the energy savings.

The hotel's design relies heavily on natural light. The big windows are operable. My room had one of the large windows—seven feet, four inches—in the bathroom. In fact, the upper half of the bathroom's outside wall was almost all window, which creates a whole set of issues both for the architect and the guest. The solution: The architect places a strip of mirror above the sink in front of the window. (Putting in contacts in the morning is tricky since there's a tendency to look out the window rather than concentrating on your eyes!)

Recycled materials play a big part in the Proximity's construction. All of its wallboard is recycled, while ninety percent of its reinforced steel is recycled. The concrete in the building contains 224,000 pounds of fly ash, a waste product from the production of electricity. Fly ash makes a fine binder for concrete. Much better than the alternative, which requires sending it to a holding pond, where it ultimately leaches heavy metals into the ground water.

Three more interesting things about the Proximity are shower heads, toilet paper dispensers, and carbon dioxide. First, the shower heads don't come out of the wall, but from the ceiling. I surmised the reason for the ceiling placement of the shower heads was to increase the water pressure so less water is used with assistance of the law of gravity. I'm probably right about those physics—but that's not the reason. Evidently, when pipes or conduit are run through the walls, the wall's effectiveness as a sound barrier is significantly diminished. So Dennis and Mike prohibited plumbing or electrical wire from being placed within the walls. The developers want a pristine sound barrier between the rooms.

The toilet paper dispensers are similarly interesting, showing the attention to sustainability in the smallest details. Rather than shiny, showy chrome fixtures made in China, all toilet paper dispensers at Proximity are simple plastic devices manufactured locally. These devices work as well as the shiny ones but are less burdensome on the environment to make and transport.

Finally, there's carbon dioxide. Have you ever wondered why you wake up tired after spending a night in a hotel or motel? Did you blame the mattress or the strange surroundings for waking up so tired? More than likely your room was so airtight in an effort to save energy that carbon dioxide levels had built-up. Literally, you are tired because you didn't breathe in as much oxygen as you're used to getting. The Proximity fights carbon dioxide build-up by circulating large amounts of outside air into guestrooms through an efficient air exchange.

All of this green stuff is nice, but how about the stay? Well, it's first-class accommodation. The rooms are pretty and well-appointed, but it's a new hotel, and that could be said about most new hotels. Most strikingly, it's quiet, real quiet. The pristine sound walls really work. And the hotel doors have very large hinges which keep doors from slamming shut. I didn't hear one door slam the entire time I was there. Another nice touch is the honor refrigerator. Rather than having a noisy vending machine on each floor, the Proximity provides a small honor refrigerator stocked with drinks.

But back again to the essential question: Why is this hotel located in the South and not New York, Oregon, or California? The main reason the greenest hotel in the country is located in Greensboro is Dennis Quaintance, an immigrant from Billings, Montana, a fifty-three-year-old son of a real cowboy. Dennis is a graduate of Hellgate High (one of the great names for a high school). He moved to Greensboro in 1978 to work in the restaurant business and opened his own restaurant in 1989 with his partner, Mike Weaver, a local Greensboro businessman. The partnership flourished and now owns and operates four restaurants and two hotels and employs 450 people. It's a big business, but it is run a little differently than other businesses.

Their employee handbook starts out stating:

We are different!

Quaintance-Weaver Hotels is an organization (a group with common objectives) that is different....We believe that success is only obtained as a by-product of worthwhile objectives. Mike Weaver and I (Dennis Quaintance) define worthwhile objectives as those that are of genuine service to the community.

Now I know that employee handbooks are propaganda pamphlets designed to rally the troops, but Dennis really does do things differently. For example, he has an artist on staff. What business hires an artist? I know that many businesses commission artists for an occasional project, but who puts them on staff? What first sounds like a radical departure from standard business practice, Dennis can easily explain. All of his businesses have walls and need wall hangings. By giving a local artist all of that work, the artist can be sustained by the regular work and he can offer Dennis a reasonable price. The cost of the original artwork may be a little more than for mass-produced art, but Quaintance-Weaver Hotels have a quality product that's local and original. More important: It's sustainable.

Dennis Quaintance, co-owner of Quaintance-Weaver Hotels

Dennis is a little different. I mean that in a nice way. What started as a one-hour interview about LEED certification turned into a day-long tour of the Proximity; the O. Henry Hotel, Proximity's sister hotel down the street; Lucky 32, one of his restaurants; downtown Greensboro; and the Historic Greenhill Cemetery. I had scheduled a forty-five-minute meeting with him to discuss the only LEED-certified platinum hotel in the country. During the first thirty minutes of our conversation, I learned about the Fibonacci sequence, the golden mean, and—my favorite—the rule about hiring midwesterners in Greensboro, which is, if someone from the Midwest applies for a job, hire them (because the smart ones leave first). To say that it was a free-wheeling conversation would be an understatement. Half of his construction contractors are Quaker, and he spoke about the influence Quakers have on Greensboro. They are honest, humble, and honorable. By their example, the Quakers raise the general ethos of Greensboro's business practices.

He also advises hiring friendly people because "competence can be taught, but niceness can't be." Dennis also said, "It's easy to do fashionable, but hard to do sustainable," and "ugly ain't sustainable." Finally, my favorite quote: "It isn't sustainable to go broke." Two or three times Dennis varied how he explained this sentiment to emphasize that his are profit-making ventures. By the end of our day together he had convinced me that the sustainability of a business depends primarily upon providing a genuine service to your community. And Dennis is all about sustainability.

I asked Dennis if he loses any money on the honor fridge, and he replied that it happens, but it's very rare. Guests intuitively understand the principal that the Proximity provides a service by not using noisy machines to dispense drinks. His guests show their appreciation appropriately because virtually everyone pays their fair share.

Obviously, people appreciate the Proximity for more than the honor refrigerator. In places like Greensboro, much of a hotel's business comes by way of local referrals, and Dennis says that the Proximity has the highest occupancy rate of any non-resort hotel in North Carolina. I concluded that's the real reason that the greenest hotel in America is located in Greensboro: Greensboro appreciates it.

Trains, Furniture, and Krispy Kreme

High Point, North Carolina, is part of the Triad, a bedroom community for the other two Triad towns, Greensboro and Winston-Salem. Most of the people I met from High Point commute into Greensboro to work. But High Point is more than an appendage of Greensboro and Winston-Salem: It's the Home Furnishing Capital of the World.

High Point's name comes from the fact that it was literally the highest point on the North Carolina Railroad line. The highest point on the line was the most convenient place to re-fuel trains during the nineteenth century, and soon a community formed around the railroad re-fueling yard. Even today, High Point has a strong connection with train travel, as three trains stop here daily: New York to New Orleans, New York to Charlotte, and a local train running between Raleigh and Charlotte. These trains depart from the old restored train station downtown.

The train station is two blocks from the International Home Furnishings Center, which houses the largest home furnishing market in the world. For the past century, people have come to High Point to discover and acquire the latest in American furniture and furnishings. Most furniture manufacturing is now overseas. Seventeen furniture plants in North Carolina have recently closed. Still, most furniture company headquarters, industry associations, and related businesses remain here or near here. High Point continues as the center of the furniture industry.

Restored train station in High Point

The High Point Market is held twice a year, during the spring and fall, bringing over 170,000 people to High Point each year. People come to market to see the newest in over sixty categories of home furnishing. The furnishings are shown in twelve million square feet of space located in over 190 buildings throughout High Point. The High Point Market buildings dominate the downtown area. Nearly 13,000 jobs are related to the High Point Market.

I was in High Point on a quiet Sunday a week before the spring intro-duction of the latest designs in furniture, accessories, lighting, bedding, and rugs. It was quiet, very quiet. The only discernible activity was the traffic from the church parking lots. I had been warned just the day before that there was no place to get breakfast in downtown High Point on Sunday morning. Perhaps there were places out on the highway—but not downtown on Sunday.

As I explored downtown High Point, I was getting hungry. When I passed a Krispy Kreme shop on Main Street, I remembered a sign quoting Ethel Waters I'd seen the day before while touring Greensboro Repertory Theatre:

> I turned again to the unholy trinity of doughnuts, pigfoot, and apple pie.

—Ethel W.

Profound breakfast words in Greensboro

I hadn't understood the significance of the sign until I turned into the parking lot for doughnuts and fried pies. (No, Krispy Kreme doesn't sell pig's feet, but two out of three is enough to make an omen.)

Krispy Kreme was founded just up the road in Winston-Salem. The store on High Point's Main Street is one of the oldest Krispy Kreme locations in the nation. A few years ago, the owners tore down the old store to build a new and bigger one. But it still had the old sign—Hot Now!—to indicate that rings of dough are being ejected from the hot oil and passing through the glazing shower. A real treat if there ever was one.

65

Until just a few years ago, Krispy Kreme was a local North Carolina tradition. Krispy Kreme parlayed its success by taking the company public, so it could open stores in New York, California, and foreign countries. Non-southerners soon learned that when the sign out front flashed Hot Now to come running: It was time to eat. Krispy Kreme cognoscenti advise to buy only (1) when the sign is on, (2) when the doughnuts are hot, and (3) no more than two doughnuts at a time because the third will get cold before you can eat it. Evidently there weren't enough non-southerners following the rules to keep the stock price up, so accounting irregularities began, and Krispy Kreme became known as much for the financial scandal as the fried dough it dispensed.

I entered an almost empty store. The only customers were an elderly couple just sitting down at a table to eat their food. She wore a nice dress, and he had on a coat and tie. Obviously they were on the way to or from church. Each had two glazed doughnuts in front of them along with a small carton of milk. I ordered the same thing but substituted coffee. As I waited for my order, I watched them. They ate slowly, very slowly, as if they were savoring their doughnuts. They ate without looking at one another or having any discussion—not a word between them. Just two folks sitting at the same table eating the same food.

A few minutes later the door opened, and a very obese man walked in and greeted the person at the counter by name. They chatted a moment and the large man ordered a dozen day-old chocolate doughnuts and chocolate milk. I assumed he was taking them home. Nope. After he paid, he waddled to the nearest table and opened the box of doughnuts. After he'd eaten half a dozen, he paused to drink some milk. I thought I might stay long enough to see who finished first, the churchgoers or the man with the boxed dozen doughnuts. I decided instead to finish my last doughnut and coffee on the road.

Towel Town No More

In 1906, James W. Cannon built a mill on his 600-acre cotton plantation. He also built a village beside the mill for the workers. At first, the village was called Cannon City, but the name was soon changed to Kannapolis. Some say the name is Greek for "city of looms." Others say that J. W. wasn't that fancy. He didn't know any Greek and most likely just changed the spelling to avoid confusion with his other business enterprises.

In time, Cannon's mill town, located some thirty miles from Charlotte, grew to become the largest towel and sheet manufacturer in the world. When J. W. died, Kannapolis consisted of twelve mills with more than 600,000 spindles and 10,000 looms, and employed over 15,000 employees, who turned out 300,000 towels daily. And the Cannon enterprises were still growing. By end of the 1930s, over 25,000 people worked at the Cannon mills in Kannapolis, producing over half of all towels and twenty percent of the sheets purchased in the United States.

The Cannons took advantage of a large pool of uneducated workers willing to work for low wages in the mills. Area agricultural workers migrated to mill work. Even though it was hard, dirty work, working for the Cannon interests was better than barely subsisting as a sharecropper.

Mr. Daniels describes Kannapolis on his Journey as follows:

Kannapolis [is] where the Cannons have a private town in which they make a good part of the towels that wipe the face of the world. As members of it, Cannons understood the Carolina race…and spent no time planting trees for a people who too often have considered them only as things to be cut down. The Cannons did their planting in one pretty little park about the mill offices and left the village itself an ugly community of dirty clapboard and asphalt shingle. One house there, I remember sat so close beside and below the unpaved lane that its whole side—even its windows—was painted with splashed yellow mud….By no material standard could Kannapolis be called a pitiful town; but by any aesthetic standards it is a hideous one.

Kannapolis was completely private. There was no mayor or city council. The streets weren't public. The Cannon Company hired the policemen. The fire department, the water company, and sewage plant were all owned and operated by the Cannon interests. Workers rented one of the 2,000 Cannon-owned houses and shopped at the Cannon-owned business district. By 1960, Kannapolis had the distinction of being America's largest unincorporated town, with some 35,000 residents. It was only after the Cannon family sold the mills that Kannapolis incorporated as a city.

Big changes started in 1971 when J. W.'s son died, fifty years after succeeding his father as president. At that time, Cannon Mills was North Carolina's largest employer. With 24,000 employees and seventeen mills, Cannon was the country's largest producer of sheets, pillowcases, and towels. Cannon Mills was doing relatively well, but the textile industry, which had come to the Carolina Piedmont from New England because labor was cheap, was on the move again seeking cheaper labor overseas.

In 1982, the Cannon family sold out lock, stock, and employee housing to a firm headed by David Murdock, a California entrepreneur, for a reported sum of $413 million. Murdock's firm moved to modernize the Cannon operations, laying off workers and selling mill houses to those workers remaining. They also began a $200 million capital improvement program to update the facilities. Within four years, the Murdock interests resold the mills and the Cannon name to Fieldcrest for $250 million.

Like the Murdock interests before it, Fieldcrest owned the Cannon mill complex only a short time before selling out to Pillowtex for $700 million. But in the post-NAFTA world, an American textile business wasn't a good investment. Pillowtex had borrowed most of the money it used to buy Cannon. By November 2000, Pillowtex tried to re-organize in bankruptcy by closing plants and shedding debt. It didn't make it. Pillowtex emerged from bankruptcy in May 2002, but liquidated fifteen months later. Barely more than two decades after the Cannon family sold the huge complex where at one time some 30,000 people labored, the mills at Kannapolis closed for good. When Pillowtex closed, fewer than 4,400 people worked the mills.

The huge, now-derelict mill complex was sold at auction. The winning bidder was one of the companies owned by David Murdock, who had originally bought the complex from Cannon family interests. Murdock paid $6.2 million for the mills, a fraction of the $413 million he had paid two decades earlier. The Murdocks demolished the Kannapolis mills, reportedly the third-largest demolition in American history. By late 2006, the 264-acre site was imploded, scraped, leveled, cleaned, and ready for the next phase—the $700 million North Carolina Research Campus.

On this now vacant property, Murdock was willing to commit a bunch of his $1.7 billion net worth to develop a biotech campus in Kannapolis. It was an ambitious project. The North Carolina Research Campus was envisioned to be a public-private partnership bringing industry and academia together to collaborate on nutrition, health, and agricultural issues. An official of the David H. Murdock Research Institute stated the mission: "Society's really big, really important problems like health and well-being are too complicated for any one person or any one group to solve....It takes a continuum." The state of North Carolina added some funding, and the venture was off and running.

The founders had envisioned a campus offering one million square feet of laboratory and office space along with 350,000 square feet of retail and residential space. When the development first was announced, the anticipated projects included a private high school for girls, a core research laboratory, the Dole Research Institute, a UNC–Chapel Hill Institute on Nutrition, and North Carolina State Institute for Advanced Fruit and Vegetable Science.

Despite the hard economic times since the announcement, four buildings and a parking deck have been built, and construction of a fifth building to house a local community college is underway. Eight universities and seven private businesses already have located to the campus.

Even though the streets are new and the buildings handsome, it's disquieting to see so much open space. It's impossible to think that this property was once a huge mill complex with thousands working there. Today it looks like farmland being consumed by a growing metropolis. Broad swaths of undeveloped land crisscross with new streets and new curbs and gutters.

Cannon Mills must have been enormous. I can't conceive of a mill ever being on the property, perhaps a clear enough indication that Kannapolis' days as a textile mill town are gone.

One can only wonder how lint heads (an old derogatory term for textile mill workers) will fit into this new order. It is clear most will be left behind. But there will always be stories of perseverance in times of change. In April 2009, the *Kannapolis Citizen* reported that Randy Crowell had been hired as a lab technician in the Core Laboratory. This hiring was noteworthy because Randy, an electrician at the old Cannon Mills, was in the final group of employees who lost their jobs when the plant closed. His return to Kannapolis was circuitous. After the plant closed, he found other factory work in nearby Lexington, North Carolina, for a few years until that plant closed. Moving to Texas, he enrolled at a local community college even though he was almost fifty years old. After graduation, Randy found work at a Texas biotech company. When the Research Center formally opened, Randy applied for a position and got it, the first former mill worker to work at the Research Center.

While Kannapolis is little more than a century old, it has seen a complete life cycle. The first one started when capitalists came looking for cheap, hardworking labor so they could make a lot of money producing inexpensive textiles. That initial life cycle ended when the capital found cheaper labor elsewhere. Kannapolis starts a second life as a center of innovation in health and nutrition. Where in the words of Randy Crowell, people are "making a real difference in human health, and alleviating suffering." Let's hope this second one lasts longer than the first one did.

Sister City

When J. W. Cannon built his huge mill complex in Kannapolis, he lived just down the road in Concord, the county seat of Cabarrus County. While J. W. and his executives commuted to work in Kannapolis, the commuter road really only went one way. No one in Kannapolis worked in Concord. Kannapolians didn't commute; they lived and worked at the Cannon complex.

Since Jonathan Daniels' visit in the 1930s, Charlotte has sprawled around both towns. Kannapolis and Concord are like siblings who share a common ancestor but took different directions in life. In Kannapolis, the mills are obliterated and huge amounts of now-undeveloped land lie fallow within the business district. Much of Concord is tract-housing, big box stores, and mall-developed suburbia. But there's more to Concord than housing Charlotte's commuters. It's a small city independent of Charlotte. Some mill buildings remain, but Concord's old textile mills are relatively small and have been adaptively reused. For instance, one primarily provides multi-family housing, as well as an antique store.

Concord claims the hottest band in the Charlotte area—and becoming so around the nation—the Avett Brothers. And Concord is the site of the Coca-Cola 600 and the largest tourist attraction in North Carolina. Now, that previous sentence might be a little unclear because it's easy to believe that the NASCAR race would be the top tourist attraction in North Carolina in this NASCAR crazy state. It's not. North

Carolina's favorite tourist attraction is about a mile down from the track, right next to the interstate: the Concord Mills Shopping Mall. That's right, a shopping mall is the top tourist attraction in North Carolina. And Concord has it. A mall, with 200 stores and an amusement park with a NASCAR theme, outperforms NASCAR with the tourists.

The mall, racetrack, airport, and NASCAR Research and Development Center are seven miles and worlds away from downtown Concord. If you take that seven-mile trip, you go from big box stores and racetracks to small town Americana. Downtown Concord still has the feel of the small county seat it once was. No tall office buildings. In fact, the old Hotel Concord—the town's tallest building—stands empty and for sale.

As in most small southern towns, people acknowledge one another on the street. Outside the courthouse, a little Victorian gem, a street vendor is set up to sell sodas and hot dogs to pedestrians. Great small-town Americana.

Because Concord was home to J. W. Cannon and his executives, it has an impressive historic district just outside the downtown commercial district. These fine early twentieth-century houses speak to money the textile industry officials made. You won't find any houses like these in Kannapolis.

There's no denying that Concord's economic life revolves around NASCAR. Concord is home to the Charlotte Motor Speedway, a venerable stop on the NASCAR circuit. Built in 1959, it's a mile-and-a-half track which seats 115,000. If you add the number of people who can sit in the infield, they can sell 150,000 to 165,000 tickets to an event. For a NASCAR Sprint event, tickets cost as much as $135. An extra hundred bucks gets you a pass to visit the pits before the race.

The Charlotte Motor Speedway is more than a NASCAR track. It's a supermarket of racing. Besides holding six NASCAR events during the year, the track hosts two racing schools, where a civilian can drive, or be driven, around the track. In 2000, the Speedway built a dirt track across the street and, most recently, installed a four-lane, quarter-mile drag strip which can seat 30,000 spectators. Then they added condominiums in the mid-1980s so people could live out by the first turn. And lights were added in the early 1990s so they could hold night racing. It's hard to imagine, however, that even with all these recent upgrades, the track is not the top area tourist attraction. NASCAR can't outstrip American consumerism.

Besides the Charlotte Motor Speedway, the Concord Regional Airport is another Concord connection to NASCAR. The Concord Airport is often referred to as "NASCAR's airport" because so many race teams and sponsors use the airport to fly to racing venues around the country. It's North Carolina's busiest non-commercial airport and, from what I've been told, you don't want to try to get space at the airport on Thursdays or Sundays when the racing teams are leaving or returning from that week's race. Across the street from the airport is a 61,000-square-foot building which houses the NASCAR Research and Development Center. This place is top secret: NASCAR parts are inspected and safety issues developed here.

Progress and optimism abound in Concord and Kannapolis. The North Carolina Research Center is Kannapolis' future, while NASCAR and shopping will drive Concord's future. Yes, the future seems bright for these two suburban cities except for one thing—water.

Kannapolis and Concord are progressive, New South towns. Suburbs are located east and north of Charlotte, both are located in the Rocky River Basin. The Rocky River Basin doesn't have much water in it—at least not enough to sustain the anticipated growth of Kannapolis and Concord. Other suburbs, Charlotte's western suburbs, don't have that problem. These suburbs get their water from a different water basin, the Catawba River Basin.

The poor Catawba River starts out as a mountain stream in the Blue Ridge Mountains and flows from the mountains into the Piedmont. It continues past Charlotte into South Carolina where it's renamed the Wateree River. As is true of many American rivers, there's really not much natural flow left in the Catawba because it has been so heavily dammed. Today the Catawba is essentially eleven lakes with small connecting streams in between. Electricity is produced by manipulating the river's flow. The river has eleven hydro-electric plants, four coal-burning plants, two nuclear energy plants, and one gas power plant on it. These dams provide electricity to over a million people.

A population base of 1.3 million people relies on the Catawba for drinking water. The Catawba is also a garbage can. There are approximately 182 discharge permits which allow people to deposit waste (pollutants) into the river. Some are small, but some are substantial, such as Duke Energy's permits which allow coal ash in the river basin. Put all of these uses together, mix in a growing population base requiring still more water, add sprawling development along the lake front—and don't forget the significant droughts of the past decade—and the Catawba becomes designated as "the most endangered river in America."

The fight over the Catawba's water is complicated: Who is allowed to take the water, and what uses should have priority? Obviously drinking water is a primary use of the Catawba. After that it's a real war over whose use is more important. It's a fight between neighbors, towns, and elected officials, who know one another and often coordinate on other regional matters.

Mostly through conservation, the war has been resolved, but a second war goes on. South Carolina has asked the Supreme Court to apportion the Catawba River's water into two shares, North Carolina's share and South Carolina's share. We'll get to that later.

They Glue Lug Nuts on Wheels

Recently Charlotte has had two things going for it—banking and NASCAR. Banking is relatively new. In 1980, only one North Carolina bank was included in the top twenty-five banking companies in the United States, and that bank wasn't headquartered in Charlotte. Twenty-five years later, Charlotte was the headquarters for two of the country's largest banks, Bank of America and Wachovia. More than a regional force, Charlotte became a national banking center. It was no longer a way station between DC and Atlanta or anywhere else for that matter. It was a destination. At one time, one of every five jobs in Charlotte was finance-related. As the center of America's modern banking industry and with NASCAR's popularity, Charlotte became a big-time, "sho-nuff" city.

By the time I visited, the banking landscape in Charlotte was decidedly different. Wachovia had gone broke and been acquired in a government-engineered takeover by Wells Fargo, a California-based bank. Though still technically present in Charlotte, Wachovia's headquarters had been moved to California. All remaining operations were being consolidated elsewhere or converted to the Wells Fargo branches. Bank of America, while still the largest bank in the United States, was around only because it had received billions of dollars in government aid and loan guarantees to stay afloat after it had been deemed "too big to fail."

Talking to bankers about Charlotte didn't have much appeal. I figured that they wouldn't be too keen about discussing how they had gone to the head of the government aid line so they would ride out the bad times they caused. The correctness of my decision hit me the first night in Charlotte. At dinner, I overheard a group of bankers discussing the day's events. Now, I want to make it clear that I wasn't eavesdropping—not that I'm above doing so—but by the volume of their voices, this party of five bankers clearly wanted everyone in the restaurant to be a part of the conversation.

What a conversation—no talking football, basketball, or even NASCAR. I'd have been glad if they'd discussed interest rates, credit swaps, or even the latest rumors about office affairs. It was a classic large organization discussion about internal processes. The discussion spoke volumes about why large corporations don't really create jobs in our modern economy. Large corporations don't excel at much except corp-speak. Here are some direct quotes: "That matter was escalated to senior management" or "We are very solution-oriented as project managers" or "I'm going to use my facilitation skill-set to answer that."

No profanity, no ribald jokes, no snappy repartee. There was, however, a detailed discussion about how to deal with "derailing behavior in a meeting"—whatever that is. One fellow, obviously a senior one, advised his managers to confront the derailer by saying, "What I hear you saying is"—then telling the managers to repeat back to the derailer what the derailer had just said. Then the manager was advised to confront the derailer directly by saying, "You've been asked to take ownership of that problem," and then finally the manager should close by asking the derailer, "Will you do that?" And these people actually get paid a salary. No wonder their banks were broke.

I wanted to stay around long enough to hear how to deal with people who had been given home loans with monthly note payments in excess of half their take-home pay: "What I hear you saying is that you can't make your payment, but you don't want me to take ownership of your house." Just then, as they ordered, one banker said, "I'm going to have the steak. We're already $2 million over budget. What can the cost of the steak hurt?" I almost choked on my salad. I'd heard enough and decided to see a little different part of Charlotte.

Now to NASCAR, the real reason to be in Charlotte. NASCAR is to Charlotte like country music is to Nashville: It's everywhere. There are three NASCAR regional offices in the greater Charlotte area. One of the major NASCAR venues, the Charlotte Raceway, is some twenty-five miles up the freeway in Concord. The $100 million NASCAR Hall of Fame is located in downtown Charlotte. Virtually every NASCAR race team is headquartered in the Charlotte area, with almost seventy racing teams located in Mooresville, a suburb northwest of Charlotte. Consider that just one racing team, Joe Gibbs Racing, occupies 325,000 feet of office and shop space and employs 450 people, and you can see that NASCAR is a huge economic force in the region.

And the fans are passionate. I met the mayor of Concord, Scott Padgett, a huge race fan. I mentioned that I planned to take the Dale Trail in neighboring Kannapolis. I hedged as I spoke when I realized I had forgotten Dale's last name. I knew Yarborough wasn't quite right, but Earnhardt wasn't coming to mind. So I just ended my response by saying that I was going to see where "Dale what's his name" lived. The look of disgust on the Mayor's face made me glad that I hadn't been talking with the mayor of Kannapolis. His response might have been violent. Padgett spit out something to the effect that Earnhardt was "a beloved name around here." He then took pity on me and advised that Dale had a son who still races and that I should always refer to him as "Junior." If you refer to him as Dale Earnhardt Jr., most people will only respond, "You're not from around here are you?" Tips like that are good for a foreigner to know.

Now, if you follow NASCAR, skip the next few paragraphs because it's an introduction to a sport that I knew absolutely nothing about until I came to Charlotte.

NASCAR is the largest spectator sport in the United States. Their tracks can seat over 130,000 spectators for a race. The circuit of races draws ten million fans throughout the year. On a typical race day, you will see plenty of people swilling beer at 10:30 a.m. But the crowd is not a bunch of drunken "crackers": Nearly forty percent of the fan base is female and fifty-three percent of them are either professionals or managers. So it's obvious why NASCAR fanatics and their brand loyalty are attractive to advertisers.

There are really just a couple of things you need to know about NASCAR to understand it. In the stands, remember that NASCAR is the only major sporting event that still begins with a prayer. On the track, here's how the race works: Go real fast and make left turns.

NASCAR stands for National Association for Stock Car Auto Racing. Stock cars are unlike Indy cars. Indy cars are specifically designed and built for racing purposes. Originally, stock cars were regular cars fitted to race. Today's NASCAR automobiles may resemble the car you drive, but those looks are deceiving. Stock cars must comply with a complex set of regulations that ensure all vehicles operate substantially equally. These cars are technologically advanced vehicles and nothing like the ones that Detroit spits out for consumers. Modern stock cars still have a few quirks. For example, NASCAR still requires carburetors on its cars (while most family vehicles today are powered by fuel-injectors). NASCAR also restricts horsepower because modern technology can make cars that just go too fast. So the NASCAR officials decreed a few years back that a couple hundred miles an hour is fast enough.

NASCAR is the big time, the major leagues of racing. There are minor leagues, regional and local circuits, where local racers can compete for smaller dollars and get experience. Within NASCAR, though, there are three leagues or series: Sprint, Nationwide, and Craftsman Truck Series. Sprint and Nationwide run in conjunction with one another at the same track each week during the season. The Nationwide Series is a slightly smaller version of the Sprint Series. Most weekends the Nationwide series races on Saturday, while the Sprint Race takes place on Sunday. The Nationwide races are shorter and offer less purse money. The Sprint Series is a thirty-six-week race season. The purses for each race are in excess of $4 million.

Just as important as the purse money are points. Points earned during the first twenty-six races determine the rankings. Points are earned for the order of finish, leading the field during a lap, and leading a race for the most laps during the race. The top twelve point-earning teams become eligible for "the Chase," which occurs during the last ten races of the season. During the final ten weeks of the racing season, these driving teams have a race within a race. These teams battle for Chase points, in addition to prize money and the standard points awarded for every race. At the end of the Chase, a winner is crowned champion and gets even more money and a cup. Now, I've tried to figure out how they distribute money, but it's just too complicated and the points system is just a little less complicated. But it is big money. The 2012 points leader, Brad Kaslowski, won $6,231,925. And he wasn't even the top money winner that year.

While I was in Charlotte, I met Heath Cherry. Heath is an employee of Joe Gibbs Racing—more specifically, a crew member of Car #11, the Toyota Camry sponsored by Federal Express and driven by Denny Hamlin. I soon learned that all you have to say around here is: "Heath is with Car #11." Anyone familiar with NASCAR understands that Car #11 is the Toyota Camry driven by Denny Hamlin in the Sprint Series.

Heath Cherry out of uniform

Heath has two jobs for Joe Gibbs Racing. Most days he's the sponsor account director. As sponsor account director, he makes sure the sponsors are being taken care of—invited to various events and provided enough tickets to the race. That kind of stuff. On race days he works on the pit crew. He carries rear tires from the infield and mounts them on the race car during the pit stops. From seven to three on weekdays, he works with sponsors or potential sponsors. Later in the afternoon, he works out with the pit crew. When I say he works out, it's exactly that— he runs, lifts weights, and practices. The analogies between a pit crew and a football team are striking. The pit crew is a twelve-man crew, seven of whom hop over a wall to work a few seconds six to eight times each race. Each person has an assigned task that must work in coordination with the others if the play (pit stop) is going to be successful.

During the race, when Car #11 leaves the racetrack to make a pit stop, Denny Hamlin steers Car #11 toward a designated space. His crew jumps into action. Basically, they do collectively what a 1970s gas station attendant used to do for every motorist during a fill up: fill the tank with gas, clean the windshield, and make any adjustments the driver wants. In NASCAR subtle adjustments make a car run faster. Things like changing the tire pressure in response to the increasingly hotter track surface during a sunny southern afternoon, making the springs tighter by sticking a wedge into a spring, or adjusting the chassis all improve a car's handling and performance. Oh yeah, the pit crew usually changes the tires during a pit stop because a stock car runs more efficiently and faster on new tires. Since the NASCAR rules make cars substantially equal, a quicker pit stop is often the only difference in the order of finish. Yes sir, they do everything a 1970s gas station attendant did—plus change four tires. In less than thirteen seconds. Unbelievable.

Twenty years ago, most NASCAR pit crews consisted of moonlighting shop mechanics. In the early 1990s a pit stop took about twenty-four seconds. Racing teams started recruiting college athletes to join their pit crews. In retrospect, it only stands to reason that you would want physically fit young people lugging seventy-pound tires around in the summer heat or pirouetting around a race car with a full twelve-gallon gas can which weighs almost ninety pounds. But back then it was kind of a radical idea to use non-racing people on a pit crew.

Heath was in the vanguard of that innovation. He graduated from Lenoir-Rhyne College in nearby Hickory, North Carolina, after being a three-year starter on the school's NCAA Division II football team. While he was familiar with NASCAR from having grown up around Charlotte, he was not really a fan. In his words, he was "a ball and stick guy," who played team sports growing up. He had no pre-existing connections with any NASCAR teams.

A race team representative dropped a business card off with the football coaches during Heath's senior year, saying there might be a need for some athletes on their race teams. Sometime later, a coach mentioned the opportunity to Heath, and Heath contacted the representative. As a result, he landed a tryout with the Bill Elliott team. To prepare for the tryout, he practiced changing tires on his own Toyota truck. The tryouts went well, and he got the job.

In Heath's career, pit stop times have dropped from over twenty seconds to under thirteen seconds. Heath says that they've cracked eleven seconds in practice. To make these times, the pit team reviews film to see how to minimize movements, for instance, determining that kneeling on a particular knee allows for a better pivot, which makes a turn a fraction of a second quicker, which allows the tire carrier to return to the wall for the second tire a fraction of a second faster. Or determining whether that move interferes with another member's movements and slows the process down a fraction of a second.

For a pit stop to be successful, the jack man must raise the car with one crank of the twenty-pound jack, the tire changer should be able to unscrew five lug nuts in one second, and it should take Heath six-tenths to eight-tenths of a second to mount the tire before he races back to the wall to get the second tire and do it again. While the gas man and catch can man can't speed up their end of the pit stop, these team members certainly can slow down a pit stop by spilling the gas.

I knew NASCAR drivers were treated like rock stars. They make millions of dollars, have their own planes, and basically get treated like Charlotte's big-time bankers were treated before the financial meltdown. I didn't know whether that celebrity extended to the pit crews. Before meeting him I wondered whether Heath would arrive in a fancy car with slicked-back hair and designer sunglasses, but he was nothing like that. He was soft-spoken and modest, arriving in the same pickup truck he owned in college. The one he used to practice changing tires on before his first tryout.

Most surprising, he was small. Later, I looked up his NASCAR statistics, which said he was 5' 8" and 175 pounds. I would have guessed 5' 6" and no more than 155 pounds. My first impression was that he looked like a slightly over-sized jockey. That's a compliment because pound-for-pound jockeys are recognized as the strongest athletes in sports.

At thirty-five and in his thirteenth season, Heath's an old-timer who has seen a lot of changes, most positive. Rather than driving to races, he gets on a private jet early on race Sundays to fly to the race. He returns the same way so that his race day is now only 18–20 hours long. (The day may take a little longer if the crew gets delayed by the post-race traffic.) During his tenure, competition for pit crew jobs has gotten significantly more fierce. Rather than leaving business cards at small colleges, race teams visit private schools that have popped up especially to train pit crew members. If Heath slows down or gets injured, there's a long line of people ready to take his job.

One of his pit crew jobs is gluing the lug nuts to the wheels. A few hours before the race, a pit crew member begins gluing lug nuts to the set of wheels to be used during the first pit stop. Gluing the lug nuts to the wheel beforehand saves time during the pit stop. There's an art to it. Pit crew members try to make sure the lug nuts are glued about three hours before the pit stop. If the glue is allowed to set longer, it becomes brittle and the lug nuts can break off. If the glue is applied too late, it doesn't have time to set and is too gooey. Gooey lug nuts slow down the process of attaching the wheel to the car. As the race progresses, Heath times the preparation of the next set of tires for the next pit stop. He then prepares himself for the next time he scrambles over the wall and sprints to the car carrying a seventy-pound tire. He races to outperform the team in the next space by a fraction of a second so that he can get Car #11 out of the pits a tiny bit faster.

Ella May's Ghost

Gastonia was the third former mill town on Jonathan Daniels' Journey. Closer geographically to downtown Charlotte than Concord and Kannapolis, it's been a part of the Charlotte metro area longer. That relationship hasn't been so positive for Gastonia. Let's put it this way, modern Gastonia could be a finalist in a contest for the Piedmont town with the most parking lot surface. In short, Gastonia has been bypassed.

When Daniels passed through in the mid-1930s, Gastonia was famous for its labor unrest. In 1934, during what later became known as the General Strike of 1934, Gastonia's main street was the location of the labor movement's largest southern protest march. Before the general strike, a strike at Gastonia's Loray Mill had made national news, and its aftermath made Ella May Wiggins a labor martyr.

Modern Gastonia retains few signs of the General Strike of 1934, of Loray Mill, or of Ella May Wiggins. Downtown Gastonia sits on the top of a hill. As you leave downtown on the old highway, you go downhill. On the left, a few blocks from downtown sits the Loray Mill, one of the most famous southern textile mills eighty years ago. A deteriorating hulk full of broken windows surrounded by large cracked asphalt and weed-filled parking lots, it's no longer impressive.

When it was built in 1900, the Loray Mill was the largest mill in the South—a six-story behemoth with 350,000 square feet of interior space. It was the first "million dollar mill" built in the South by northern interests seeking to take advantage of the cheaper labor force. It immediately drew the organizing interest of the labor unions, and attempts at organizing Loray's labor force began almost immediately. The first strike occurred by 1907.

Loray Mill today, in search of a new use

In 1921, the mill expanded with an 85,000-square-foot addition so it could produce cord for tires for the automotive industry. By the late 1920s, the Loray Mill was owned by people from Rhode Island. They instituted the "stretch-out." A stretch-out occurs when management requires production-based workers to "stretch-out" and work more machines or work machines faster to produce more without a corresponding increase in wages. Responding to a stretch-out announcement, the American Communist Party targeted the Loray Mill for a strike.

The Loray Strike provided a perfect setting for an epic event. Classic characters were present: out-of-state mill owners, exploited workers working longer hours for less money, mothers and their children walking a picket line, communists, and law enforcement officials harassing the strikers and their families.

The 1929 strike began when management fired five people for engaging in union activity. Labor walked out. Management refused to negotiate, but within a few weeks they had the mill back running with former strikers and replacement workers. Management then evicted strikers from the mill-owned housing. The ousted strikers began a tent city at the edge of town and maintained the picket line in front of the mill. The picket line was "manned" mostly by women and children because the men went elsewhere to find work. On June 7, 1929, a private security force attacked and broke up the picket line. Later in the day, Gastonia's police chief and his deputies went to the tent village, and a shoot-out followed between the police and the strikers. In this skirmish, the police chief was killed. Authorities rounded up seventy-one people and ultimately tried sixteen union members for murder. After a mistrial was declared on the murder charges, things got worse.

Private security forces began harassing strikers and running them out of town. One unionist of particular attention to the vigilantes was a woman, Ella May Wiggins. Ella May was an uneducated hill person who had moved to the Piedmont with her husband to work the mills. Her husband abandoned her, and she began working nights as a spinner in the mills to support nine children, earning about nine dollars a week. Her brood came down with the whooping cough, and she asked to be transferred to the day shift so she could tend to her children. When this was refused, she quit and, with no money for medicine, four of her children died. Radicalized, a few months later, she joined the union. Over the next few years, she became a union organizer and the union's bookkeeper. She also became versed in strike tactics. She had a talent for one particular tactic: the protest ballad. Singing ballads gave strikers an effective outlet for their discontent. As the strike's leading balladeer, Ella May became notorious: one of her ballads concerned the death of Chief Aderholt; another celebrated the strikers being released from jail in June. Sung to familiar tunes, these ballads were important in maintaining morale.

On September 14, 1929, unknown assailants attacked a truck carrying twenty-two strikers on the way to a rally in Gastonia. Ella May Wiggins was shot in the chest and died at the scene. The strike collapsed shortly thereafter. No one was ever convicted of her murder, although it occurred in broad daylight in front of dozens of witnesses. Five men later were charged. They were found not guilty after a jury deliberated less than thirty minutes.

For a short time, Ella May was a national labor martyr. At her funeral, her most popular ballad, "The Mill Mother's Lament," was played:

We kiss our children good-bye,
While we slave for the bosses,
Our children scream and cry.

And when we draw our money,
Our grocery bills to pay,
Not a cent to spend for clothing,
Not a cent to lay away.

And on that very evening
Our little son will say:
"I need some shoes, Mother,
And so does Sister May."

How it grieves the heart of a mother,
You everyone must know.
But we can't buy for our children,
Our wages are too low.

Now listen to the workers
Both women and you men
Let's win for them the victory
I'm sure twill be no sin.

In death, Ella May made the cover of national magazines.

The Loray Mill survived Ella May's killing but not the stock market crash. Within a year of Ella May's death, the mill filed for bankruptcy. By 1936, the Loray was back in operation as a Firestone tire plant. It continued to kick out tires until 1992 when it closed. It has not been in operation since.

LABOR DEFENDER

Oct. 1929   10¢

ELLA MAY—
MARTYR FOR AN ORGANIZED SOUTH

Ella May Wiggins (courtesy of the University of North Carolina at Asheville)

A dozen years after the tire plant folded, developers tried to re-develop the Loray. But it's a big building in a not-so-nice part of town. Re-developing what once was the largest single mill in North Carolina would be difficult. It would require finding lots of funding sources and coordinating mixed uses to create a viable twenty-first-century project. An Atlanta developer proposed turning the half million square feet of former mill space into a mixed use project which would include 172 apartments, office space for private business, office space for the city and county, self-storage space, and 40,000 square feet of school space for a charter school. The developer also promised to develop a number of market-rate condominium units.

Things looked promising for a revitalized Loray until 2008. When funding looked ready, Wachovia Bank, which had committed to be one of the primary funders, collapsed. Wells Fargo Bank took over Wachovia and pulled its financing commitment. This stopped the project. In June 2012, the developers announced that they had procured financing for a scaled-back project—190 loft-style apartments. However, many months later, construction has yet to start. You have to wonder whether the ghost of Ella May is exacting her revenge.

America's First Civil War Battle

I left the city behind. Besides the traffic, one of the problems of spending a few days in a metropolitan area is how quickly you lose connection with the land. Charlotte is part of the Piedmont, but traveling around in the center of the city, you lose appreciation of the area's natural beauty. Once you leave the city's tall buildings and concrete, the natural beauty of the Piedmont reintroduces itself with rolling green hills and azure sky. Soon I exited the interstate at the Kings Mountain Military Park exit. This National Park memorializes the Revolutionary War battle fought here.

About three miles from the park is a restaurant located in a former convenience store—Ronda's Kitchen—"Come Hungry and Leave Hooked."

Ronda's has only five booths and two tables; they must do a great carry-out business. Late on a Saturday afternoon, a dozen or more people picked up carry-out orders, while only three booths housed diners. Ronda's restaurant is a family operation. The owner's wife, Ronda, handles the cash register. Their daughter is a waitress. And the owner-father's job is to make sure everyone is happy. His job isn't very difficult because the hamburgers are handmade, as are the onion rings. And the fried fish is good.

The menu offers shrimp baskets—fantail shrimp, calabash shrimp, and green shrimp. I had never heard of shrimp with those names. Since I had been headed southwest for a while, I didn't know how far Ronda's was from the coast. Leery of seafood dishes offered by inland restaurants, I questioned Ronda about her shrimp: Were they local shrimp? Georgia shrimp? Or were they from the Gulf? Really, were green shrimp actually green or just prepared that way? Inquiring minds wanted to know.

Ronda's Kitchen near Kings Mountain

Ronda was hazy about the origin of her shrimp, but she cheerfully assured me they were all prepared the same way—fried. Most important, the green shrimp didn't start out or finish green. The only distinction between dishes was the size of the shrimp. The fantail shrimp were the smallest and the green were the largest, with calabash somewhere in between. I knew Ronda was giving me her best information so I ordered the green shrimp. Ronda then informed me they were out of green shrimp. I asked if she had any calabash. She said yes. So I settled on a basket of them.

Ronda said it would be awhile before my order was ready, so I sat at one of the two tables. This was small-town America at its best. Everyone entered with a smile and said hello to everyone but me, the stranger. Everyone spoke with a soft Carolina lilt: "fiine jes fine—hi u doowin." Familiar discussions centered mainly on who was hiring and the next day's NASCAR race. Economic opportunities may be plentiful in the city but not so much here. The calabash shrimp basket came soon enough, and I directed my attention toward it. Afterward I needed to walk off the meal of calabash shrimp, french fries, and iced tea. Luckily, I was only minutes from the Military Park at Kings Mountain.

The park has been in public ownership for over 100 years, and except for the paved road, there is no evidence of the twentieth century and little of the nineteenth.

Don't feel bad if you're not familiar with the story of the Battle of Kings Mountain. It's not as well known as Revolutionary War battles like Concord, Saratoga, and Valley Forge fought up north. But make no mistake, Kings Mountain was an important battle, a true turning point in the war. Many scholars consider it the single most important battle of the war. It stopped the British advance and started the series of events which led directly to the Redcoat surrender at Yorktown. Without the victory at Kings Mountain, the war could have gone in a decidedly different direction. The English could have sued for peace, content with keeping the southern colonies and retaining the output from their tobacco, cotton, rice, and indigo plantations. So there would have been no United States— just some Yankee states and Britain's southern colonies.

In the early years of the revolution, the War for Independence in the Carolinas had the feel of a civil war. There was no invading English army and little formal fighting. Many locals were sympathetic to the Crown. These sympathizers, Tories, outnumbered the colonial patriots who were known as Whigs. The Whigs, under the command of Francis Marion and Thomas Sumter, engaged in guerrilla activities harassing the Crown's men. The Crown's forces, mainly Tory militia, dealt with these guerrilla activities by summarily hanging "traitors" and getting their Indian allies to kill women and children back home. These harsh responses caused a number of Tories and undecideds to move into the patriot camp.

In May of 1780, Charleston fell to the British, and within weeks the British army subdued most of South Carolina; the Redcoats swept into

Charlotte ready to neutralize North Carolina. The British organized the area Tories into a militia under the command of a Scotsman, Major Patrick Ferguson. In September 1780, this militia chased the patriots up into the mountains of North Carolina where Ferguson issued an ultimatum to the patriots. If they did not give up opposition, he would "march his army over the mountains, hang their leaders, and lay waste their country with fire and sword."

In response, these backwoodsmen decided to take the fight to Ferguson and his troops. Beginning in southwestern Virginia, 200 militiamen crossed into Tennessee and picked up 500 militiamen in present-day Tennessee. As they marched over the mountains of North Carolina, more men responded to the call to arms. A few days later, this militia now called the "overmountain men" reached the Carolina Piedmont almost 1,400 men strong. When news of these movements reached Ferguson, he posted another message to the area colonists:

> Gentlemen: Unless you wish to be eat up by an inundation of barbarians, who have begun by murdering an unarmed son before the aged father, and afterwards lopped off his arms, and who by their shocking cruelties and irregularities, give the best proof of their cowardice and want of discipline, I say, if you wish to be pinioned, robbed, and murdered, and see your wives and daughters, in four days, abused by the dregs of mankind—in short, if you wish or deserve to bear the name of men, grasp your arms in a moment and run to camp.
>
> The backwater men have crossed the mountains; McDowell, Hampton, Shelby, and Cleveland are at their head, so that you know what you have to depend upon. If you choose to be pissed upon forever and ever by a set of mongrels, say so at once, and let your women turn their backs upon you, and look out for real men to protect them.
>
> —Pat Ferguson, Major, Seventy-first Regiment.

This message, presumably, was an attempt to recruit more Tories. To say that the message did not have its desired effect is an understatement. On October 6, the backwoods group combined with militia from South Carolina and Georgia. Speed and surprise were essential to the mission's success. The American militia sent a group of 900 men racing through the night to surround Ferguson's force at Kings Mountain before he could rejoin Lord Cornwallis in Charlotte. These forces surrounded and then surprised the Tories and destroyed them in about an hour's time. Of the 1,050 men under Ferguson's command, at least 250 died in battle and the rest were captured. The victory was so complete that, after receiving news of Ferguson's defeat, Cornwallis left Charlotte, the next step in a series which ultimately led to his surrender at Yorktown.

Except for Major Ferguson, all of the combatants at Kings Mountain were Americans—brother against brother, neighbor against neighbor—America's first civil war battle. The day after the battle the families of the fallen, many of whom were neighbors, came to view the carnage. In the weeks after the battle, many Tories changed sides and fought with the Americans. Others left the Piedmont.

One little postscript: The route the Overmountain men took through the Blue Ridge Mountains to catch Major Ferguson is now a National Historic Trail. It starts in Abingdon, Virginia, continues through extreme eastern Tennessee, over the high mountains in North Carolina, and down to the Carolina Piedmont where it terminates at Kings Mountain. Each year in September, re-enactors retrace the trek of these mountain men racing to catch their countrymen in Kings Mountain. The trail is now known as the Overmountain Victory National Historic Trail.

Hub-Bub in the Hub City

Spartanburg, South Carolina, is edgy. Not at all what I thought I would find here in upstate South Carolina. Spartanburg lies a few miles from the intersection of Interstate 85 and Interstate 26 some seventy-five miles west of Charlotte and thirty-five miles from the North Carolina state line. Some of Spartanburg's edginess may come from directional confusion. Generally, interstate highways ending in even numbers run east/west, while those with odd numbers go north/south. But going from Spartanburg west to Atlanta requires taking I-85. But if you want to go north to Asheville, North Carolina, or south to Charleston, South Carolina, take I-26.

Coming into Spartanburg from the interstate, you can't help but notice the sprawl. Technically, it's not urban sprawl because Spartanburg isn't big enough to qualify as urban. Local musician Baker Maultsby, who wrote—but sadly did not become famous for—such songs as "Bingo=Sin" and "Fatback & Egg on Bun," captures these changes to Spartanburg and other small towns with his song "Four Wal-Marts":

> We got four Wal-Marts
> In the Tri-county area
> An outlet mall
> It's bargain hysteria

We got a BP with a cappuccino machine
An Exxon attached to a Dairy Queen
Cause it's small town, mall town America
It's small town America

Strip malls on both sides of the street
Asphalt on top of concrete

Downtown Spartanburg is picturesque, sitting on high ground, with rolling hills in the background. Traffic slows when the five-lane road ends at the old downtown. The corporate headquarters of Extended Stay Hotels and Advance America anchor the west (or is it the north?) side of Morgan Square, the town center.

Just south (or is it east?) of Morgan Square is the home of Hub Culture, as well as its subsidiaries, Hub-Bub and the Hub City Writers Project. Spartanburg was called Hub City in the early twentieth century because a number of railroad lines intersected there, and these organizations take their names from the old nickname.

The Hub City Writers Project started in 1995. Three writers, who hung out in one of Spartanburg's first coffee shops, established it to support local writers. The organization was patterned on the Depression-era Federal Writers' Project—but without any federal funding. The Hub City Writers Project began with a collection of first-person essays about living in Spartanburg. To finance the book's publication, these three writers solicited $100 contributions from local residents. When they secured enough money to print the book, they threw a party at the deteriorating train station to celebrate. They booked a local band, and 1,500 people showed up. The book was a success and the party was, too. Not only was it a good party, but partying at the old train station kick-started efforts to restore the derelict building, which now houses the Spartanburg Visitors and Convention Bureau.

For years, the Hub City Writers Project operated from Betsy Teter's kitchen table. The group has published almost 250 authors to date, with no signs of slowing down. While they once struggled to produce one or two books a year, now they do five. One of the three founding members, Betsy is now the executive director. When I visited, she had an office (or at least a desk) on the second floor of their 1928 building which originally housed the Spartanburg Nash Rambler Dealership. The office was shared with eight or nine employees of the umbrella organization called Hub Culture and had an art exhibition space. The first floor is a multipurpose venue for events.

Betsy Teter, Hub Culture's CEO

The Hub Culture building is three stories tall—big time in a small town. Hub Culture is advertised as the "frontline of creative culture in Spartanburg." Betsy told me that they hold 100 music, film, and literary events a year in the building.

The third floor houses one of Hub Culture's new programs: Artists in Residence. Each year, four young, aspiring artists are selected to the program—three visual artists and one writer. Each receives a free apart- ment, studio space, and a stipend. To qualify, the artist must be single, under thirty years of age, and willing to help out at Hub Culture doing things such as taking tickets or pouring drinks at Hub events. Artists come from other parts of the country: a writer from Kansas; a printmaker from Louisville, Kentucky; and two painters from north of the Mason/Dixon Line. Betsy reports that this program has been a great success, and they have 180 applicants for next year's class.

Hub Culture's building

I asked if any stay in the area, and she replied that two recent former AIRs (artists in residence) received adjunct positions at one of the six Spartanburg colleges. She then mentioned that three of these six colleges have creative writing programs. Three college-level creative writing courses in a town of 40,000 people—I think that may be an answer to the question of how a writers' project has flourished in Spartanburg. One local college, Wofford College, offered a year-long course called "Cornbread & Sushi." During the fall semester, students read and discussed southern writings in a formal classroom setting. In a short January term, they traveled throughout the South eating, visiting authors, and visiting sites related to southern authors. During the spring semester, the students write, edit, and publish a large paperback book of the essays.

Spartanburg's economy evidently is tough on small, independent coffee shops, as they open and close periodically. The Hub-Bubians believed that this trend might change if a coffee shop was operated in conjunction with a non-profit bookstore with volunteer staffing. To that end, they cut a deal with the local Masons to lease the ground floor of the Masonic Temple a few blocks away. (The Masons still occupy of the top two floors.) The Hub-Bubians installed a coffee shop on one side and a bookstore on the other. One feature of this bookstore is a central display titled "What Spartanburg Reads," where local leaders and readers recommend books. The offices of the Writers Project have moved to the Masonic Temple building two blocks west—or is it north? If I had seen a sign toward Interstate 26, I could tell you which.

Downtown New South

Greenville, South Carolina, is a surprisingly large southern town with a stated population of 71,000. Apparently South Carolina has stringent laws concerning annexation, so a lot of development has occurred outside of Greenville proper. Greenville's population figures don't really reflect its metropolitan area or character. The metro area is estimated to be over 600,000. Neither of these population figures prepared me for the sight of downtown Greenville on a late winter Saturday night.

So let me set it up. I was ten or twelve miles away from downtown Greenville a few minutes before 8:00 on an early spring Saturday evening. Tired and hungry, I made a strategic decision to push on to the Hotel Poinsett where I had a room reserved for the night. I figured that it would take less than fifteen minutes to arrive at the hotel. After a quick check-in, I would find something to eat. In a town of 71,000, what could go wrong? I was less than a mile from my destination when my GPS directed me to turn left onto Main Street. I couldn't make the turn onto Main Street because it was barricaded and closed to vehicular traffic. As I drove past Main Street, I noticed that stores were open and groups of people walked down the middle of the street. I didn't think too much about the situation until I tried to make two left turns to return to Main Street. Traffic toward Main Street was snarled, so I continued on in the dark, looking for a way to get back on Main with the GPS voice repeating "recalculating" every thirty seconds.

One problem was that I was in a strange city after dark. The one-way streets were a compounding problem. I knew I was only a few blocks from the hotel. But every time I found a one-way street taking me back to Main Street, it was completely backed up—gridlocked in downtown Greenville on a Saturday evening. After waiting through one light, I finally pushed my way onto the cross street and traveled two blocks back to Main where I faced an even bigger line of traffic.

It took almost thirty minutes to negotiate the last few blocks to the hotel. Despite my hunger, I was now curious about the downtown crowd. At the check-in desk, I inquired about the special event causing the traffic jam. The nice receptionist looked surprised at my question and said that nothing special was going on but surmised, "It's just the first nice weekend evening in a while and people are out to enjoy it." I found later that her statement was slightly inaccurate because the University of South Carolina Gamecocks and the Clemson Tigers had their annual rivalry baseball game at nearby Fluor Field. (Fluor Field is a great minor league baseball park, a smaller version of Fenway Park complete with its own "Green Monster.") But the game didn't explain the traffic problem because the ball park is located a few miles on the other side of downtown from where I was, and, more importantly, it was being played as I arrived.

I hit Main Street to see what was happening. At 9:00 on a Saturday night, there were people everywhere—families with children, groups of young people hanging around outside of some stores, old people shopping—but there didn't seem to be anything special happening. A few blocks later, I arrived at a public park, Falls Park on the Reedy River. I couldn't say when I last went into a public park after dark, but it's been a long time. I saw fairly regular-looking people making the turn into the park right in front of me, so I decided to follow them. After I turned, I saw a sign that I'd never seen before.

I must admit that my initial thought was not a good one. The sign was there either to hassle bored, young Greenvillians with nothing better to do, or there was a gang problem. Either prospect made me leery of walking through a public park in a strange place after dark. But I continued into the park. I soon saw old people strolling through the park, and moments later families with young children in strollers, even families with teenagers. Can you imagine a father with three teenagers on Saturday night saying, "Come on, kids. Let's get your mother and all go downtown and see what's happenin' at the Falls Park." Or as they would more likely say around here: "Hey y'all—go get Momma, 'cause we're gowen to the Park."

Park sign in Greenville

Late the next morning, I headed to the closest coffee shop on Main Street and struck up a conversation with Tre, the counter person. Tre related that he came to Greenville from Charleston for college. He loved the area and decided to stay. A bright, articulate young man, he laughed when I asked if he had gone to school at Bob Jones University. Bob Jones is the conservative university which proudly advertises that forty percent of the student body was home-schooled. It was pretty obvious: Tre didn't look like a Bob Jones alumnus.

Tre, serving coffee in Greenville

Tre explained that Main Street Greenville was "extremely cool." The extreme coolness arises from the diverse cultures which exist here. (When was the last time you heard that about a southern town?) In the past few years, the Greenville area had developed significant Hispanic, Asian, and European communities along with the traditional African-American and white ones. "The blend is pretty cool," he said. He noted that within a few blocks, downtown Greenville offers Thai, Indonesian, Green, Italian, Asian, sushi, and Dutch food—not bad for a town of 70,000. "It's all on Main Street," Tre said. With coffee in hand, I strolled down Main Street on a Sunday morning.

It was a lot quieter on Sunday morning than it had been on Saturday night. But there were still a lot of people walking on Main Street. In the daylight, I retraced my route from the night before. The Park at Reedy River is a great example of the change in Greenville. Until some fifteen years ago, the Reedy River was a garbage dump with trash and whiskey bottles strewn along the banks. Years before that, Reedy was little more than an exhaust system for the textile mills located on the banks. During those years, the color of Reedy reflected the color the local dye plant had used that day. The dye plant is gone, replaced with condos and a new hotel by the river rapids. As I left downtown Greenville, another crowd was forming on the river bank. A band was setting up to play for the street festival that afternoon. I wished I could stay.

Rapids of the Reedy River in Greenville

Jerusalem Artichokes
and Robert Kennedy

The ambient temperature changes dramatically where the Carolina Piedmont gives way to the Appalachian Mountains. It is estimated that temperature changes three degrees for every thousand feet of elevation change. So Greenville, which sits at about a thousand feet above sea level, is much hotter and more humid than the mountain towns as close as forty miles away because the nearby mountain towns sit over 3,000 feet above sea level. In early spring, when it's pleasantly warm in Greenville, the mountains are chilly. In July and August, when Greenville reaches 100 degrees with plenty of humidity, the dry, cooler mountain air is a welcome respite.

The Blythe Shoals Produce store stands in the shadows of the mountains, a few miles from Caesar's Head State Park. A former gas station, it has signage that advertises "Produce, Homemade Can Goods and Boiled Peanuts"—what a place. The sign outside doesn't even begin to describe the food inside.

Walking up to the store, even the untrained eye can tell that Blythe Shoals Produce isn't a tourist establishment. The owner was out front talking with a friend and just waved as I walked from my car and into the store. To say he was casually dressed would be an understatement. He was wearing an old plaid shirt and cuffed blue jeans that needed to be washed. His face hadn't seen a razor blade for a few days. I followed him inside the store and started looking around. Boiled peanuts, known as "Piedmont caviar," are sold here. Besides boiled (pronounced "bawled"), there were also roasted or fried peanuts. I'd never heard of fried peanuts. Lucky for me the owner's friend left and he wandered in to see how I was doing. The owner introduced himself. He spoke with a classic southern drawl and gave me his name, a classic "cracker" name, Lester Galloway. Since I was the only customer around, I peppered Lester with questions. Frying peanuts in their shell lends credence to the notion that southerners will fry anything. However, as Lester explained, the nut itself doesn't get fried in the process, just the shell. He offered me a handful and said they're a real treat: "Jes pop 'em in yo mouth, shell and all. If'n you don't eat the shell, fyin 'em ain't worth it." Lester continued to explain that fried peanuts are a low country delicacy brought to the Hill Country by tourists. "The first time I saw dem people from Chaarlston popping them things in—shell and all—I thought they dun come from goats."

Besides peanuts, Blythe Shoals Produce carries all types of canned goods: pear butter, sweet potato butter, very berry butter, peach jelly, muscadine jelly, banana strawberry jelly—and that's just listing items from a small portion of two of the five shelves of canned goods that Lester carries. One jar simply said, "Pumpkin." I asked if it was a type of jelly and Lester patiently replied, "No it's just pumpkin; the parts you want if you were to make pumpkin pie."

He also carries a full line of pork rinds—plain, sour cream-n-onion, and vinegar-n-salt. He has ciders to drink—apple, blueberry, and the ever favorite muscadine. The brittles were my favorite—peanut, cashew, and bee. "Bee brittle?" I asked. "Yeah, dey's got honey in 'em. Real good, too. You ought to try 'em." So I did. The rest of the afternoon, I munched on a bag of fried peanuts and bee brittle. Munched to excess, I should mention. Fried peanuts are addictive.

But I'm getting ahead of myself. After I bought my provisions, Lester gave me a tour of his establishment—out front he has empty wooden shelving for the vegetables—"too early for 'em now." Over to one side, he showed me a wooden box on the ground with a wire bottom where he had been working as I arrived. I asked what those little brown root-like things were. He said, "Thay's Jerusalem artichokes. Ain't you ever seen Jerusalem artichokes afore?" I replied that I had not ever heard of them, let alone seen them before, and that I had no idea what they were. He explained that they weren't real artichokes but tubers, like Irish potatoes. "It's a health food," he said. With that, we went back inside so he could show me a health food catalogue and how much "them scudders" cost if you ordered them. He showed me the catalogue to prove his point. Lester doesn't order them but grows them out back. I asked to see his field while he explained the process of growing Jerusalem artichokes. He was happy to oblige.

Lester and his canned goods

After touring his garden, we returned to my car. I had been talking with Lester over thirty minutes by that time. I felt like we had become friends and perhaps I could ask more personal questions. I asked him about his business prospects. He said that last year hadn't been a good one, that he'd lost money. He admitted, "I can't have another year like last year or I'll have to give it up." Thinking back to the bankers in Charlotte and how they were buying steaks even though they were two million over budget, I refrained from asking if he was still ordering steak when he went out to eat. After a few more minutes, I left this friendly unshaven shopkeeper and Jerusalem artichoke farmer and headed toward the mountains.

How does Robert Kennedy figure in this story? After being in South Carolina, perhaps the most Republican state in the Union, the most memorable thing about Blythe Shoals Produce is the sign that hangs by the front door:

Bobby's admonition

Some men see things as they are and say, why.
I dream things that never were and say, why not.

— Robert Kennedy

The Mountains

M unching fried peanuts as I left Lester's place, I looked at the straight, flat highway ahead of me. A few miles from Lester's place, a dramatic rock outcropping known as Caesar's Head came into clear view. Apparently this rock feature looked to early travelers like Julius Caesar's profile protruding from the mountain, thus the name. Caesar's Head marks the beginning of the Blue Ridge Escarpment and the Appalachian Mountains. As you head into the mountains, the road, the land, and the people change. No more straight roads for a while.

I contemplated leaving the Piedmont portion of the Journey. Jonathan Daniels observed when he passed through here: "The road rose almost precipitously from Greenville. From making textiles the country turns abruptly to taking tourists for a living."

Many things have changed in the years since Jonathan Daniels made that observation. The textile industry no longer dominates the Piedmont; computer-making, car-making, and banking have taken the place of textiles. But tourism remains the engine of the rocky North Carolina mountain country.

In the 1930s, Caesar's Head was the site of a 100-room hotel which burned in 1954. It now is an 11,000-acre state park. The state park headquarters is built on the grounds of the old hotel and has the best views. The southern view from the park headquarters is dramatic: The Piedmont looks like a broad valley below. The park has fifty miles of hiking trails. It is also known as one of the best places to watch hawks. In the fall, migrating hawks take to riding the thermal updrafts at the base of the escarpment.

Ascending to Caesar's Head, the road changes. No longer are there places to pass, and one camper van can create a long line of traffic as it struggles to negotiate the severe curves. Travel feels much more isolated. Trees canopy the roadway and block the afternoon sun, which sets sooner behind the high hills. It gets dark early in the mountains.

Local legend has it that the highway from Caesar's Head to Brevard was originally cut by Solomon Jones, a local farmer. Farmer Jones would take his pig, Sue, up the mountain and would chop a path down the mountain on the route the pig took returning home. Eventually, Solomon and Sue's trail linked Transylvania County, North Carolina, with the Caesar's Head area.

At the outskirts of Brevard, a mountain town of fewer than 7,500 people, a historic marker notes that the site of the Walton War lies just to the east. Not so much a war as a battle, the Walton War might well count as America's second civil war battle—the first one being the battle of Kings Mountain during the American Revolution. In the early nineteenth century, the states of Georgia and North Carolina tussled over a twelve-mile strip of land where present-day Georgia, South Carolina, and North Carolina join. Under a 1798 treaty, the Cherokee Indians abandoned some land which everyone erroneously thought had once been part of South Carolina. In 1802, Congress gave this land to Georgia and it became Walton County, Georgia. The land actually lay north of the 35th latitude, the true boundary between North and South Carolina, so it should have been North Carolina's land all along. When peaceful efforts to address the surveying error failed, North Carolina called out its militia to oust the Georgia government from the area.

Militia from the two states met at McGaha Branch just outside of Brevard's present city limits. The North Carolina militia killed an unknown number of Georgians and took about twenty-five prisoners. The Georgia survivors later re-engaged the North Carolina militia some three miles away. Here, the rest of the Georgia forces were either shot or taken prisoner. The North Carolinians suffered only one casualty in the fracas. After that beating, Georgia made no serious attempt to retake the area.

Many years later, Georgia reignited the dispute. In 1971, a Georgia legislative commission claimed that the accepted boundary was in error. The Georgia commission claimed that the state line was actually a mile or more south of the 35th parallel and indicated that it should get that land back. In response, the North Carolina legislature passed a joint resolution authorizing the governor to mobilize their state militia once again to "protect, defend and hold inviolate the territorial border of North Carolina against the spurious claims by the State of Georgia." Neither state took any further action.

Now that you know the extent to which North Carolinians will battle their neighbors in property disputes, you get a whole new appreciation for Brevard's fight to be claimed the "White Squirrel Capital of the World." According to local history, white squirrels came to Brevard when a carnival truck overturned near Brevard in 1949. The squirrels escaped and soon bred in the wild. Some forty years later, the Brevard City Council voted to declare Brevard a sanctuary for these little creatures. For whatever reason, these albino-looking squirrels roam all over Brevard. They aren't really albino, though. They have a white coat but dark eyes. While I didn't see any of them running around the park, versions of them abound in the local gift shops. Despite Brevard's history with this furry creature, other places—Marionville, Missouri; Kenton, Tennessee; Olney, Illinois; and a town in Canada—have the temerity to claim the title of White Squirrel Capital.

In 2005, the mayor of Brevard challenged these other towns to debate their claims during Brevard's annual festival honoring the little varmint. As Mayor Harris said, "I will have an open mike here during the White Squirrel Festival and I challenge any other city to send their mayor to debate the hard facts." As Mayor Harris sees it, the "hard facts" backing Brevard's claim are these:

> The largest white squirrel population (25%-30% of their squirrels are white)
> Real white squirrels—no albinos need apply
> A festival dedicated solely to white squirrels each Memorial Day weekend
> A commissioned white squirrel marble sculpture in front of city hall
> An official white squirrel weather vane at the county courthouse

A White Squirrel Shoppe on Main Street
An official white squirrel theme song
An official White Squirrel Day
The national headquarters of the White Squirrel Research Institute
Future home of the international White Squirrel Museum

No mayor accepted Brevard's challenge. Perhaps they were afraid that the North Carolina militia would be called up to protect Brevard's honor.

Cashiers

I t's not a mountaintop, but a valley. It's not an incorporated town, but a community. It's not pronounced "Cashears" but "Cashurs." Despite its strange name, Cashiers—along with its neighbor town, Highlands— caters to the high end of the mountain tourist trade.

The name Cashiers is derived from a bull owned by South Carolina's most famous citizen, General Wade Hampton. A Civil War hero at First Manassas, Hampton later became South Carolina's governor and finally its senator. General Hampton owned most of the land in the valley. He also owned two bulls, Brutus and Cassius. Cassius ran away, got tangled up in a thicket, and died. In the beast's honor, Hampton named the valley after it. Years later, when map-makers came through and asked the natives the valley's name, due to the local twang, the Roman name Cassius was understood and recorded by the cartographers as "Cashurs."

Even more than Brevard, Cashiers relies on the tourist trade. During the summer months, it's crowded, but during the cold weather, it's very isolated. Cashiers has about one thousand year-round residents. In summer, the local population swells to ten to fifteen times that number. Making a left turn onto U.S. Highway 64 is a five-to-ten minute endeavor because of traffic congestion. But in the winter, with only an occasional vehicle on the highway, ingress and egress is easy.

A few days before I arrived, a storm had come through. The mountains are a collection of mini-environments strung out through the hills, so storms are very different weather events from town to town. Cashiers had received rain mixed with ice. A few miles south of Cashiers at the South Carolina border, the storm had been much worse because the precipitation was mostly ice. In fact, the roads to the south were still closed. Back east in Brevard, the storm brought snow but no ice, and north of Cashiers, virtually no snow or ice fell. It was just rain.

The roads around Cashiers were clear and drivable, but piles of branches downed by ice were everywhere. Entrance to the High Hampton Inn and Country Club lies about a mile from Cashiers' main intersection. It was late afternoon, and I wasn't really prepared for the quiet of High Hampton. The inn, closed since Thanksgiving, wouldn't reopen until April. The golf course was covered in snow. There were a few cottages on the grounds, but except for mine, none of them were occupied. The wind moving through the trees was the only sound as I got out of the car. I looked up and the stars were much brighter and clearer than at any other time on my Journey. With no competition from artificial lights, the stars popped out in the night sky.

Since the early twentieth century, High Hampton has been the mountain vacation spot for many southerners. I asked my host, Will McKee, why. He says three reasons: location, location, location. Within the Appalachian Mountain chains, the Blue Ridge Mountains are considered the prettiest. The prettiest part of the Blue Ridge Mountains is the Blue Ridge Escarpment, and the prettiest part of the escarpment is the southern end of it. And High Hampton is the center of the southern end of the escarpment. He noted that the area around Cashiers has more biodiversity than all of Europe, and that it also has the largest North American waterfall outside of Niagara. Finally, High Hampton is the closest mountain resort to low country southerners. Will's father was fond of saying, "No self-respecting southerner would allow his wife, and certainly not his elderly mother, to suffer in the severe summer heat of Savannah if he could help it."

Will is the third generation of his family to operate High Hampton. His grandfather bought the 1,400-acre resort in 1922 from Senator Hampton's family. In 1932, the inn and the lodge were destroyed by fire. At the depth of the Depression, Will's grandfather began reconstruction.

Many locals avoided starvation with the wages earned rebuilding the 120-room inn. It was completed within a year using mostly local materials, the cheapest way to reconstruct the inn. Those local materials are not so cheap today. For example, the inn's exterior sheathing is chestnut bark. Try pricing a pallet of that stuff for your next construction project.

Will McKee, owner of High Hampton

Neither the exterior nor the interior has changed much since 1933. The interior is pine plank and local stone. The rooms have not been retrofitted with air-conditioning, televisions, or telephones. The lobby has a phone and a television for the use of the guests, but there are no phones or televisions in the rooms. I forgot to ask about wi-fi, but I noted that my cell phone worked only intermittently even outside the inn.

Nope, you don't go to High Hampton for a twenty-first-century experience, more of a 1940s one. Besides your room, the lodging rate includes all of your meals—a pricing system once known in the travel industry as the American plan. Meals are served family style. High Hampton serves mostly traditional southern food, such as fried chicken, along with local fish and vegetables, to over 300 people every day of the summer. Guests still dress for dinner—dresses for ladies and a coat and tie for gentlemen. In a concession to modernity, for two nights a week, a jacket and collared shirt constitute suitable dress for the weekly low-country boil and barbecue dinners.

Chestnut bark exterior of High Hampton

There is a golf course. During the original construction of the course during the late 1920s, the architect presented Mr. McKee with an interim billing after completing eleven holes. Mr. McKee, after paying the bill, promptly stopped construction. Until the 1950s, High Hampton had the only eleven-hole course in the world. In 1958, the noted golf architect George Cobb redesigned the course. He added seven holes to give the tract the traditional number of holes.

Besides golf, High Hampton offers guests six clay tennis courts, hiking trails, and a thirty-five-acre, spring-fed lake for bass fishing. Mountain hiking, whitewater rafting, and trout fishing in the local rivers are additional diversions for the guests. In a quaint touch, guests are allowed to cut blooming flowers from the garden to brighten their guest rooms.

Apart from a few changes, the High Hampton experience is largely the same as it was in the 1940s. Their clientele is also largely the same as it was in the 1940s—just different generations. Will estimates that ninety percent of his guests are repeat customers. During the high season, between June 15 and August 15, the inn is filled with families who come annually and who coordinate their stays with other families. Last year saw the passing of an era because the last of the "grand dames" who came for the full summer season passed away. Now most guests come three or four times during the spring and summer, generally staying for a week at a time.

Besides the inn, there are 230 private homes on the resort. Most of these homes are second homes and many have been in the same family for generations. Cashiers' real estate is clearly feeling the effects of the economic slowdown. Will noted that it's not a good time to be in the real estate business—the phone had not rung once while we talked. But he noted that even in these difficult economic times there was a market for houses at High Hampton, and houses still sold when they came on the market. I guess the old adage about the three rules of real estate—location, location, and location—remains true.

Franklin

The drive from Cashiers to Franklin is remarkable. It's about ten miles from Cashiers to the next town, Highlands. During those ten miles, the altitude rises about 700 feet through a two-lane mountain road. From Highlands, it's twenty miles, mostly downhill, to the town of Franklin, the county seat of Macon County, North Carolina. On this stretch, Highway 64 literally twists around the Cullasaja River Gorge. The North Carolina Highway Department conveniently constructed vehicle pull-off areas so drivers can leave the highway and let faster traffic pass or simply enjoy the waterfalls at the highway's edge. This is hard mountain driving with no straightaways and no places to pass. The thirty-mile trip takes a full hour of hard driving.

Somewhere on this short stretch, I made an important crossing—the eastern continental divide. West of the divide, rivers flow toward the Gulf of Mexico; east of it, they flow to the Atlantic Ocean. During colonial times, the area west of the continental divide was known as backwater because the rivers flowed "backwards" (away from civilization and the Atlantic Ocean).

During the American Revolution, the backwater men lived a little north and west of here but in the same type of country. They passed just east of here racing to meet the British at Kings Mountain. Seeing how rugged this land is, I appreciate the feat of the Overmountain men who walked 330 miles in less than two weeks, carrying guns and provisions, to get to Kings Mountain. And I feel like a wimp complaining about how hard it is to drive on the mountain roads.

Located in a broad valley, the town of Franklin has a brand-new McDonald's and a bypass. Hard to believe, but a town of less than 4,000 people has a bypass. This is rural America. The nearest cities are Greenville, South Carolina, and Asheville, North Carolina, but they are not convenient. Franklin is remote. It is the largest town in Macon County. Macon County has a large land mass of 519 square miles, but much of the county is publicly owned land. The Nantahala National Forest, the largest of North Carolina's four national forests with over 500,000 acres of forested park land, covers much of the county. Only 32,000 people reside in the county.

After that thirty-mile stretch of mountain driving, I was ready to eat. Rather than stay on the outskirts of Franklin, I headed downtown. No McDonald's for me, I went downtown to the Peddler Restaurant and got the vegetable plate—a generous plate of four vegetables for $4.58 including tax. You've got to like the pricing out here in the country.

Historically, this is Cherokee country. Franklin is the site of an ancient Cherokee town called Nikwasi, "center of activity." Nikwasi was first described by the British explorer Sir Alexander Cumming as the place where in 1730 thousands of Cherokee came from all over to meet him. Evidently things didn't go real well at the meeting because the British returned to burn the village. The Cherokee rebuilt, but the American colonists destroyed it again because they feared that the Cherokee would join with the British in the American Revolution. The only remnant from the Cherokee days is the Nikwasi Mound in the center of downtown Franklin. The mound is probably 600 to 800 years old. When the Cherokee ran things, the mound was a spiritual center and had a building at the top along with a sacred eternal fire. The mound has never been excavated or farmed.

Franklin caters to two types of tourists. The first are rock hunters: Franklin advertises itself as the "gem capital of the world." The area historically produced corundum and gem-quality rubies and sapphires. But by the early twentieth century, the mines had lost their commercial viability. Since then the mines operate for the tourist trade. Franklin is known as one of three main locations in the world for hunting gem stones; the other two places are in Burma and Thailand. Here, tourists can search for gem stones at a half dozen locations.

The second type of tourist arrives on foot—hikers on the Appalachian Trail. The Appalachian Trail, known as the AT, is the 2,172-mile trail running from Georgia to Maine. Macon County has forty-seven miles of AT trail. It is estimated that four million people visit the trail every year. The southern terminus of the trail is about one hundred miles from Franklin or, in terms of travel time, about a one-week walk. Franklin is the second town that AT thru-hikers reach as they travel north.

Now you might not think of hikers as a great class of tourist. In fact, after a week in the wilderness, they are a fairly nasty-looking and nasty-smelling bunch. After a couple of weeks on the trail, most hikers want a clean bed, a laundry facility, and a few good meals. Ron Haven caters to these tourists.

Ron is a Franklin native. He's a big man. He left Franklin after high school to become a professional wrestler. He wrestled professionally for Georgia Championship Wrestling from 1975 to 1981. He returned to Franklin with a wife, who had grown up in Los Angeles, and twin boys. Ron is also a hiker. He first hiked the AT up to Harrisburg, Virginia, as a

Ron Haven, friend to AT hikers (courtesy of Ron Haven)

sixteen year old. Now he and his family spend time hiking the AT together.

A Franklin real estate mogul, Ron owns three motels downtown. And a few apartment buildings and other real estate. But catering to AT hikers is his niche. He owns a bus and two vans which are used to pick up hikers from the trails some ten miles away. Pick-up and drop-off are complimentary for his guests. He estimates that from mid-March to mid-April, he will house forty to forty-five hikers a day. From the end of April through the rest of the summer, his occupancy averages a hundred hikers a day.

Ron sponsors the Hiker Fool Bash, an annual celebration for northbound hikers held every year on the weekend nearest to April Fool's Day.

It's held at Ron's Sapphire Hotel. Close to 3,000 people attend the event, which starts on Friday evening with the music of Loafer's Glory Bunch, a local group. According to Ron, the group took the name of a Porter Wagoner song about the Saturday swap meet which once took place at nearby Kaiser's Grocery. A local celebrity, the former crew chief for NASCAR driver Richard Petty, serves barbecue to the crowd.

On Saturday of the Hiker Fool Bash, vendors set up booths to display the newest in sleeping bags, tents, and other hiker paraphernalia. Entertainment continues throughout the day with music and clogging. For the uninitiated, clogging is hillbilly tap-dancing, a type of step dancing where the heel of the foot keeps the beat and the female dancers wear frilly, puffy dresses. Ron reports that there may be some moderate consumption of adult beverages, but drunkenness is a definite no-no. After 9:00 p.m., music cannot be amplified but can be played as long as the crowd stays, sometimes until 3:00 a.m. In December, Ron sponsors a similar event, the Hiker Christmas Party, for the south-bound hikers, who are a week away from completing their thru-hikes. It's much smaller but with the same vibe.

This relatively new tourism industry is important to Franklin's economy. Ron's motels are not the high end of the industry. For example, Ron advertises a single-occupancy room for $39.99 at his Budget Inn. It has onsite laundry facilities and high-speed Internet. Local business people estimate that over sixty percent of the thru-hikers are over forty-five years old and they spend $200 each day they stay in Franklin. As Ron says, "The money from these hikers is like a circle going around and around the community. It helps the restaurants, it helps the grocery store, and I don't have to lay off employees during the year."

The Smoky Mountains

The Great Smoky Mountains National Park is reputed to be within a day's drive of sixty percent of the United States' population. I don't know if I believe this factoid: I guess the critical element would be how one defines a day's drive. These people might be coming from St. Louis, Cleveland, and Washington DC, which I guess you can make in a day's drive. But those cities sure seem a long way away.

Proximity to the country's population centers is the reason given for why the Great Smoky Mountains National Park is the most visited national park in the nation. Almost 9.5 million people visit the park annually. The park covers 816 square miles and 522,419 acres. It straddles two states: North Carolina and Tennessee. The range of altitudes within the park is dramatic—Clingmans Dome is the highest point at 6,300 feet above sea level, while the lowest parts of the park are only a few hundred feet above sea level.

U.S. Highway 441 bisects the park. It enters the east side of the park at Cherokee, North Carolina, and exits on the west end at Gatlinburg, Tennessee. The route through the park is slightly more than thirty miles long. In the off-season with virtually no traffic, my trip took about an hour. I'd hate to think how long it takes during the summer, when the traffic is bumper-to-bumper with flat-land tourists negotiating the hairpin turns. The Park Service advises crossing before 10:00 a.m. or after 5:00 p.m. during the summer months.

Cherokee, North Carolina, the east end of the park, lies within the Eastern Cherokee Indian Reservation. To be part of the Eastern Band of the Cherokee, you basically had to be a descendant of someone who wasn't deported in the nineteenth century on a forced march now known as the "Trail of Tears." Most of them got to stay only because the adopted son of Chief Yonaguska was a white man and he devised ways to allow some 600 Cherokee to become citizens of North Carolina. As citizens, they could not be deported but simply placed on a reservation. They were also considered "colored" citizens under North Carolina's Jim Crow laws, so for a long while they weren't considered full citizens of North Carolina.

Cherokee stands out from the other towns in the area: Cherokee is poor. It's in the same county as Cashiers but really bears little resemblance to it. The topography is the same but little else. Before 1995, this poor little band of Eastern Cherokee had only a few ways of making a living. They enticed a few tourists off the interstate with black bears in "zoos" and a dramatic outdoor play, *Unto These Hills*. Most residents worked during the six months that the tourist trade could support them. During the off-season they relied on welfare.

Gambling changed all that. In 1995, Harrah's opened a casino owned by the Cherokee. Since it's the only casino in the eastern part of the South and convenient to Interstate 40, it has done real well in Cherokee, North Carolina. Now that gambling has arrived, the Cherokee are doing somewhat better. First of all, the casino provides much needed service jobs tending to this new type of tourist. Second, the tribe, as the casino owner, receives the profits. Half the casino profits are required to go into tribal coffers for community projects. These profits, for example, funded the construction of the really fine Museum of the Cherokee Indian. The other half of the profit goes directly to tribe members. With profit distributions in excess of $6,000 a year to each member of the tribe, it is now "cool" to be Cherokee, or at least eastern Cherokee. So long as the casino remains profitable, people will search the Internet for a Cherokee ancestor or attempt to tie an ancestor to the Baker Roll of 1924, the baseline for proving lineal ancestral certification as a Cherokee.

Still, being Cherokee in North Carolina isn't easy. The signs of poverty are pronounced: bad teeth and run-down mobile homes abound in Cherokee. Even though it still wouldn't be confused with Cashiers or even Franklin, Cherokee is doing better today than it did twenty years ago. Recently, the Cherokee instituted liquor sales at their casino, which increased their take. The casino business is doing so well that the tribe built a twenty-one-story hotel with 1,108 rooms. It also built a championship-caliber golf course nearby as a diversion for the gamblers.

Call me a cynic, but I doubt that casino gambling will help the toothless ladies at the gas station, the poor children living in the worn-out mobile homes, or the broken-down busboys at the restaurant. While casino gambling has been here for only a few years, these poor people have been getting cheated for centuries.

I left Cherokee and entered the park on a bright winter day. An hour later, I left the park and arrived in Gatlinburg where it was gray and overcast. This type of weather change is not unusual in the mountains.

But what a spectacular drive through the Smokies.

The view of the Smokies from U.S. highway 441

Gatlinburg is redneckville. The quiet and solitude of the national park masks the American ingenuity lying just outside the gates and its incalculable ways of separating tourists from their money. First are the food peddlers selling tacos, pizza, and other modern junk foods. My favorite is the Ogle Dog—the "fresh dipped" corn dog—no stinking pre-dipped dogs here. Other stores sell fudge—buy three, get the fourth piece for free—though most of the people I saw waddling out of these "shoppes" didn't need the first piece, let alone four. Next are the souvenir shops. Trinkets, badges, pottery, and art are all sold in these shops. Black bear items seem real popular. And I've only walked a few blocks of Gatlinburg.

Redneck Central: Gatlinburg

When Jonathan Daniels traveled through here in the 1930s, he noted, "Gatlinburg is a town for tin can tourists." I'm not sure what a "tin can tourist" was, but I suspect it was the budget tourists who ate from tin cans rather than visit restaurants. If so, things haven't changed that much since Jonathan Daniels' time. Gatlinburg brags that it can sleep 30,000 guests a night. That doesn't mean it has 30,000 motel rooms. Instead, tourist camps, campgrounds, and camper parks get added to the number of motels and upscale condominiums to determine how many guests Gatlinburg can accommodate.

Fresh-dipped corn dogs: a Gatlinburg treat

The saleslady at the visitors' center was an Arkansas native from the Delta town of Blytheville. I asked her if she missed the humidity of the flat land. Her reply was short and direct: "Not for a minute. I love Gatlinburg. It's so much fun and there's always something to do." She cautioned that Gatlinburg had really felt the drop in the economy, but a lot of people still came to Gatlinburg. She told me that I was a few weeks early for the Santa Claus convention. Santas come from all over the United States for the Santa convention. The festivities end with a parade of Santas marching down Gatlinburg's main street. "It's a sight to behold. And they have so much fun. They're coming back again this year," she noted.

The now annual gathering of Clauses includes more than Santas: Mrs. Clauses and elves and reindeer are also invited. The convention is more than socializing; it now includes continuing education seminars for the modern Santa and Mrs. Claus. The seminars include instruction on the following subjects:

Beyond the Beard and Red Suit—Improving Santa's Image
The Characteristics and Traits of Santa
Children's Impression of the Jolly Old Elf
Santa's Body Language and Communication Skills
Being Santa 24/7 and 365 Days a Year
Mrs. Claus' Wardrobe
Media Relations for Santa
Booking Mrs. Claus
Santa Magic Basics—Communicating Effectively With Children
Creating a Santa Launch Plan
Santa Roundtable

If I only had more time.

Good Old Rocky Top

To get from Gatlinburg to Knoxville, you pass Pigeon Forge, the home of Dolly Parton's theme park, Dollywood. Pigeon Forge's tourist attractions seem to be on steroids, much larger and flashier than Gatlinburg's, which seem downright old-fashioned in their trashiness. Forget about the quiet of High Hampton and the quaintness of Ron Haven's Budget Inn. Pigeon Forge is all about flash, outlet malls, and four-lane highways. After Pigeon Forge, the mountains and mountain tourist industry are in the rearview mirror. It's a return to the real world.

Knoxville is Tennessee's third-largest city and the capital of east Tennessee. Every time I'm in east Tennessee I remember my father, a proud graduate of the University of Tennessee, saying that Tennessee is one of the most important states in the Union—parts of east Tennessee are closer to Canada than to Memphis. His characterization of Tennessee's importance is pure opinion. But he was geographically correct: Bristol is a few miles closer to the Canadian border near Windsor, Ontario, than it is to Memphis.

Knoxville and Memphis have little in common. Memphis—west Tennessee—is Democratic-controlled flat land, while east Tennessee is Republican-dominated hill country. That's not to say that Knoxville is like most of east Tennessee. It isn't. With a population center numbering over a million people, it's certainly more urban, making it different from the rest of east Tennessee. It may be the lack of elevation: Knoxville sits in a valley only 900 feet above sea level. Knoxville's summer humidity reminds me more of the Deep South than of the mountain air forty-five miles to the east. Unlike most other mountain towns, Knoxville has an African-American community. Most probably though, the difference is the influence of the over 27,000 young people who come from all over the country to attend the University of Tennessee. One of them was my son, Will. During the half decade of his college matriculation, I got to know Knoxville, my birthplace.

Yes, Knoxville's different. Knoxville is the center of east Tennessee, and the University of Tennessee is the center of Knoxville. College football is the center of the University of Tennessee. Beginning late summer and throughout the fall, activities in Knoxville revolve around the university football team, the Volunteers, generally referred to as the "Vols." In that regard, Knoxville is not any different from any other college town in the Southeastern Conference. Oxford, Tuscaloosa, and Columbia, I'm sure, are the same.

The Vols play their home games in Neyland Stadium—pronounced "Nayland"—the largest stadium in the conference and third largest in the United States. The record attendance for a football game occurred in 2006 against the Florida Gators, with 109,061 spectators viewing the game. The stadium's capacity has been reduced the past few years due to the installation of box seats for the well-heeled athletic supporters. Since 2006, a mere 102,037 spectators completely fill the stadium.

In one of our son's senior years at Tennessee, my wife, who has little interest in football, concluded that we had violated some collegiate obligation by not attending a parents' football weekend. So we went to see the Vols play the University of Alabama (the one from the Birmingham campus, not the Crimson Tide). That other University of Alabama, the one from Tuscaloosa, was the number one ranked team in America and was slated to play my alma mater, the University of Arkansas, that same afternoon.

Neyland Stadium sits on the north side of the Tennessee River. The river bank is only yards from the stadium. Because of the stadium's riverside location, the Tennessee Vols have a unique group of supporters at each home game—the Vol Navy. The navy consists of approximately 200 boats that tie up on the river bank for each home game. Some come for the day, some for the weekend, while some boats are a fixture on the river throughout the whole football season.

Vol Navy, boat supporters of the Tennessee Vols

The Vol Navy has a hierarchy. The earliest boats tie up to the dock. Late arrivers tie on to the earlier ones, thereby creating strings of boats. The outer boat owners then walk across the closer boats to get to the game. Now some of these boats are small, but most are not. One boat in the Vol Navy, listed for sale, was 164 feet long and worth $38,000,000. The night before the game you can walk along the river bank, look into the boats, and watch boat occupants entertain, grill, or watch TV. Yes, watching TV in the darkened cabins—on flat screen TVs connected to satellites. Most were tuned to ESPN so that the occupants could also watch other college football games.

When members of the Vol Navy are not watching TV, they make their way to Calhoun's On The River, a nearby food and beverage establishment. Calhoun's has a large outside deck. On nights before football games, Tall Paul entertains Vol fans. Tall Paul—Paul Bobal—is a 6'6" gentle, middle-aged musician from Virginia. He sports long blond hair and favors tie-dyed shirts. Tall Paul is a local favorite who has played the "strip" for the past twenty years. Every university has a strip adjacent to the campus which has bookstores, t-shirt shops, and bars, even though a few universities call it something different. (Hear that, UVa?) The strip is where Tall Paul makes his living.

He's normally a solo act, just a guitar, but on this night he was accompanied by a group called Ramajay. The back-up band featured a Rastafarian-looking fellow playing the steel drum. By the way, the steel drum is not a really a drum but a pan made from a fifty-five gallon oil drum. It makes the distinctive sound of Caribbean music. So the night before the big game we sat by the Tennessee River on a pleasant early fall evening listening to Tall Paul and his buddies play island music. From our seats we could look out over the river, over to the boats of the Vol Navy, or up to the hulking shadow of Neyland Stadium.

At 10 p.m., the band played "Rocky Top." "Rocky Top" was written fifty years or so ago about a guy who left Tennessee and longed to return to it and to simpler times. Over the past fifteen years, "Rocky Top" has become the unofficial fight song of the Tennessee Volunteers.

"Rocky Top" isn't the official fight song; that's a little ditty called "Down the Field." Few wearing Tennessee orange know the lyrics of "Down the Field," but everyone knows "Rocky Top." If you didn't know the lyrics before game weekend, you will by the end. It is played throughout game weekend and every few minutes during the game. That night, as the first few notes clanged from the steel drum, everyone began singing:

> Rocky top, you'll always be
> Home sweet home to me.
> Good ole rocky top,
> Rocky top Tennessee, rocky top Tennessee

Between the last two lines, everyone gives out a short "woooo": "Good old rocky top—WOOOO—Rocky top Tennessee, rocky Top Tennessee." After a rousing, extended rendition of the island-based version of Rocky Top with lots of wooooing from the crowd and tinging from the steel drum, the band took a break and we left.

The state of Tennessee is known as the "volunteer state" because of the role that General Andrew Jackson and his Tennessee troops played in defending the "lower country" from the British and their Indian allies during the War of 1812. During the football game, an undergraduate reprises the role of the backwoods volunteer by wearing buckskin and a coonskin cap and running around with a shotgun. (Unloaded, I assume, but since this is the South, you can't take that for granted.)

When the Vols score a touchdown, this Daniel Boone character runs around with a coon dog, Smoky. Smoky is the official team mascot, not the Daniel Boone–looking fellow. Evidently the university's marketing opportunities for selling stuffed hound dogs outweigh those for marketing a stuffed, crazily-dressed redneck holding a shotgun. Just outside the stadium, fireworks explode, while inside, 100,000 people (there were a few UAB fans in one corner) dressed in hideous orange and white stand up and sing "Rocky Top." I don't want to disparage the song because my wife really got into singing the woooo. During the song's refrain, she placed her left hand on her hip, while her right hand shot up into the air as she wooed:

Good ole rocky top,
Woooo
Rocky top Tennessee, rocky top Tennessee

The first dozen or so times she sang it, I was fine. But let's say about midway through the first quarter, "Rocky Top," and particularly its woooo, started wearing thin. By the beginning of the second quarter, I was officially "Rocky Top" tired.

Let's talk about Tennessee orange. Tennessee orange, while a truly ugly color, is at least real orange, not that watered-down burnt orange that the other UT (Texas) uses. No, Tennessee orange is a bright orange, a color most people can't wear well. I think it's sometimes called "blaze orange." If you live anywhere other than Tennessee, you can locate Tennessee orange in most any clothing store. Go straight to the bargain bin and find any orange color garment that's marked down at least fifty to seventy-five percent—this garment will be Tennessee orange. People say that Tennessee orange is a very versatile color. On Saturday, you can wear it to the game, Sunday out to the deer woods, and on Monday back to the correctional center.

At half-time, the Vols were safely ahead 24-7. Early in the second quarter, the sun broke out and, with no breeze and tens of thousands of human beings in close proximity, it was uncomfortable, even though it was probably only eighty degrees. I can't image how uncomfortable the stadium had been the week earlier when it was ninety-five degrees. We (or should I say I) decided that we should find a place where we could watch the Arkansas-Alabama game on TV. So we went to the strip.

At the strip, we located the Tin Roof, which had cold beer, good food, and big TV screens. Only one problem, the TV was set to the game we had just left. We arrived just in time to watch the Dragons from UA–Birmingham stage a dramatic second half comeback against the Vols and tie the game at the end of regulation. To say that the Tennessee fans were distressed would be an understatement. The game was exciting for a disinterested observer, but it was interfering with the game that I really wanted to see. As the orange-clad locals cheered the Vols to a double overtime victory, the loyal Arkies in the house missed seeing the first two scores of the truly important game occurring in Fayetteville, Arkansas.

As the Arkansas game progressed, it looked like the Hogs might upset the #1-ranked Crimson Tide. Since Alabama is a mortal enemy of the Vols, more and more orange-togged people began to cheer for Arkansas. I bought a pitcher of beer for one group of Tennessee students who stood up and "called the hogs"—Arkansas' famous "wooo, pig sooie" cheer. The wooo in the Arkansas cheer is much longer than the wooo the Vol fans interject into "Rocky Top" and is also a better cheer for a football game. But that's not germane to this story. One of the young men in the group stood up, thanked me for the beer, and announced loudly to the crowd, "I hate Alabama!"

Later a dispute broke out in the booths behind us. A young man in one booth saw an older Tennessee fan in the other booth openly root for Alabama. The young man jumped up and confronted the wayward Vol saying, "You're wearing a Tennessee shirt. I saw you root for Alabama. How can you wear orange and cheer for Alabama? I hate Alabama!"

When the truant fan didn't apologize fast enough, the young man turned to the truant's female companion and said: "Did you see what he was doing? Your husband was rooting for Alabama. You're wearing orange, too. How could you let that happen? How could you marry a guy like that?"

The young man wasn't angry or threatening, merely incredulous. He turned back to his table and remarked to his companions, "I don't get it. That guy's wearing orange and cheering for Alabama. What's the world coming to?"

Norris, the Planned Community

Remember Lester Galloway, the friendly, unshaven seller of honey bee brittle and fried peanuts? From his name, I knew he was a probably a "cracker"—that particular strain of upland South white people who emigrated from the Celtic areas of Great Britain and populated the mountainous backwoods of early America.

As Grady McWhiney noted in *Cracker Culture*, crackers migrated to east Tennessee and other areas of the Appalachians:

> Such a region was ideally suited for the clannish, herding, leisure-loving Celts, who relished whiskey, gambling and combat, and who despised hard work, anything English, most government, fences and any other restraints upon them or their free-ranging livestock.

Lester turned out to be a fairly typical cracker—friendly, generous, a wonderful storyteller. I spent nearly an hour at his produce store.

The first use of the term *cracker* is found in a letter to the Earl of Dartmouth:

> I should explain to your lordship what is meant by Crackers, a name they have got from being great boasters; they are a lawless set of rascals on the frontiers of Virginia, Maryland, the Carolinas and Georgia who often change their abode.

The *Oxford Universal Dictionary on Historical Principles* defines *cracker* as follows: "A braggart, liar (1681). One full of conversation (Scottish). A name for poor whites in the southern United States (1767)."

In modern parlance, they are wisecrackers who lounge (oftentimes drinking whiskey) and "crack" jokes. The cracker culture was readily distinguishable from the Puritans of New England, the Quakers of the Mid-Atlantic, and the English Cavaliers of Virginia. Crackers are also known as rednecks, white trash, or Scots-Irish.

It's easy to over-generalize cultural characteristics, but I've found crackers to be generally like Lester—open, friendly, and welcoming. Vernon Louis Parrington described them in *Main Currents of American Thought* as "a vigorous breed, hardy, assertive, individualistic, thrifty." But cracker culture is not always sunlight and roses; they're also known to be clannish, extremely suspicious of strangers, and quick to take offense. In Norris, I met the darker side of cracker culture.

Norris, Tennessee, is a twenty-minute straight shot north up Interstate 75 from downtown Knoxville and a similar distance due east of the Oak Ridge National Laboratory. While most of the surrounding county has been engulfed by Knoxville's sprawl, Norris retains a quiet, rural character. It is no typical suburb. There are neither McMansions nor fast food franchises in Norris. Norris doesn't have the feel of a small Tennessee hill town. I guess that's a credit to the TVA planners who built the town some eighty years ago for the workers constructing the first TVA dam during the Great Depression.

The Tennessee Valley Authority, TVA, was one of President Roosevelt's first and most significant New Deal programs. It was highly controversial because it was this country's first experiment with government-owned electrical generation facilities. It was socialism. In Arkansas, it's long been recognized that the Arkansas River valley was the better place to start such a program. But Senator Joe T. Robinson of Arkansas had a good constituent who was the private provider of electricity in Arkansas. Senator Robinson, who had been the Democratic Party's nominee for vice president in 1926, prevailed on the Democratic administration that the Republican-dominated Tennessee valley was a better place for a radical experiment with public ownership of utilities. So TVA came to the Tennessee hills, bringing good jobs and electricity during those hard times.

The TVA staff designed Norris to be a model community in TVA's secondary purpose of raising the standard of living in the area. Before

TVA came, less than five percent of the area residents had electricity, but Norris was fully electric. Norris was the first town in Tennessee to have dial telephones, and the Norris Creamery was the first electric milk-producing plant in the world. The TVA planners used a central commons in the center of town and reserved a band of rural land around the edge of town—a green space. They designed it to be a self-contained town with a small business area originally containing a grocery store, gas station, and post office. The TVA built all the houses, offering twelve models all with porches and native building materials. By the end of World War II, the TVA had finished its development. After the war, Congress designated the town surplus property and ordered it sold.

Today, approximately 1,500 people call Norris home. In the center of town, the gas station and the grocery store still remain open and appear to be doing well. The commons sits across the road from the old high school, now a grade school. Watching children leave school and walk across the commons calls to mind simpler times when most children walked to neighborhood schools.

City roads amble through the hilly terrain. It's easy to get turned around because there are no city blocks, just rural lanes with four or five houses grouped together in a semi-circle like an off-road cul-de-sac. These housing groups appear at irregular intervals along the road. While there are some newly constructed houses, most appear to be original TVA houses. Many TVA houses have been modified, though not so dramatically that they lose their original character. Most of them appear well maintained.

Over one hill or around a bend, I decided to get out of the car to document one of the housing semi-circles. As in many small southern towns, the roads in Norris don't have curbs, gutters, or sidewalks. The roadside was not wide enough to allow me to get my car entirely off the road. So I did the next best thing and turned into a driveway far enough so my car would not impede traffic. I walked away from the car to get a better angle for a picture. I had taken only few pictures when I noticed a man walking down the driveway toward my car. I had been out of my car for two or three minutes.

With camera in hand, I returned down the road toward him. I smiled, extended my other hand, and said hello. The man, a fair-skinned white guy, was wearing khaki pants and a blue buttoned-down collar shirt which had the letters TVA embossed above the shirt pocket. He looked to be in his mid-forties. He didn't extend his hand; he only looked at me unsmiling and said, "Who are you?" I dropped my hand as I introduced myself.

As we stood at the intersection of this rural lane and the common driveway to these few old TVA houses, I quickly explained that I was from Arkansas. I was visiting my son who was a student at the University of Tennessee. I told him that I had heard that Norris was the original TVA-planned company town and wanted to see it while my son was in class that day. The Norris cracker, while staring at the Arkansas license plate above the rear bumper of my car, asked whether I had registered with the chief of police before driving around town. I smiled and replied quizzically: "Register with the police just to look around your pretty town?" He turned to me with an unsmiling one-word response—"Yes."

My smile vanished when I realized that his nostrils had flared and he looked like he was ready to fight. I took a step back to get a better view of him and see if he was carrying a gun. Seeing no evidence of one, I relaxed slightly. I decided I'd better leave before his anger escalated. I said I was finished with my picture-taking and was going to go to the Norris Grocery (which I knew was across the street from the police department) to get a soft drink.

The man then ordered me to stand where I was while he took down my license plate number. He then handed me the pen and paper and demanded my name and telephone number. Without a word, I took it and wrote my name and gave him the telephone number of my least favorite person in Little Rock. As I wrote, he said, "If anything turns up missing around here, you will be hearing from the chief of police." While I had a number of choice comments for him, that tiny voice in my head told me to say nothing. I returned the paper to him and walked to my car.

Perhaps he realized how rude he had been because as I walked away from him, he explained that Norris had undergone a crime wave. The thieves had hit him and stolen his dog. He said that Norris residents couldn't be too careful with strangers. He suggested that I go talk with the chief of police about it. I didn't turn around or respond. I got in my car and drove away without saying another word.

As I got my Coke at the Norris Grocery, I thought about asking the grocer behind the meat counter about the man, or the Norris crime wave, but instead we just talked about the weather. Later I wished I had gone to see the police chief just to discuss the Norris crime wave. I would have invited the chief to speculate about whether the cracker's dog had really been stolen—or had just run off looking for a kinder environment.

Hard-bitten Land

Tennessee's Copper Basin is only a few miles south of U.S. Highway 64. It's not so much a basin as a broad valley lodged between a series of hills near the junction of North Carolina, Tennessee, and Georgia. The Copper Basin has two small towns, Ducktown—named after Chief Duck of the Cherokees—and Copperhill. It's also home to one of the prettiest rivers I've seen. It's such a beautiful river that it has been given two names. In Georgia, it's the Toccoa River. When it crosses the state line into Tennessee, it becomes the Ocoee. A river so pretty one name won't do.

The movie *Deliverance* was filmed not far from here. It starred Burt Reynolds as one of a group of four city dwellers wanting to get away from the city on a float trip. Going up to rural north Georgia, they encountered strange people and had some strange adventures. I began thinking about the movie when I arrived.

I stopped at a convenience store to get a cup of coffee. A typical convenience store, it had large coolers with cold soft drinks and beer on one side. The middle of the store contained racks of convenience foods—nuts, candy, and a few travel supplies. I didn't notice any souvenirs. Against the back wall was the coffee. Large containers with labels denoting the variety—regular, decaf, and strong—sat on a cabinet. Next to these coffee containers, a hand-written sign announces: "Stirrers, napkins, and creamers are purchased by the store owner for coffee drinkers. If you take them without buying coffee or take more than you need, you are stealing and subject to arrest." Customer satisfaction must have a different meaning to these hill people.

Since I had an appointment later in the day with the mayor of Chattanooga, I decided that caution was the best policy. I left the coffee stand, went to the wall cooler, got a Coke, paid for it, and moved on without saying a word to anyone.

After a couple of stops and walking the streets of Copperhill, I realized that the convenience store owner's attitude was not uncommon in these parts. The people in Copperhill and Ducktown were simply not friendly like people had been in the other small towns I visited. I wouldn't want to make broad generalizations based on limited observations, but people there didn't smile or acknowledge people on the streets or in the stores. It can't be a racial thing because I am a middle-aged white guy, and all these people look a lot like me. I thought of the man in Norris— the guy who had been so unpleasant. Perhaps he had relatives there. A nice spring day and all I saw throughout the day were blank stares and hard glances as people passed me on the street or in the stores.

Maybe this distrust of strangers is understandable because outsiders have not been kind to this area blessed with beauty and natural resources. The history of the Copper Basin is a microcosm of America's relationship with the land. In the 1930s, Jonathan Daniels noted that some eighty years before his travels, Frederick Law Olmsted came through the pretty valley of the Ocoee, "where hemlocks and laurel grew together in perfection he had nowhere else seen." Daniels visited a completely different landscape:

> Hemlock and laurel and every other tree and plant and shrub are gone now. Miles away from Copper Hill and its neighbor, Ducktown, the trees begin to look sick and small. They become sparser and between them run deeper and wider ditches through the dry cracking earth. But where the true desert starts all is ditch or the color and consistency of dry ditch bottoms. The whole earth is washed down to clay, red, white, yellow, and the whole looks cancerous and diseased. Only 50 miles from the Great Smoky Mountains National Park and near neighbor to the Cherokee National Forest, this desert in the mountain forests is a terrifying picture of what man can swiftly do to his earth.

The famous photographer Marion Post Wolcott took these pictures during the 1930s which show how Copperhill looked like the far side of the moon.

Copperhill in the 1930s (courtesy of the Library of Congress)

Copperhill pits in the 1930s (courtesy of the Library of Congress)

The history of this area is the history of copper extraction. The Cherokee first mined and smelted the copper found in the area. After the Indians, the English attempted to develop the copper industry. But not until the late 1800s did the copper mining become commercially viable. Because the copper ore contained high concentrations of sulfur, early operators placed ore on layers of wood called "roast piles." These roast piles burned the foreign matter from the copper ore. This open-air burning process also released a great deal of sulfur dioxide into the air. The sulfur dioxide was not beneficial to the things living in the valley. By 1878, the hills were stripped completely of trees. Without trees and undergrowth, the topsoil eroded, forming large gullies.

Modern environmental law sprang from this destruction. Three local landowners, seeking to enjoin the emissions from the smelters, filed a lawsuit in Tennessee alleging that they had been

> ...annoyed and discommoded by the smoke so that the complainants are prevented from using and enjoying their farms and homes as they did prior to the inauguration of these enterprises. The smoke makes it impossible for the owners of farms within the area of the smoke zone to subsist their families thereon with the degree of comfort they enjoyed before. They cannot raise and harvest customary crops, and their timber is largely destroyed. *Madison v. Ducktown Sulphur, Copper & Iron Co.* 113 Tenn. 331, 83 S.W. 658 (1904).

The Tennessee Supreme Court expressed sympathy for these small landowners and found that they were entitled to damages. But the court would not stop the smoke. The court stated:

> In order to protect by injunction several small tracts of land, aggregating in value less than $1,000, we are asked to destroy other property worth nearly $2,000,000 and wreck two great mining and manufacturing enterprises, that are engaged in work of very great importance, not only to their owners, but to the state, and to the whole country as well, to depopulate a large town, and deprive thousands of working people of their homes and livelihoods, and scatter them broadcast. The result would be practically a confiscation of the property of the defendants for the benefit of the complainants—an appropriation without compensation. The defendants cannot reduce their ores in a manner different from that they are now employing, and there is no more remote place to which they can remove.

For all their litigation, these three landowners collected a few hundred dollars, and the copper-smelting operations continued.

Carbon dioxide from these smelting operations also drifted across the state line, killing area plants and trees in Georgia. The State of

Georgia commenced an action directly with the U.S. Supreme Court. This lawsuit settled when the smelters agreed to discontinue open roasting and use furnaces with taller chimneys. The settlement of the initial State of Georgia lawsuit only made matters worse. Using taller chimneys created a larger area of destruction and soon the state of Georgia was back asking for an injunction against the further dispersal of sulfur dioxide from the smelting operations. Even though the Supreme Court's decision largely favored the State of Georgia, the parties settled by restricting the plants' production. But continuing the smelting activity, even at a reduced level, continued degrading the environment. This environmental damage continued until 1987, when copper mining ceased altogether in the Copper Basin.

Now some seventy years after Jonathan Daniels visited, the area has changed again. It's been reclaimed. Since the 1980s, approximately 32,000 denuded acres of Tennessee hill country have been reforested. Besides reforestation efforts, contaminated soil has been removed and the area's acidic water is now being treated. Today the Copper Basin no longer looks like a moonscape, but rather like other places in the region.

Copperhill today

Land that was once the Copperhill pits

Today over 250,000 visitors annually enjoy the area's main attraction, rafting and canoeing on the Ocoee River. Like the Catawba River in North Carolina, the Ocoee is a working river; its primary purpose is the generation of electricity. Most of the time, the Ocoee is a largely dry, rock-strewn riverbed. But when the TVA releases water, the Ocoee is transformed into the foremost white-water river in the eastern United States.

White-water racing events have been held on the Ocoee since 1978. The first ever event for freestyle kayaking, Ocoee Rodeo, was held on the Ocoee in 1983. The Ocoee Whitewater Center was built to host the 1996 Summer Olympic kayaking events, and a section of the river was constructed boulder by boulder for the Olympic kayaking events.

White-water rafting occurs in sight of the U.S. Highway 64 roadway that winds alongside the narrow rock-filled riverbed toward Chattanooga. In the summer, you can drive and watch canoeists as they dodge the rocks in the river. Where the river slows and empties into

Ocoee Lake, traffic signs warn of traffic congestion. They seem out of place on an early spring weekday when no one is around. As I passed the signs, I couldn't help but wonder whether the people in Copper Basin acknowledge or speak to tourists.

Chattanooga Rebound

I took Anita Ebersole's advice about traveling from Ducktown to Chattanooga, even though it made no sense at the time. Anita sent me an e-mail saying:

> Ducktown is approximately 70 miles from Chattanooga. Due to the beautiful scenery which you will want to slow down to admire, it will take you about an hour and a half to two hours.

Anita is an aide to Chattanooga's mayor. I thought she was being very conservative about the travel time. With over half of the trip on four-lane highway, averaging thirty-five to forty miles an hour seemed awfully slow. But she was right. It's not just the scenery that causes the slow pace, but the traffic on the four-lane portion of the trip.

Once I got to the four-lane roads, I thought traffic to Chattanooga would move faster, but it didn't. Even though it's not a big city, Chattanooga traffic jams must be fairly common occurrences. It's Tennessee's fourth-largest city—only a little larger than it was sixty years ago and just slightly larger than Neyland Stadium's seating capacity. One reason for traffic problems is Chattanooga's geography. It's located on a 180-degree bend in the Tennessee River. You have to cross bridges to get almost anywhere, and bridges tend to delay traffic. Also, Chattanooga is nestled in a valley along the foothills of the Appalachian Mountains, and the combination of bridges and hills is particularly brutal on the pace of travel.

The hills surrounding Chattanooga are famous to Civil War buffs: Signal Mountain, Missionary Ridge, and, of course, Lookout Mountain. Geography and the fact that it was the Confederacy's railroad center made Chattanooga strategically important. A number of significant battles occurred here during the war.

After the Civil War, Chattanooga rebounded, quickly becoming the center of southern manufacturing. A number of Yankees aided Chattanooga's re-development when they returned after the war to make their fortunes. Iron foundries and furniture factories located in Chattanooga, and it soon became known as the "Dynamo of Dixie."

But neither relocated Yankees nor new industrial concerns gave Chattanooga its biggest boost. A newfangled soft drink sparked Chattanooga. In the early twentieth century, two young Chattanooga lawyers took a train to Atlanta and convinced the owner of Coca-Cola to sell them the national rights to bottle Coca-Cola. Asa Candler, the developer of Coca-Cola, didn't place much faith in their production method. So he sold the bottling rights for a nominal sum to these two young Chattanoogans and kept the syrup-making part of the business. As a result of that single transaction, Coca-Cola created more millionaires in Chattanooga per capita than it did in Atlanta. Boosted by Coca-Cola bottling wealth, Chattanooga's economy matured during the first half of the twentieth century as a diverse center of banking and insurance as well as the manufacturing center of the South.

Throughout the 1940s, '50s, and early '60s, highly industrialized Chattanooga was an economic anomaly in the South. Chattanooga consistently ranked among the ten most industrialized cities of America along with the likes of Allentown, Pennsylvania; Detroit, Michigan; and Gary, Indiana. When America's industrial and manufacturing sectors faltered in the 1970s, Chattanooga slid from its perch as one of the most vibrant southern cities.

Even though it was weakening, Chattanooga's industrial base created another problem: pollution. In 1969, Chattanooga was declared the country's "dirtiest city." Chattanooga was so dirty that people often drove with their lights on during the day so they could see through the haze. The nearby hills were not visible from downtown, and office workers often changed soot-stained white shirts during the day. During the 1970s and early '80s, Chattanooga lost jobs and residents at a fairly steady rate. Its economic prospects were about as good as its air quality.

"America's dirtiest city" in 1969: Chattanooga (courtesy of Chattanooga-Hamilton County Air Pollution Control Bureau)

But Chattanooga avoided the fate of the other cities like Allentown, Detroit, and Gary and reinvented itself as a vibrant small city. How did it avoid being a southern version of Gary or Allentown? What changed its fortunes? How did Chattanooga come out of its free fall? These were the questions I had for the mayor of Chattanooga, Ron Littlefield.

Mayor Littlefield isn't a native; he came to Chattanooga in the late 1960s from Georgia (by way of Auburn University). In other words, he's a Chattanoogan by choice and not by birth. Working as a city planner, he saw the decline and rise of Chattanooga from the front lines. He held a number of positions, including head of Chattanooga's Public Works and later the first executive director of Chattanooga Ventures. He also was a member of the Chattanooga City Council before becoming mayor.

Chattanooga's rebirth began in 1982 with the creation of the Moccasin Bend Task Force. Moccasin Bend is where the Tennessee River makes its big curve between Lookout Mountain and downtown Chattanooga. It's a part of the twenty-two miles of Chattanooga's riverfront. The task force recommended that the river be considered an amenity and made cleaning the riverfront the first priority for the community's rebirth.

About that same time, a broad cross-section of Chattanoogans visited Indianapolis, Indiana, to see the work of the Greater Indianapolis Progress Committee, founded as a public-private partnership in the mid-1960s. Seeing what Indianapolis had accomplished, Chattanooga Ventures, a community-based, non-profit organization, was created. As its first project, Chattanooga Ventures began Vision 2000, a public goal-setting exercise to determine what Chattanooga could and should look like at the turn of the century. It involved 2,000 citizens in a series of public discussions. Vision 2000 identified forty community goals and nearly two hundred projects and programs designed to revitalize Chattanooga by the end of the century. Mayor Littlefield noted that in 1984 the end of the century seemed a long way away, but sixteen years wasn't that long to plan and implement fundamental changes in a municipality.

Mayor Littlefield is personable, confident, and straightforward. He was quick to give credit to others, especially to the Lyndhurst Foundation. The Lyndhurst Foundation kick-started Chattanooga's revitalization efforts by largely funding the Moccasin Bend Task Force and being a major funder of Chattanooga Ventures and Vision 2000. Mayor Littlefield specifically credited the leadership of Jack Lupton, whose family—Coca-Cola heirs—had founded the Lyndhurst Foundation. Mayor Littlefield was impressed that while Mr. Lupton had his own vision for the project, he insisted on involving as many "smart people" in the decisions as possible. He believed that people would be less interested in being involved if the people thought that he alone controlled the outcome.

In this and other ways, Mr. Lupton made clear that he did not want undue influence on the process or the conclusions, even though he and the family's foundation were providing the funding. Mr. Lupton saw the process as a marketplace of ideas. The goal was to identify the best achievable ideas and projects for Chattanooga. All of the ideas, even his, needed to compete in the process.

Scholars and writers who have analyzed "the Chattanooga process" tend to focus on the community involvement aspect of Vision 2000 and relegate the Lyndhurst/Lupton influence to the role of having simply provided seed capital. But Mayor Littlefield credits Mr. Lupton for having the wisdom to take a hands-off approach to the process, allowing a competition of ideas to direct the priority of projects and ultimately the city's direction. This free market, community-involved approach is what probably sets the Chattanooga Process apart.

Modern-day Chattanooga

Largely because of the decisions and projects from Vision 2000, Chattanooga is again re-industrializing. When Volkswagen looked to open its new American plant, it chose Chattanooga. In announcing its decision, Volkswagen stated:

> Like many other cities with an industrial past, changing times once threatened to leave Chattanooga in rust and decline. But, unlike some other cities facing the same fate, Chattanooga's leadership and citizens chose to restore, reinvest and reinvent....The people of Chattanooga took responsibility for their city's future and made great things happen.

As jobs return to the area, Chattanooga continues to move forward. The city-owned electric utility, EPB, has developed the world's fastest municipal Internet service, which is attracting tech entrepreneurs. The city is coordinating the development of 755 acres along the river, the Moccasin Bend National Archeological District, into a national park, which will further improve the quality of life.

It's difficult to talk with Ron Littlefield and not be excited for Chattanooga. It avoided being a Detroit, Michigan; Anderson, Indiana; or virtually any other industrial-based American city that stagnated and then declined in difficult economic times. Today, Chattanooga's future is bright.

A Civil Misunderstanding

Just up from the Tennessee Aquarium in Chattanooga, there are two bookstores: one bright and well lit, featuring new books by regional authors; the other dark, dusty, and severely over-crowded with shelves of old books and stuff overflowing onto the floor. The owner of the latter bookstore, a woman I later discovered was seventy-five years old, greeted me and asked if she could help. I declined her offer, saying that I just wanted to browse. The next customer, a young woman with a child, requested books for homeschoolers. The proprietress confirmed that she sold such books and added, "It's your responsibility to educate your children, not the state's." A few moments later, the owner said to the child, "Homeschoolers will save America."

That last part raised my hackles, but I said nothing. First, I was a guest in her store. Second, I knew that the lady wasn't really interested in my view that quality public education may well be the singular reason for America's continued greatness. And I didn't want to debate. I merely wanted to hang out and browse through the stacks of books. So I said nothing and moved toward the aisles of books.

As I browsed, I noticed the books on the Civil War were located behind one counter. I sought out the owner and asked her permission to go behind the counter to view the books. She followed me back to the area and asked if I was interested in anything in particular. I mentioned that I was interested in anything having to do with the Immortal 600.

She said that she was not familiar with them and asked who they were. Because her accent was southern, I felt like I could establish some *bona fides* by telling her the story of the Immortal 600.

I first said that my great-great-grandfather was one. He was a Yankee POW, having been captured in an attack on Knoxville and sent to a prison on the Delaware River near Philadelphia. In the winter of 1864, the Yankees took him and 600 other captured Confederates to the barrier islands outside of Charleston and used them as human breastworks in retaliation for the treatment of Union prisoners at Andersonville.

I added that until Abu Ghraib in Iraq a few years ago, the treatment of the Immortal 600 was the last time the United States' official policy on the treatment of prisoners of war conflicted with that of the rest of the civilized world. An inflammatory ending to the story, I know, but I really wanted to see her response now that I had established myself as a son of the Confederacy, and, more important, had two books tucked under my arm to buy.

Her response was curious. She coldly said that the Yankees had starved her grandfather to death in a POW camp in Ohio. Her people figured that such were the ways of war. She continued by saying that the southerners hadn't mistreated the Yankee prisoners at Andersonville— because there was widespread starvation and the Yankee POWs starved along with the southerners. She asked if I thought the Iraqis held at Guantanamo Bay had any rights.

I was taken aback because she hadn't responded as I assumed she would. She wasn't treating me as a home boy but more like an intruder. "I'm not sure they have rights, but as a civilized nation, by taking and imprisoning them, we have an obligation to show the world how to act by treating them in a fair and humane manner," I replied. She harrumphed, clearly not satisfied with my response. She then turned on her heel and left me alone to finish my browsing.

I finished looking at her books and wandered back to the cash register to buy my two books. As she checked me out, we made small talk about the two books I was buying. Handing me a receipt, she smiled and said: "Come back and we'll straighten your politics out." Again taken aback, I smiled and said nothing but thank you.

Heading toward Alabama, I reflected on my exchange with the book lady. I realized that her attitude toward me changed at the beginning of the story about the Immortal 600. It then occurred to me that she quit listening when I referred to my great-great-grandfather as a "Yankee POW." She misunderstood him to be a Yankee held prisoner by southerners, not the other way around. I don't think she heard the part about the Yankees taking him from Philadelphia back to the South to stand as fodder for Yankee cannon fire. From her perspective, she was confronting some Yankee descendant looking for confirmation of his ancestor's mistreatment. I suppose under those circumstances, she was being as nice as she could be. After that exchange, I decided to leave politics alone—even nineteenth-century politics.

Alabama Retail

Alabama is about thirty miles from Chattanooga. It's not the nearest neighboring state to downtown Chattanooga—that would be Georgia. The route to Alabama takes you through northwest Georgia. Traveling through three states in thirty minutes is a record for the Journey.

Jackson County is the corner of northeast Alabama. Scottsboro, a town of 15,000 people, is the county seat. Locals here are tired of being reminded of their claim to fame. Back in 1931, nine African-American youths were convicted and sentenced to death for raping two white women, fellow hobos, in a freight car running between Chattanooga and Memphis. The initial convictions of the "Scottsboro boys" were regarded throughout the country as a prime example of the racist nature of the early twentieth-century southern judicial system. The American Communist Party then got involved and hired lawyers for the boys. Soon, the story of the Scottsboro boys went international. The boys continued to receive national and international attention for years mostly because two of their appeals reached the U.S. Supreme Court. Both decisions were significant. The first one established a criminal defendant's right to the effective assistance of counsel and the second one held that people may not be excluded from juries solely because of their race. Supposedly the novel *To Kill a Mockingbird* is based in part on the Scottsboro boys' story.

A 2001 *New York Times* article "Scottsboro 70 Years Later, Still Notorious, Still Painful" reviewed the PBS documentary *Scottsboro, An*

American Tragedy and found that the present-day Scottsboro residents were leery of reopening the past. The article described the town:

> Today Scottsboro is a pretty place of about 15,000 people, nestled in the hills of northeast Alabama along the Tennessee River. It is the home of the Unclaimed Baggage Center, which sells unclaimed baggage from airlines. The town still celebrates First Monday, a monthly gathering in the courthouse square, a flea market and swap meet that has existed for more than 100 years. Schools are now integrated, although blacks and whites still live mostly in separate neighborhoods.

Except for the housing part, I found this description to be a pretty good assessment of Scottsboro. African Americans comprise about five percent of the area's population, and it seems a little harsh to suggest that Scottsboro's housing patterns are any different than those elsewhere in the country.

Downtown Scottsboro looks like a prosperous small town even though the new four-lane highway bypasses it by a couple of miles. Scottsboro appears to be one of only a handful of small towns in the country, southern or otherwise, which have maintained a vibrant town square after Wal-Mart or K-Mart locates on a bypass. The square looked much the same as during the 1950s: lots of activity, few vacant stores, and virtually no empty parking places, even on a rainy weekday afternoon. I was disappointed that Payne's Soda Shop was closed for the day. Established in 1869, Payne's is the oldest ongoing business in Jackson County, and I'd been told they still make a pretty good milkshake.

One store dominates the east side of the square, occupying four store fronts. A modest sign hangs over the second storefront that reads Hammer's. On a whim, I decided to enter. Did it bring back memories! If you spent any time in a small town during the 1950s or 1960s, Hammer's transports you back to that time. Hammer's describes itself as a department store, and I guess that's technically true, but it's more like a general store.

Rather than leave downtown, Hammer's expanded by taking over its immediate neighbors. Merchandise hangs from the walls or sits in old-fashioned bins. Hand-printed signs inserted into chrome-plated frame sign holders advertise bargain prices. No new-fangled merchandising here—mostly bins full of stuff. Lined up in one bin were women's shoes—one of each pair. You pick out the shoe and hand it to a sales clerk. She goes to the stock room in the back, finds the mate, and then returns to watch the customer try on the pair. If the customer doesn't like them, she hands them both back to the clerk and repeats the process.

You can get pretty much anything at Hammer's. One storefront displays Oriental rugs. The second store contains women's shoes, bathing suits, and undergarments. The third one carries men's clothes, hunting clothes, work clothes, and boots. I understand jewelry and home accessories are in the final store.

I'm sure I didn't see everything that Hammer's offered, but I did go through the men's department. Everything was first quality, though some items were closeouts, overruns, or discontinued. I was about ready to walk out when I spotted a pair of brown cords that I remember men wearing years ago—probably described today as "old-school." Anyway, they were my size, and only fifteen dollars.

I took my old school pants to the checkout line. While standing there, the cashier lady, with a soft southern cadence to her speech, remarked to a customer, "You're lucky to get those pecans. We just can't keep bagged nuts in stock. We put them out and they're gone within fifteen minutes. I don't know why." The next customer tried to pay with a credit card and she pleasantly asked: "Would you mind if I saw your driver's license? I just want to make sure that it's your credit card that you're using." I don't remember anybody being that nice when asking for an ID. I was paying with cash. She gave me a smile, handed me the change from my twenty-dollar bill, and said she hoped I wouldn't get too wet from the rain falling outside the store.

The Unclaimed Baggage Center, located a few blocks from downtown Scottsboro, was my next stop. UBC has been in business since 1970 in Scottsboro, maintaining contracts with airlines to dispose of unclaimed baggage. Airlines spend up to ninety days attempting to return luggage to the rightful owners. After that time, they consign the baggage to Scottsboro's Unclaimed Baggage Center to sell the contents.

UBC's motto: "From lost treasures around the world."

Have you ever wondered what happened to the sunglasses you left on an airplane? They're probably for sale in northeast Alabama for five bucks, unless they are the designer-kind, which cost fifteen dollars—one price for all. Clothing—golf shirts, shorts, and dresses—fills most of the store. UBC claims to stock 7,000 items daily and that you never know what you might find. High-end items like fine jewelry, Hermes scarves, Versace dresses, and Burberry raincoats are known to come through, but I didn't see bargains like that. I did see lots of reading glasses for $3 and CDs for $4. Innumerable iPods, suitcases, travel bags, and noise-canceling earphones rounded out their inventory. I'm not sure the prices are bargains compared to what you get on eBay, but the thrill of a bargain overpowers some people.

Leaving the store I noticed that UBC's main entrance contained an alcove which housed the Museum of Unclaimed Treasures. An old violin was its most notable item. The violin was in good shape and displayed with its original case. The case was open with inscriptions inside noting the dates and places where the violin was made and subsequently repaired. Not many stores have their own museum.

While in Scottsboro, I attended the First Monday Trade Days, an event held around the Jackson County courthouse square since 1902. First Mondays originated with James Armstrong, owner of the local newspaper, who called it Horse Swapper's Day. Beginning in 1925, the local newspaper gave free advertising to any farmer who wanted to sell, trade, or buy anything on the first Monday of the month. As Scottsboro's economy changed, First Mondays changed. The modern First Monday begins on the weekend before the first Monday of each month because today most vendors are not farmers but people with full-time jobs. Most of the shoppers are also.

On an overcast Sunday afternoon, First Monday shoppers fully occupied but didn't crowd the Jackson County courthouse square lawn. Adult shoppers visited leisurely with one another on the courthouse lawn, while children played nearby. A leashed beagle puppy jumped at soap bubbles from a child's bubble-making machine as they floated by on a gentle spring breeze. It was an all-American scene.

Around the square, vendors displayed the typical categories of swap-meet merchandise: plants, rocking chairs, crafts, sunglasses, used books, pottery, and DVDs. A number of dealers sold, for lack of a better term, juntiques—cheap used furniture and personal goods. I later discovered that many vendors leave their wares out, but covered, overnight. One or two vendors sleep in their trucks for protection. Between them and the attentions of the police, there aren't any thieving problems. I told you this was a small town.

About forty-five minutes after I arrived, some vendors began packing up. It was early afternoon with still plenty of daylight left. I sought out a departing furniture vendor to ask why he was leaving so early in the afternoon. I stood around waiting while he paid a young man, the grandson of another vendor, twenty dollars for his help in packing goods into the nearby van. The furniture man, Philip Chandler, told me the vendors had heard about some rain sixty miles away and he was afraid it was coming this way. He had been afraid of the weather so he had set up early this weekend. He reported that shoppers were out by 8:00 a.m. both days and business was steady both mornings. Now with the threat of bad weather, shoppers wouldn't come out and there was no reason for him to stay.

Mr. Chandler lived in rural Jackson County and was by my estimation seventy years old. He was formal, consistently addressing me as sir. He explained that he had been selling furniture for a number of years—first, in a swap meet near Acworth, Georgia, a northern suburb of Atlanta over a hundred miles away. The past few years, he'd been selling his furniture only at First Monday. He sold furniture made by his wife's uncle in nearby Tennessee. He said he could pretty much get whatever you want within a week.

Without much prompting, Mr. Chandler explained the process of becoming a First Monday dealer. At the beginning of every year, he buys an annual permit for three spaces—parking places around the square. They go for $5 per day per space. So he pays $180 for Saturdays and $180 for Sundays. (I completely forgot to ask him if he buys spaces for Mondays.) Then he's ready to go for the year. He's usually here every month but often doesn't attend the January or February trade days because of the weather. He invited me to come back Labor Day weekend, saying that the biggest trade days occurred in September. As he said, "People don't work anymore on Labor Day."

As we parted, he shook my hand and said, "It is surely my pleasure to meet you, sir." He then advised that if I had any further questions about First Monday, I should see the city officials. He gave me detailed directions to City Hall, just a few blocks away. Mr. Chandler could not remember the name of the lady at city hall that I needed to see about First Mondays. He suggested that I call the telephone operator at city hall and tell her I needed to talk to the lady about First Monday. She would take care of me, Mr. Chandler assured me. Then—even though he never asked what I sold—he said that he would be pleased if I would take the space next to him.

Alabama Wholesale

Traveling across the top of Alabama, the first real city that appears is Huntsville. When Jonathan Daniels arrived during his Journey, Huntsville was a quiet little community that led the state in cotton production. Today it is well-populated: About 180,000 people live within the city limits and another 250,000 in the area.

Cotton has taken a backseat to something more modern. Huntsville is "Rocket City." For the past two generations, Huntsville has been a big cog in this country's space program. Beginning with the arrival of Dr. Wernher von Braun, at the end of World War II and through the development of the George C. Marshall Space Flight Center at Redstone Arsenal, Huntsville has become central to America's space program. With the U.S. Space & Rocket Center Space Camp for Kids, Huntsville remains a key city for the future of America's space and aviation industries.

It's also home to one of the longest "fast food, big box" roads I've ever seen—maybe in the country. Coming in from the east, Huntsville transitions quickly from rural Madison County. But leaving Huntsville heading west, the town sprawls toward the interstate thirty miles away with one familiar franchise food joint after another, numerous small retail strips, and a mall. A student of modern America land-use planning or contemporary culture would do well to study the Lee Highway out of Huntsville past Athens, Alabama.

After putting Athens, Alabama, in the rearview mirror, the quiet character of the Alabama hill country returns. This is part of tornado alley, and spring storms turn deadly here. On April 3, 1974, during the "super outbreak," two tornadoes, classified as F5 and F4, hit rural Limestone County within thirty minutes of one another. These two tornadoes followed almost the identical path for fifty miles, killing fifty people and injuring 500 more, not to mention inflicting millions of dollars of destruction on a very rural area. Tornado watches were posted for the evening I was there, but thankfully only thunderstorms occurred.

Florence, Alabama, is located in the northwest corner of Alabama, a dozen miles from Tennessee and not much farther from the Mississippi state line. Florence is a small city of 35,000 people. It's a college town—home to the University of Northern Alabama. My mother is a graduate of that fine institution. Despite the college influence, Florence is still one of the many buckles in the Bible Belt. Liquor by the drink didn't come until the late 1980s, and draft beer wasn't available until 2007, an astounding fact for a college town. In the 1930s, Florence was one of the tri-cities, which included the nearby towns of Tuscumbia and Sheffield. As the music of Muscle Shoals became nationally known, "tri" became "quad," and, finally, the whole area became known as "the Shoals."

Until a few years ago, the area was known mainly for the "Muscle Shoals sound," a type of popular music. It's hard to believe, but this little corner of Alabama was a "Ginnin' Gussie" of music. From the late 1950s through the end of the century, FAME Studios (Florence Area Music Enterprises) and the Muscle Shoals Sound Studio recorded such artists as Wilson Pickett, Aretha Franklin, Joe Tex, the Staple Singers, Percy Sledge, Bobby Purify, the Rolling Stones, Paul Simon, Willie Nelson, Boz Skaggs, Cher, Rod Stewart, Lynyrd Skynyrd, and the Allman Brothers. And, later, other artists including Levon Helm, Eric Clapton, Glenn Frey, the Oak Ridge Boys, Alabama, Sawyer Brown, Etta James, Faith Hill, Melissa Etheridge, and Joe Nichols became part of the Shoals' music scene.

The reasons given for world-famous musicians coming to a place without high-end hotels, restaurants, or nightlife during the last forty years of the twentieth century are not entirely clear. The lack of outside influences, which allowed for music-making with minimal distractions, was the primary reason. Another reason for the Shoals popularity with recording artists was the unique music environment, which is occasionally called "honky soul."

The roots of honky soul began with WLAY, an AM radio station in Florence, which has played a "variety format" since the Depression. For years, it was the rare southern radio station that broadcast different genres of music: southern gospel, country music, and "race" music (music by African-American artists) throughout the day. Additionally, the station sponsored live performances of bluegrass and Delta blues musicians in the area. In the early part of the twentieth century, northern Alabama had an unusual practice for the South: black and white musicians felt free to collaborate. These collaborations created a melting pot of blues, gospel, bluegrass, and country.

While FAME Studios still exists, the Muscle Shoals Sound Studio has closed. WLAY still broadcasts on AM and now on FM 92.3. Known as "the Sound," it plays primarily Shoals music. Artists with some connection to the Shoals, by having grown up, written, played, or recorded there, get airtime on the Sound. For those who like to hear this eclectic genre of modern music, the Sound is now available on the web at www.wlaythesound.com.

Florence's population has not grown appreciably in the last thirty or forty years; most of the growth has occurred outside the city limits. The metropolitan area, which covers the two counties of the quad cities, Lauderdale and Colbert, now has a population of about 150,000. Florence has two lakes near it—Wilson Lake and Pickwick Lake—where the newer and higher-end housing is located. Though it is not as vibrant as downtown Scottsboro or Chattanooga, Florence's downtown is bustling. When I asked for a downtown restaurant recommendation for dinner, most locals hesitated. Luckily, Billy Reid, owner of the New York City men's store of the same name, asked if I was up for an old-school steakhouse. Since I had taken it easy at lunch I thought, *What the heck, I'll bite*, which led me to Dale's.

Dale's Steakhouse is down by the river in a building obviously built in the 1960s; it has that skinny, light-brown, rough-edged brick that was a popular building material back then. The owner of Dale's, Chuck

Tompkins, is a lifelong resident of Shoals. Originally from Tuscumbia, Chuck moved across the river to Florence after graduating from college. As a high schooler, Chuck saw Mick Jagger at a hamburger joint when Jagger was recording "Wild Horses." Chuck said that the incident is noteworthy now even though it wasn't such a big deal at the time since sightings of big-name artists were common.

Today, when people ask Chuck where he's from, he tells them Tuscumbia, not Florence. It irritates his wife, who was born in Florence. He said the river still has meaning. While the Shoals area is one economic engine, the towns compete with one another. Take liquor by the drink—in this Baptist-dominated area, liquor by the drink did not arrive until the late 1980s. But once one locality allowed it, others changed their laws so that they wouldn't lose business to their neighbor.

Dale's was a local Alabama steakhouse chain founded after World War II by two GIs. These fellas swore that if they ever got out of the Pacific theater alive, they would start a steakhouse in Birmingham selling steaks flavored like the ones they had tasted in Hawaii. Over the years, Dale's succeeded and in time expanded to seven locations throughout Alabama.

When the original owners and their wives died or left the business, the seven locations were sold piecemeal. The Florence location is the last remaining Dale's Steakhouse. It's a family business, literally. Every member of Chuck's immediate family has worked in the restaurant, and most of the wait staff and kitchen help go back a couple of generations. He hasn't hired any wait staff for fifteen years because there has been no turnover. Once he had three generations of the same family on the same shift. Local deaths are a scheduling problem for the restaurant in this close-knit community. Dale's might have to shut down one afternoon every few weeks for a funeral, but the employees take shifts going to the visitations or funerals.

Chuck isn't worried about the long-term prospects of his business or the Shoals because the area is such a desirable place to live. He said there are a lot of people who live in the Shoals area but make their money else-where. One lawyer has an office in Nashville but spends most of his time on Pickwick Lake. With the Internet and telephones, no one knows he isn't in his Nashville office. And many people from the music industry maintain a presence in Nashville, two hours away by car, but really live in the Shoals area.

Besides the refugees from the Nashville music industry, little Florence, Alabama, is home to two top clothing designers, Billy Reid and Natalie Chanin. Billy is a clothing designer who sells through his stores in Charleston, Charlotte, Nashville, Dallas, and Houston. And—get this—the East Village of Manhattan. *New York Magazine* selected his Manhattan store as the best men's store in the Big Apple. Oh yeah, his main store is in Florence.

Billy Reid at his Florence store

Billy has been described as a "whiskey-sippin' William Faulkner and Buddy Holly rolled into one." While I concede that his glasses make you think of Buddy Holly, I'm not sure where they come up with Faulkner. Unless it's because he occasionally offers customers sips of small-batch bourbon in his New York store.

Natalie designs a collection called "Alabama Chanin." It is high-end handmade women's clothing sold through stores like Barney's and Bergdorf Goodman in New York. In Natalie's words:

> We craft limited-edition products for the individual and the home. Our products are made by hand using a combination of new, organic, and recycled materials. Each piece is constructed with care by talented artisans who work and live in communities in and around Florence, Alabama.

> Our products come numbered in a one-of-a-kind or limited edition series and are signed by the artisans that made them.

Given my limited understanding of the fashion industry, I really had one question for both of them: How can you anticipate the whims of the fashion industry from the boondocks of Florence, Alabama? Both of them had the same reaction: It's not difficult. With the advent of the Internet, fashion information is transmitted instantaneously. You no longer need to be in New York to know the latest goings-on in the fashion business.

After that, the rest is easy. Both of them are small business people who, like small business people everywhere, have to wear a number of hats to be successful. Both seem more comfortable talking about the business aspects of their operations than the creative side. (Or maybe it's that I understood the business side better.)

Billy has moved his corporate headquarters from Dallas to downtown Florence. The second floor of his shop houses the administrative offices and includes a design studio for hand-tailored, made-to-measure clothing. The front of the first floor is the retail space and has enough room to showcase his entire men's and women's collections. The back of the building is devoted to warehouse operations. When was the last time you heard of a distribution facility moving to a place where the nearest interstate is an hour away?

Natalie's corporate headquarters have been located here for some time—in an old t-shirt factory north of Florence. The factory is actually hard to find, but as in most small towns, when I went to the wrong place, the men in the warehouse asked who I was looking for. I told them Natalie Chanin. They pointed out a nearby building and said that she'd be behind the gray door. The factory had been vacant before Natalie took it over, a victim of the textile business having been shipped overseas. When the factory closed, the jobs went away. The skills of the textile workers did not.

Just a few months later I was in New York City, getting out of a cab in midtown. I looked up and saw Natalie's fashions in a store window. A few days later, I went to Billy's store in the East Village. It has the same feel of the Florence store with Shoals music playing in the background and southern memorabilia on the walls. I told the young sales clerk that I had recently been in the main store in Florence and took some satisfaction when she said enviously that she hoped one day to be able to go there. It shows how far the South has come in the past few generations when a person in Greenwich Village dreams of one day seeing Florence— meaning Florence, Alabama.

Driving the Natchez Trace Parkway

If I were leaving Florence to catch a plane, I'd travel to Nashville the same way as Billy Reid does every couple of weeks. I'd start back the way I came: east on Alabama Highway 72, the famous Lee Highway, to Interstate 65, which I'd then take north to Nashville. It's a distance of 150 miles and takes less than two and a half hours, if you're lucky with Nashville traffic.

Since I wasn't catching a plane, I took roughly the same path Jonathan Daniels did: west toward the state of Mississippi and the Natchez Trace Parkway. Rather than fight the trucks on I-65 at seventy miles per hour, I cruised the Parkway at fifty. OK, I'm lying. I'd drive about eighty on the interstate, but on the Parkway, I could only push fifty-five.

Most people believe that the Natchez Trace started as a buffalo trail. These creatures migrated from their grazing pastures in what is now central Mississippi to salt deposits in present-day central Tennessee. The local Indian tribes, the Choctaw, Chickasaw, and Natchez, followed the "traces" of these animals, creating foot paths as they traveled. The local paths developed into America's first national "road" in the late 1700s, linking the wealthy city of Natchez to the United States. The trace was especially helpful for those frontiersmen like Abraham Lincoln who floated produce and merchandise down the Mississippi River to New Orleans. After arriving in New Orleans, they sold their flat boats for lumber and walked back home via the Natchez Trace.

In the early 1800s, the trace got promoted from path to postal road. General Jackson marched his army of volunteers from Tennessee down the trace to the Battle of New Orleans. By the 1820s, the importance of the trail declined as pioneers developed new roads. More importantly, the new-fangled steam boat allowed river traffic to travel upstream on the river. As a result of these two developments, the Natchez Trace became obsolete as a national road and devolved into a series of local roads. For over a hundred years the trace didn't change much; it remained a collection of local roads. During the Great Depression, though, Congress decided to build two national parkways as public works projects. The Natchez Trace was to be one of the two. In 1939, the acting superintendent of the project wrote:

> Congress has authorized the construction of a parkway along the general route of the old Natchez Trace, designed for tourist and passenger car traffic. Presumably the Natchez Trace Parkway eventually will be one section of a national parkway system of arterial routes for passenger cars. A parkway is an elongated park containing a road, and a parkway as part of a comprehensive recreation and conservation program would make available to the traveler certain areas along its route of a scenic, scientific and historic importance. On the Natchez Trace Parkway historical features will be emphasized although final plans for preservation and development are far from complete.

This last sentence indicating that final plans were "far from complete" was a slight understatement because the last twelve miles of parkway didn't get finished until some sixty-six years later, in 2005.

The Parkway is 444 miles from beginning to end. I was traveling about 120 of them getting to the Nashville terminus. As they say in north Alabama, "leaving out" on the Parkway, the road crosses the Tennessee River at the former Colbert Ferry. At this crossing in 1811, Mr. Colbert charged General Jackson the incredible sum of $75,000 to ferry the troops across the river to meet the British in New Orleans. Seems war profiteering has been around for a while.

On the Parkway, you can go miles without seeing another car. I estimate that I drove a stretch of about thirty minutes on this weekday afternoon without seeing a car coming or going. There's not much else on the Parkway. Driving the Trace at night has been described as eerie because modern travelers are not used to the complete darkness with no light pollution. Where the roadway is not canopied by trees, wide shoulders of the right-of-way create a park-like grassy lawn.

Welcome to the Parkway

The only signs on the Parkway are mile-marker signs or Parkway signs directing you to 356 archeological sites, thirty-six cemeteries, twenty-one properties listed on the National Register of Historic Places, and sixty miles of National Scenic Trails. Besides restricting signage, the Parkway prohibits gas stations, businesses, and trucks.

At fifty miles an hour, the trip should take a little more than two hours. But because I became a sucker for the Parkway signs, the trip took a lot longer. I stopped to see the grave of Meriwether Lewis (of Lewis and Clark fame). Poor Meriwether was either murdered or committed suicide while traveling the Trace in 1809. I also stopped to walk a portion of the original trace, a wide dirt path following one of the many ridges in the south-central Tennessee hills. Standing beside the Parkway, the only noise I could hear was the rustle of the summertime breeze through the trees. Even though I was a long way from the Blue Ridge Mountains and Cashiers, North Carolina, the quiet and solitude were the same.

Stretches of the Parkway are very remote. Wild turkeys typically stay away from humans as much as possible and are generally seen only in unpopulated areas, but a few miles after stopping to walk part of the original Trace, I had the first of seven wild turkey sightings. These birds feed on the Parkway's right-of-way. After traveling the Parkway, the number of wild turkeys I've seen in my lifetime totals nine.

Traffic picks up as the road nears the Parkway terminus. There was now a car coming in the opposite lane every few minutes. Most of the Parkway had been relatively straight, but for the last few miles of the parkway, it wound and turned. In a line of three cars, traffic poked along at thirty-five or forty miles an hour toward Nashville's west side.

The Natchez Trace Parkway Bridge on Tennessee Highway 96 is a pretty double-arch bridge with a unique engineering design. To appreciate the bridge I'd need to leave the Parkway which I didn't do. I wish I had, because the exit is near the town of Leiper's Fork. Leiper's Fork has a general store named Puckett's which I've been told is a great live music venue. The Leiper's Fork area is also reportedly home to a bunch of country music stars like Keith Urban and his wife, Nicole Kidman; John Hiatt; and the Judds. But I was ready for the city and soon reached Highway 100. Here the Parkway ends and civilization rudely begins. As you turn onto Highway 100, gas stations, traffic lights, and billboards quickly end the reverie of the Parkway drive. A highway sign points to Interstate 40 and the concrete and the tall buildings of downtown Nashville.

Nashville Hootenanny

Loveless' Café sits just outside the Natchez Trace Parkway terminus. People who went to school in Nashville swear by Loveless'. To be honest, it looked like one of those chain country restaurants with rocking chairs out front, the ones you see on interstate exits. I later discovered that it had expanded recently—opening a live music venue. Locals say that, while not all the changes are for the better, Loveless' Café is still a pretty good place to get what they call a "meat and three."

To be precise, the Natchez Trace Parkway doesn't end in Nashville, but rather in Belle Meade, Tennessee, an independent city within metropolitan Nashville. Belle Meade is famous as the home of Al Gore and the location of Belle Meade plantation. Gore is, of course, the former vice president of the United States, Nobel Peace Prize winner, and credited by some as inventor of the Internet. Belle Meade plantation gained fame in post–Civil War Nashville as a horse-breeding facility. Times got tough in the early twentieth century and Belle Meade's owners borrowed money they couldn't repay. Sadly, the horse-breeding industry left Belle Meade via a foreclosure sale.

That doesn't mean horse racing is completely gone. Since 1941, at the public park a few miles from the beginning of the Parkway, Nashville holds one of the biggest days of steeplechase racing in America—the Iroquois Steeplechase. The Saturday after the Kentucky Derby finds a seven-race card of steeplechase races culminating in the Grade I Calvin

Houghland Iroquois Steeplechase, a three-mile race. Steeplechase racing requires horses to jump over obstacles, as opposed to flat races in which horses run as fast as they can. (The Kentucky Derby is an example of flat racing.) While steeplechase racing is not as popular as flat racing, it is also not dependent on wagering (which is illegal in Tennessee, though not in Kentucky). Since there's no sanctioned wagering, the Iroquois Steeplechase is now a charity event, raising money for the local children's hospital. It's also a society event, with folks picnicking and visiting decked out in their finest spring clothes. Men wear seersucker suits and ladies wear hats.

Remember that the Natchez Trace was a historic road and doesn't end at the Parkway. After leaving the Parkway, you can wander around on streets named Natchez Trace almost to the center of metropolitan Nashville. But you won't mistake it for the Parkway. It's now just a series of city streets through neighborhoods, some of which are not so nice.

Back in the first real city since Charlotte, North Carolina, let's take a minute to review where we are. Nashville is the state capital of Tennessee, so there is a large governmental presence in the city. Set on a hill, the state capitol building is one of the prettiest in the South. The state legislature makes laws for the entire state, but Nashville rules only middle Tennessee. The hills of east Tennessee and the flat land of west Tennessee are decidedly independent.

Nashville is the undisputed world capital of country music. The Country Music Hall of Fame is touted by the Chamber of Commerce, "You should spend as much time as possible at the Country Music Hall of Fame—it is the jewel of our city—the heartbeat!" Country music is everywhere. If you're looking for live music, the city has placed signs outside venues so that visitors can more readily find live music venues.

Country music in Nashville is literally ubiquitous. Every restaurant and hotel plays country music indoors and out so you can hear it from the time you get out of the car. After a while you want them to turn off the music, especially the songs with a heavy emphasis on the steel guitar. A little note here: The steel guitar is not native to country music. The instrument was invented in Hawaii in the late 1800s and imported into hillbilly music in the mid-1920s.

Live music here!

The Gibson Guitar Company also got into the act with its Guitartown Project, a public arts project featuring ten-foot-tall sculptures of Les Paul or Chet Atkins model guitars honoring famous artists and events. Today there are over thirty of these sculptures throughout the city.

Country music just keeps coming—even in your hotel room. In most cities, the in-room hotel magazine is little more than a catalogue of local tourist-related businesses. My hotel selected *American Songwriter: The Business Issue* for its guests' reading pleasure.

This is still the South, where on any fall Saturday, you can watch Southeastern Conference football on television for about twelve consecutive hours. But after this run of football games, in Nashville the next television show was—you guessed it—a documentary about country songwriters. Pretty interesting, but seriously, what about some *Saturday Night Live* reruns as a change of pace?

Guitartown on Music Row

The next day, I scheduled a meeting with Tom Shinness, my college roommate's younger brother, at Doak Turner's "Third Sunday at 3:00" event. Since 2002, Doak opens his house for songwriters and musicians on the third Sunday of each month for a potluck. Everyone brings a dish or a drink, and, no, chips are not a dish. Doak provides the main course, often barbecue, but on this night it was fried chicken. People come late in the afternoon, eat and visit, then play music together through the evening.

Doak's place is located in west Nashville. Technically, the town is called West Meade, and it lies just north of Belle Meade. A rainstorm passed through as I drove to Doak's get-together. As instructed, I parked in the parking lot at a nearby Baptist church and walked a long, wet block to Doak's 1970s-era ranch-style house in the suburbs. No one stood out front, so I followed the driveway to the back of the house. From there, I spotted people standing at the openings of the double garage.

I arrived very wet. I thought I would be early, but at least two dozen people were already there. In better weather, food and lawn chairs would have been stationed outside. Because of the rain storm, everything had been brought inside. Chairs and tables covered with food dishes lined the walls of the garage. Drinks, mainly iced tea and beer, sat in pitchers and crowded coolers. My contribution to the potluck was a bottle of iced-tea flavored vodka from a local beverage shop. Since I wasn't sure of the protocols, I placed it on the dessert table—not with the iced tea.

From the garage, I stepped into what originally had been the basement. At some time in the house's history, two rooms had been created with low seven-foot ceilings. The low ceiling made the spaces seem small and crowded. A keyboard player talked with four or five friends while he set up his instrument. In the other room, musicians sat on couches with plates and drinks, eating and kibitzing. None of these people looked like the picture of Tom I had seen on the Internet.

I continued upstairs into the house to continue my search for Tom. When I found him, he suggested that we go back downstairs for food. As we stood and ate, Tom told me his story. Originally from Anderson, Indiana, he'd lived in Nashville for the past six years, moving from Dallas, Texas. I knew from his brother that Tom has been supporting himself as a full-time musician for a few years—no easy task. One of his three children is a struggling Nashville musician, who sings with Tom on occasion.

Most people arrived, as I did, through the garage in back. Almost everyone had a guitar case or some type of musical instrument. Sooner or later, things got so crowded around the food that guests migrated to the upstairs rooms. Even though we ate quickly, the return trip upstairs was much more difficult, as little groups of people were camped throughout the basement, on the staircase, and upstairs in the kitchen. Tom was a regular at Third Sunday. He was like a good politician, keeping his feet moving as he made his way through the crowds. He moved easily through the small groups of people, acknowledging everyone with a hello or a friendly glance, but not really stopping to talk with anyone.

In one room, a kind of enclosed sun porch, Doak set up a video camera linking the event to the Internet to broadcast the music. But it was still early in the evening and musicians had not begun playing the room. Tom and two musicians ducked into this room and talked shop. One of the musicians described his recent experience of performing four gigs in two days. The other, Kurt Fortmeyer, had released a new CD. He and Tom, who has six CDs to his credit, discussed the business side of music: the cost of production time; musician friends who can be counted on for help with a recording session; the problems of CD jackets (where to get them made); and how to cop a few extra copies in production overruns. The tricks of the trade you need to know when you don't have a recording contract or management taking care of such details.

Later in the conversation, Kurt confessed to the small group that he'd applied for a day job as airport security with the TSA. Taking a day job is obviously a step back for a musician, but as Kurt said, "It offers health insurance." The group nodded in a sad, unspoken understanding of why day jobs are necessary. When I heard his disclosure, I had a slightly different thought. Now don't get me wrong, but I guess one reason I don't feel much safer flying today than before all of the new security measures is that I don't believe that Kurt is the first musician hired by the TSA.

I'd been there a couple of hours and Third Sunday now had become a free-form event with music coming from a half dozen rooms. Musicians flowed through the rooms and filled the chairs or sat on the floor waiting their turn to play. Their audience was one another; only a few people were mere spectators like me. In the living room, close to a dozen musicians sat in a circle and played music—one after another. Most were singers and guitar players. Some were quite mediocre; some pretty good. But everyone was supportive and encouraging.

As I stood in the living room watching, Tom reappeared saying that two musicians from east Tennessee had arrived and that I didn't want to miss them. He said he needed to retrieve his gear. I followed Tom back downstairs again to get his instrument, and then back upstairs toward a bedroom. It was now about 6:00 and there were a lot of people in the house. It felt like there were sixty to eighty people. Most occupants carried guitars or guitar cases with them, which made traveling through the house even more difficult. My frame of reference was the crowd in the two downstairs basement rooms, as this was my third or fourth trip through them. The rooms were now completely packed with players, most of whom were not drinking iced tea.

Tom walked down to the end of the hallway and turned on the light in a small empty bedroom. I assumed I would meet two guitar players, but only one tall fellow followed Tom into the room. He and Tom unpacked their equipment. Tom had a cello. Big Boy had a case which held a bassoon. The bassoon has various parts that go together about as simply as the parts of an automobile transmission. As he assembled his instrument, Big Boy and Tom talked. Big Boy had grown up in Nashville, had moved away a few years before, and had moved back to town a few weeks ago. This was his first Third Sunday experience.

Tom Shinness on the cello and Big Boy on the bassoon

Big Boy started tuning his bassoon, and Tom followed on his cello. They began playing together in earnest. The music was significantly different than what was being produced in the other rooms, and curious spectators soon crammed into the small suburban bedroom. People out in the hallway craned their necks to see the music being made. Tom and Big Boy played for a little more than five minutes. The two instruments blended well together. When they stopped, the crowd cooed appreciatively. I sat on the floor cross-legged with my back against the wall trying to remember the last time I had heard a cello solo. College maybe. But more likely high school. I could safely say I'd never seen a live bassoon performance.

They took a very short break for Tom to swap his cello for his harp guitar. Now don't ask me about the harp guitar. They are rare instruments. The harp guitar has two necks: The bottom one looks like a standard guitar; the top neck carries a bunch of strings like a harp. The two players began playing again—this time alternating, like two old friends swapping stories in a conversation. When the second instrumental ended, Tom softly announced to the assembled that it was the first time the two had ever played together. The small crowd of a dozen or so murmured its appreciation.

As Tom and Big Boy repacked their instruments, three guitar players filed into the small room, making a crowded situation even worse. Two of the guitarists constituted a group that I assumed were the guys from east Tennessee. One of them sang his song about how America had become a society of victims—pretty right-wing politically—but well-written and well-received. I would have figured a crowd of musicians to be left-wing or liberal. But this is country music country, not Hollywood, and not all musicians are liberal around here. Many of the small crowd nodded in agreement with the song's sentiments about not complaining during hard times. None of these people could be considered wealthy by any means. I suspect that most of them struggle to pay their bills each month. But trying to break into Nashville's country music scene, they work without a safety net like regular paychecks or jobs with paid health insurance. Theirs is a long-shot struggle for success.

Success in the music business requires talent. But talent isn't enough—because the next song was a wonderful, moving song, one so good it should be a hit. It was a story about whether someone could be lucky enough to have two great loves in life. The song was so sad that when it ended, one of the guitarists confessed that he had hoped to play it this one time without crying. The song's author, a young man, spoke up and confessed the story was a true story. It was about a woman with whom he'd fallen in love, a war widow. She had lost her first husband, the love of her life. In the song, and in his life, the writer wondered if he could be lucky enough to become the second great love of this woman's life. If the song hadn't gotten to you, the author's story surely did.

I left soon afterward, but I have no doubt that they played late into the evening at Doak's.

Mississippi Embayment

The rolling hills of middle Tennessee transition to flatland just east of Memphis. Welcome to the Delta. The Mississippi Embayment is the fancy name for the lower Mississippi Delta. According to University of Memphis professors Roy B. Van Arsdale and Randall Cox, this embayment formed about 95 million years ago when the earth's crust warped upward from southeastern Missouri south to Louisiana and east from the present-day Tennessee River, and west to Little Rock, Arkansas, possibly rising two or three kilometers above sea level. Later, 24-to-85 million years ago, the area which had been lifted started going the other direction so that the crest fell and formed a trough that was eventually filled by waters from the Gulf of Mexico. As the seas receded, the trough formed the Mississippi River. If you are interested in the causes of this prehistoric warping, see the January 2007 *Scientific American* article Van Arsdale and Cox wrote.

The lower Mississippi Delta begins around Sikeston, Missouri. The Delta extends mostly southward through eastern Arkansas and western Mississippi, ending in the middle of Louisiana near Alexandria. With its widespread poverty, high infant mortality rates, and terrible diabetes and obesity statistics, the Delta is the United States' "third world." Just mention any unwelcome standard you use to define a depressed area and the Delta either leads in that statistic or is right up there at the top. (Or one should probably say the bottom.) Things are so bad in the Delta that it has its own federal improvement bureau, the Delta Regional Commission.

Despite all these terrible problems, the National Park Service has noted, "Much of what is profoundly American—what people love about America—has come from the Delta, which is often called the 'the cradle of American culture.'"

Historian James Cobb once described the Delta as "the most Southern place on earth." The Delta is hot, flat, and muggy. It is home to the blues, the Tamale Trail, and cotton fields which still dominate this flatland. This is an agricultural area, to be sure. The economy rises and falls largely on the fortunes of the area's farmers. Historically the Delta was all about cotton and, to a large extent, still is today, though corn, rice, and soybeans now occupy substantial Delta acreage. The Delta also leads the nation in the production and processing of pond-raised catfish.

It's flyover country: Most outsiders only see the Delta from an airliner. Looking down out of a plane's window you see a checkerboard of various shades of brown and green—large squares of farmland spread out in all directions. From the perspective of 10,000 feet, an occasional speck of a car travels a very straight ribbon of road passing patches of buildings in small and remote towns.

It's easy to lose perspective when driving the Delta. Because there are very few towns and no hills, it's hard to judge distances out here. Approaching cars appear from a long way away; they seem close but take a long time to get to you. If you are trying to pass a car on these very straight and flat two-lane highways, the flatness takes some getting used to. Not that traffic is a big problem. With about one person per square mile, the Delta is one of the least densely populated areas of the South. Once you get your bearings though, passing on the two lanes becomes easy because visibility is so good and there's so little traffic.

Travel Notes:
What's a Julep?

Negotiating the 200 miles from Nashville to Memphis can create a thirst, and in the capital of the most southern place in America, what better way is there to quench a road thirst than with a mint julep? I came to know the mint julep on the Journey. Jonathan Daniels mentioned that he drank juleps during his travels and took great care to note the regional variations in this classic beverage. Solely to make the book more authentic, I did the same, though I did make a slight detour into Sazeracs while visiting New Orleans. But that's a whole different story.

The term *julep* comes from a Persian word meaning "rosewater." In the Middle Ages in England, it was a term to describe sugary syrup often mixed with foul-tasting medicines. The mint is an American addition, adding the plant's own medicinal qualities to the mixture. The mint julep is thought to have originated in Virginia where mint was used to mask the "kick" of rough whiskey. A hardworking man might need the occasional mid-morning invigoration of a toddy of water and whiskey. It's now considered a truly southern drink and the forerunner of the present-day mojito. During the Journey, I experienced both the rough whiskey and the need for invigoration.

Some people taste their first julep at the Kentucky Derby, but the track at Churchill Downs is no place to get your first mint julep—because they make a pretty bad one. One reason the drink has fallen into disfavor during the past few generations is that too many people first sample a mint julep at Churchill Downs.

The center of high-class Delta culture is the Peabody Hotel in Memphis. As David Cohen observed in 1935:

> The Peabody is the Paris Ritz, the Cairo Sheperd's, the London Savoy of this section. If you stand near its fountain in the middle of the lobby...ultimately you will see everybody who is anybody in the Delta.

So how good is the mint julep at the center of the Delta? After I checked in at my hotel (not the Peabody, by the way), I headed to the

Peabody to check out the lobby bar. Like most downtown hotels throughout the country, the Peabody hit hard times during the 1950s when central cities deteriorated and suburbs boomed. It closed in the early 1970s, but reopened in 1981. When it reopened, the new owners reinstituted a Peabody tradition—the duck march. Each morning, ducks parade from their rooftop home to the lobby by way of the hotel elevator. The ducks swim in the lobby fountain throughout the day. The cocktail hour starts with the ducks, led by the duck master, marching to the elevator with a pomp and circumstance to return to the roof. I missed the duck parade, but I didn't care. I wasn't there to watch ducks waddle from the lobby pond into an elevator. I was there to test the Peabody's claim of having the best juleps in the Delta.

The lobby bar at the Peabody is a pretty place. At 8:00 p.m. on a weekday, it was fairly crowded with businessmen crouched over drinks and engaged in high-level discussions. Tourists sat gawking at the stained glass and the beamed ceiling. A piano player entertained, while I waited a long time to be served. I placed my order and, after another fairly long wait, the mint julep arrived. It was made with a premixed bourbon and sugar mixture and served in a glass with cubes of ice. It wasn't much—mediocre at best. About the only thing that kept it from being "pure-dee lousy" was the fact that they at least garnished the drink with fresh mint. Otherwise it was a just an $8.00 headache-maker.

Even though my experience at the Peabody was not particularly positive, I've continued my field research on the mint julep. The mint julep is not a complicated drink, but it does require forethought. First, get some fine—really fine—spring water. Then make what's called "simple syrup" or sugar water by boiling the fine spring water with cane sugar. While the sugar water is hot, put it in a mason jar and add a bunch, and I mean a whole lot, of mint leaves. No stems, just leaves please. Let the concoction cool for two to twelve hours. Take the leaves out and leave the mint-infused sugar-water in the refrigerator for the next time you face a day when it's going to be 90 degrees at 9:00 a.m.—or p.m., it makes no difference.

One of those hot days, at or near 5:00 p.m., take out a fancy pewter or silver cup—if you don't have one of those, a glass cup can be substituted—and a few mint leaves. Muddle the leaves. (*Muddling* is a bar term for squishing the leaves against the side of the cup.) Don't be shy: muddling requires some squishing. I must add here that there is some controversy on muddling. Some believe that over-muddling releases bitter inner juices from the mint leave. I respectfully disagree with mini-muddling. Finally, get good bourbon. You can use cheap bourbon, but the drink's not as good if you use cheap stuff.

Now here's the hard part. Some people put the ice in first and add the bourbon and simple syrup. Others pour the bourbon in first, then add the simple syrup, stir the liquids together, and finally fill the container with ice. Either way is fine. My advice is if you put ice in first and then add the liquids, serve the drink with a straw so the drink will seem less strong. When I say fill the container with ice, that's the critical part. Get the best crushed ice you can find and pack it in. In the old days, people had house servants who gained reputations for their mint juleps. Some say that the quality of the bourbon is the most important ingredient; others would say it's the spring water. But the servants gained their reputation on how well they could beat a block of ice into little bitty pieces. Like many other things in our modern society, that task is now performed by a machine. But it's important to get really well-crushed ice to make a truly fine mint julep.

After making the drink, go outside, preferably near a fan. It's cooler and the moving air keeps mosquitoes away. (I understand that mosquitoes are not good flyers and they don't do well in a breeze.) Find a comfortable chair in the shade and take a seat. I find that looking west toward the sunset is good. I swear that after a few sips, you will be relaxed. I can't say whether it's the ice, the sugar, or the bourbon, but no matter how hot the weather, you soon will be re-invigorated.

That's not my only advice. If your host asks you if you would care for a second julep, you might respond as my grandfather did when asked if he wanted a refill: "A bird don't fly with one wing, does it?"

Day Trip to Arkansas

Leaving downtown Memphis, you immediately climb skyward toward the expanse of steel and cable crossing the Mississippi River into Arkansas. The bridge is high, the river wide. And every time I cross it, I think of the New Madrid fault, the seismic scar which runs from southern Illinois through southern Missouri and northeastern Arkansas. From December 1811 until February 1812, the region recorded four of the largest earthquakes in North American history. These earthquakes were so severe they rang church bells in Boston—and caused the mighty Mississippi to change its course. Whenever I'm on the bridge, I wonder what poor souls will be caught there when those tectonic plates shift again.

It's a concern today because my trip is to the "sunken lands" of eastern Arkansas. These sunken lands are swamp lands and standing water lakes created during the New Madrid earthquakes. The sunken lands area is one of the country's last frontiers. Because the land was wet most of the year, it was wild and untamed until the first two decades of the twentieth century. Levees were built to control flooding, and drainage districts built ditches which allowed the swamps to dry. Once the swamps dried, timber was cut and the soil below was some of the most fertile land in North America. Now it's mostly used to grow cotton and rice. What remains undrained is prime hunting land.

On his Journey, Jonathan Daniels visited Tyronza, Marked Tree, and Lepanto, the three major towns in eastern Poinsett County, Arkansas.

He came to see firsthand the tenant farmer problem. During the Great Depression, an overproduction of cotton caused the price to fall precipitously. One government program paid cotton farmers not to farm cotton. Conventional thinking assumed that reducing cotton production would cause cotton prices to increase and thereby help return them to a level where remaining producers could make a living.

The first problem with this plan was that much of the cotton crop was raised by sharecroppers, but the government required no assurance that any part of the relief payments be paid to sharecroppers. Not surprisingly, few landowners shared the government checks with their sharecroppers. Moreover, since they weren't planting as much cotton acreage, landlords let a number of sharecroppers go, causing an increase in the number of homeless. Due in large part to the unintended consequences of this federal aid program, the country's first fully integrated union, the Southern Tenant Farmers' Union (STFU), formed in eastern Poinsett County in 1934 to help the tenant farmers. Jonathan Daniels came to see this unique union movement.

Agriculture has changed dramatically, and the STFU died out in the 1960s. Cotton is no longer picked by hand. Today the process is mechanized. Fields that once took hundreds of human beings weeks to pick by hand are now done in days by three or four men using huge farm machines. Multi-row machines pick cotton bolls which are then packed in large truck-sized modules in the fields. These modules contain approximately 16,000 pounds of cotton which yields thirteen bales of ginned cotton. At harvest time in the Delta, these green-topped modules dot the countryside.

Tyronza, Marked Tree, and Lepanto, along with Trumann, still remain eastern Poinsett County's major towns. Tyronza is a town of fewer than 1,000 and lies about thirty miles from downtown Memphis, close enough to be a suburb of the big city. But it's not. Memphis developed eastward away from the river. Few Memphis commuters venture west across the bridge each afternoon; it's almost like the river is a barrier. Tyronza is about the same distance from downtown Memphis as Collierville, Tennessee. Collierville is a suburban paradise, with a small old downtown surrounded by housing developments, fancy eating establishments, a couple of private schools, lots of big box merchandisers, and the limited-access Nonconnah Parkway which allows commuters quick access to downtown. Tyronza has none of this. A branch bank, a public grade school, and a restaurant that serves breakfast and lunch—that about sums up Tyronza's amenities.

Cotton crop in the Delta

Tyronza is home to the Southern Tenant Farmers Museum. Now affiliated with Arkansas State University, the museum is located in a restored dry-cleaning establishment and gas station which once shared a common wall with the Bank of Tyronza. In the 1930s, the owners of the dry-cleaner and the gas station were socialists and their establishments were known as "Little Red Square." Local legend holds that the common wall with the bank saved the socialists from having their places bombed. The Federal Deposit Insurance Corporation hadn't been established, and apparently the plantation owners were afraid they might blow up their own money getting rid of the socialists.

The modern cotton bale

Other than the museum, Tyronza last made the news as a speed trap. Though not as infamous as its neighbor Gilmore, Tyronza raised most of its city revenues by targeting travelers on nearby Highway 63, the four-lane, divided highway between Memphis and Jonesboro. Arrests got so bad that the Arkansas General Assembly passed a statute that prohibited a city from receiving a majority of its revenue from traffic tickets. Any excess money went to the state. If the city didn't get the funds, it wouldn't use valuable police time writing tickets for minor infractions. It's no small credit to that statute that I was able to drive around Tyronza and Marked Tree without getting a ticket. Flat land, straight roads, and little traffic—a recipe for fast driving.

North of Marked Tree and east of Lepanto lie the 26,000-acre Sunken Lands Wildlife Management Area and the Hatchie Coon Hunting and Fishing Club. Hatchie Coon is one of those great southern names. You can tell if someone's from the South by the way they pronounce it. It's not like an Indian or Scottish name with a bunch of syllables that can be mispronounced. Just say these simple words, and the cadence and the emphasis confirm a speaker's regional identity. Get a Chicagoan or Pittsburgher to pronounce "Hatchie Coon," and any southerner will respond, "You're not from around here, are you?" Pine Bluff and Turrell are other local examples of regional identifiers.

Tyronza today

Anyway, the club is an old one. It was founded in 1892 by a bunch of rich fellows from Memphis who crossed the river to hunt and fish. Hatchie Coon acquired its land directly from the State of Arkansas in an original land grant of 700 acres. In 1932, the club became an Arkansas not-for-profit corporation. Still today most of its members are doctors, lawyers, and business magnates from Memphis.

Later, the Arkansas Game and Fish Commission acquired 25,000 acres of land for the Sunken Lands Wildlife Management Area. The

Game and Fish Commission's acquisition made Hatchie Coon's holdings even more valuable because the club now has the only access to the river within three miles north and two miles south of its property. If you think Tyronza is rural, you "ain't seen nutten yet." Hatchie Coon is really the boonies. But the hunting and fishing are great.

In rural America, hunting land is important and when disputes arise, they are serious matters. Hatchie Coon was recently involved in a great one. The Hatchie Coon Hunting Club claimed ownership of a forty-five-acre island in the St. Francis River as part of the original grant from the State. To be precise, the club claimed ownership of a *former* island. The island had been covered with water since the 1970s when the Game and Fish Commission raised the minimum water level of the river. For years, a man by the name of Hancock maintained a floating duck blind in the middle of the island. Hatchie Coon sought to have the duck blind removed. In 2001, Hatchie Coon filed a complaint to prevent Hancock from hunting on that duck blind because his hunting club claimed ownership of the submerged island. Defendant Hancock asserted that he owned the right to the duck blind, that he had received it from his father who had bought the rights to the blind during the 1960s. Furthermore, he testified that others had owned the blind many years before his father.

The trial court and the Arkansas Court of Appeals agreed with the Hatchie Coon Hunting Club that it had title to the submerged island. The matter was appealed further to the Arkansas Supreme Court. The Arkansas Supreme Court disagreed with the lower courts. It held that since the island had been submerged for more than seven years, the submerged island now was part of the river bed and therefore owned by the State. As a result of the litigation, Mr. Hancock lost his duck blind, reputed to be the best or second-best blind on the river. The Hatchie Coon Hunting club lost title to the island. But because the island is still under water, the public has a right to use it.

Jonathan Daniels ended his side trip to Arkansas in Dyess, or Dyess Colony, as it is still known to the locals. Dyess was a planned community developed in Arkansas by the Federal Emergency Relief Administration about the same time the TVA developed Norris as a model community in the hills of east Tennessee. In 1934, Colonization Project Number One was established in southwestern Mississippi County with the purchase of approximately 16,000 acres of uncleared bottomland from private interests. Interviewers traveled throughout Arkansas, evaluating farm families on the state's relief roles to find potential colonists. In the fall of 1934, these pioneers relocated and began the task of clearing land.

Now think about the situation during the Great Depression. There was a surplus of cotton land and too much cotton production. So what's the government's response? Pay people not to plant cotton. When sharecroppers are laid off because they are not needed for the unplanted fields, the government relocates the laid-off workers to another area. The first thing these new residents do is start clearing land for more production.

Project Number One grew to include approximately 500 individually owned forty-acre farms. The town was named Dyess. It was formed to support these former tenant farmers. The experiment was designed to show how former tenant farmers and sharecroppers could become self-sufficient. A few years later, World War II came. Many of these pioneers saw better non-farming opportunities in the war industries, so many people left Dyess for the factories.

Dyess' high point was 1936 when it had 2,500 inhabitants. In 2010, the last official estimate was 433, down 52 residents from ten years before. The only commercial activity in the town was a convenience store located about a block from a white-columned administration building which had seen better days. But the administration building was doing a darn sight better than the buildings on either side of it—one burned beyond repair and the other, a former movie theater, fallen down except for its front exterior wall.

With deteriorating streets and houses, Dyess is a depressing place. It's not at all like Norris with its well-kept streets and houses. None of the inhabitants appear prosperous or tidy, and virtually all of the homes are in some state of disrepair. And when I got out of the car to take a picture, the stench from the standing water made me get right back in.

Dyess does have a claim to fame—country music star Johnny Cash grew up there. His parents were sharecroppers in southern Arkansas but moved to Dyess in 1936; Johnny graduated from Dyess High in 1950.

He wrote the song "Five Feet High and Rising" about the evacuation of Dyess during the flood of 1937.

Dyess Administration Building

Dyess is now on the rebound. Arkansas State University created a master plan for Dyess. The university is restoring the exterior of the administration building and stabilizing the shell of the theater. It acquired Johnny Cash's boyhood home. The university and the Cash family hold an annual Johnny Cash Music Festival to raise funds to restore the house as a museum. Even though the house is not scheduled to open until 2014, the festival has created enough interest that tourists have started coming to Dyess in busloads from as far away as Ireland and Finland. Working with the community, the goal is to make Historic Dyess Colony: Boyhood Home of Johnny Cash an international tourism destination.

A look back at Dyess

The Delta in Mississippi

Graceland, home of Elvis Presley, is just a few miles from downtown Memphis. It's reportedly the most visited house in the country, outside of the White House. The house is about 17,000 square feet, surprisingly modest compared to the mansions of modern music stars. It sits prominently on fourteen acres of land. Even those who aren't fans of Elvis need to visit Graceland once. You might be surprised how Elvis' music and story grow on you.

Less than four miles south of Graceland is the Mississippi state line. Signs direct travelers to Tunica, the Las Vegas of the South. To get the gamblers from Memphis to Tunica quicker, the roads to Tunica are the newest and best in the state. It wasn't always that way. Only a few decades ago, Tunica County, Mississippi, was not just the poorest county in the Delta but the poorest in the entire United States.

That all changed in 1990 when Mississippi legalized casino gambling on river boats. Since Tunica is the closest county to Memphis, this part of the Delta got an economic shot in the arm with riverboat gambling. A couple of casino boats were brought in and proved to be so popular that the owners were able to charge an admission fee for the privilege of getting on the boat. Even with an admission fee, customers lined up and waited for the gambling boats to dock. Within a decade, the casino boats morphed into an area now called Tunica Resorts—an area of nine large Las Vegas–style casinos and 6,000 hotel rooms. Tunica Resorts also has a couple of golf courses, an outlet mall, and other stuff for gamblers and their spouses. The casinos no longer charge fees to get in but still seem to be doing all right. The sight of cotton fields giving way to the bright lights of the casinos and the nearby thirty-one-story hotel is strange.

The casinos have had a profound effect on the Delta. As the locals would say, "They pay good"—meaning not the slot machines but the jobs. The casino jobs pay much more than the minimum wage. With over 15,000 jobs, the casinos became an economic force in the Delta, and the casinos had their pick of the best workers in the area. There are also other direct benefits from casino gambling. Taxes from the casinos' activities paved virtually every road in Tunica County, and every county building is practically brand new and much finer than those in surrounding counties. Area promoters point to the relocation of the new Mid-South Coliseum as proof that the gaming creates sufficient economic activity to attract other businesses, to the benefit of all. Detractors say the indirect social costs are huge. Bankruptcies and child support delinquencies rose dramatically after the casinos arrived. They contend that housing and school achievement are the truer measures of whether the casinos have a positive effect, and according to these measures, they haven't.

Continuing south from the casinos, huge fields of cotton and soybeans stretch uninterrupted. An occasional house or sign announcing the plastic pipe used by a particular farmer's irrigation system breaks the flat agrarian landscape.

The famous Blues Highway, Highway 61, is four lanes around here and carries a bit of traffic. You leave most of the traffic behind when you turn off Highway 61 toward Friars Point. The fifteen miles to Friars Point pass through Coahoma, Mississippi, a depressing little community of a couple hundred African Americans living in shacks. These small Delta towns are overwhelmingly black; census data puts the white population at less than ten percent. There is no industry, no commercial district— just an occasional, worn-down convenience store and a collection of substandard houses. The dire poverty of the inhabitants is staggering, even if you only glance at it traveling fifty miles per hour.

The only memorable aspect about arriving in Friars Point on a gloriously sunny fall day was the foot traffic. There is virtually no automobile traffic. I passed only two or three cars on the road while I explored this tiny Delta town. But I came upon at least a dozen groups of people on foot. With no sidewalks, groups of two or three pedestrians ambled down the road. If I was driving toward the pedestrians, they stared—intently and impassively—into the car. As I passed, no one smiled or waved. It was spooky. I began looking in the rearview mirror to see if the they looked back to catch a glimpse of my license plate. They didn't; they just kept walking. The same scene played out repeatedly as I drove through the town—and since Friars Point is such a small place, I drove through most of the town. All of the pedestrians were African American. I knew from my research that less than 100 white people lived in Friars Point. Maybe they were looking to see if I was familiar to them. And since I wasn't, they didn't bother to acknowledge me. They just walked—staring as if I weren't there.

I had received this treatment before in the hills of Tennessee. Perhaps Friars Point is the black equivalent of Ducktown.

Metropolitan Friars Point runs north and south for about a block and a half. The area contains the Friars Point municipal building, a bank branch, a couple of vacant commercial buildings, and a small museum which was closed. Right by the post office stands a World War II tank. The west side of the commercial district backs up to the levee which protects Friars Point from the Mississippi River.

The levee is a large, sloped earthen wall at least two or three stories tall. This earthen wall is thick enough that the top of the levee is a dirt road. Even though it's a one-lane path, it's plenty wide for two pickup trucks to pass one another. On the town side of the levee, all is quiet—no automobile traffic, no children playing, no sounds at all. You can hear the wind blow through the trees. As I got closer to the top of the levee, the noise level from the river side of the levee increased. Sounds from crickets, frogs, birds—I'm not sure what all—but lots of different noises came from the wild, swampy land on the Mississippi River side of the levee.

Looking up and down the levee road, there is absolutely nothing to see but the dirt path. Looking west from the top of the levee, the river is not visible because the brush, which houses all those noisemakers, has grown so high that it blocks any view of the river. The levee must be the highest point in the county. From this vantage point, I looked back toward the tired little town of Friars Point and the fields beyond it. In this very rural setting, I thought about how far I was from anywhere. If I wasn't in the middle of nowhere, I was pretty close to it. It was easy to wonder why anyone still lives here.

Levee road at Friars Point

Mississippi Highway 1 runs about five miles east of Friars Point. At that intersection, I turn south toward Sherard and Hillhouse. Sherard is a small former plantation community, and Hillhouse is only a memory. You can drive fast on Highway 1. There's no traffic and the road is straight and completely flat.

Some fourteen years after Jonathan Daniels visited in the 1930s, the African-American plantation workers honored the owners of the Sherard Plantation—Mr. Holmes Sherard and his sister, Mallie Rawles—with an "appreciation hour." The story of this celebration gained national attention at the time and is thought to be unique in the Delta as the only true worker-inspired celebration of Mississippi plantation life. Speaking at the celebration, Mr. Sherard said, "We are all dependent upon each other, and here we all seem to have taken our obligation to each other for granted. I am wondering, could this lack of obligation to our fellow man be the trouble with places where we hear of unrest?"

Today virtually all of the descendants of the interdependent celebrants have left the area. The Sherard plantation commissary is the only remnant of the plantation era. The commissary sits at the intersection of Highway 1 and the highway to Clarksdale, the county seat ten miles away. A well-built building, it's obsolete now that agriculture is so mechanized. Peering in the window of the handsome building, you can see reminders of the plantation days: Old tables and post office letter slots stand dusty and unused. Sherard has a few houses and still retains its elementary school, but the school board has plans to close it. Once the school goes, I guess the plantation building will soon be all that's left of Sherard.

With its few remaining buildings, Sherard is better off than Hillhouse. Hillhouse, a private-enterprise, Depression-era experiment in communal farming, is completely gone. The sole evidence of this grand experiment is a street sign.

The Delta Farm Cooperative at Hillhouse was started by Sherwood Eddy, Reinhold Niebuhr, and H. L. Mitchell, an inhabitant of Tyronza's Little Red Square. Mr. Eddy received a contribution of $20,000 from an admirer with the instructions to use the money where it would do the most good. He bought almost 2,200 acres of buckshot land. Buckshot land is rock-filled Delta land. The rocks make the land less productive. With this purchase, Mr. Eddy began a farming cooperative. Initially, the cooperative had some thirty families. Most were black, though a substantial minority was white. Housing was separated according to race, but the accommodations were similar for both.

Each farmer signed a contract which provided for a joint operation of the farm and a division of the profits and losses in accordance to their labor. Mr. Eddy reported that in the first year of operation, the members received almost $9,000 in cash dividends, an average of almost $330 per family, fifty percent more than the average sharecropper made. It was discovered later that the farm operations were not profitable, and charitable contributions were the real source of the tenant farmers' dividends. The next two years, farm production and contributions dwindled and the experiment failed. In 1938, the trustees moved the farming operations to another farm eighty miles away. Soon the Delta reclaimed the buildings. Now nothing remains of the socialist experiment at Hillhouse.

Cosmopolitan Helena

In the 1930s, Jonathan Daniels had a hard time getting to Helena from Sherard. It must have taken most of a day because there were few paved roads and no bridge across the Mississippi, only two ferryboats. Today it's a short thirty-minute drive to Helena crossing the river by way of the bridge at Lula, Mississippi. Beside the bridge is a casino. Passing it on the highway, the casino appears to be a small one. By the looks of the parking lot, it must be popular with commercial truck drivers.

The Mississippi River Bridge lands in Arkansas at about the same place Hernando de Soto held the first Christian service west of the Mississippi. This is also near the site of the battle of Helena, fought on July 4, 1863, in the western theater of the Civil War. The Rebels tried to retake the high ground near Helena but were rebuffed by the Yankees. On the day that Vicksburg fell, the Rebels' failure to retake Helena allowed the Yankees to keep the river open to traffic and gave them a base from which they could subdue the rest of the state.

Helena sits at the very southeastern tip of Crowley's Ridge, an unusual geological formation. Crowley's Ridge begins in Cape Girardeau, Missouri, and extends all the way to Helena. The only hill in these parts, the ridge rises 300–500 feet from the Delta floor and is three to twelve miles across. Evidently, it's the remnant of a prehistoric mountain range. Some call it America's largest prehistoric sand bar because the tops of the ridges would rise occasionally above the prehistoric seas which covered the area between Memphis and modern Little Rock.

With Crowley's Ridge in the background, Helena (technically called Helena-West Helena since Helena and West Helena merged into one municipality in 2006) doesn't look like your typical Delta town. But Helena has the problems of the typical Delta town: high unemployment, widespread poverty, and the attendant health problems that systemic poverty brings. Even though there is no question that Helena has significant problems, a sense of optimism pervades Cherry Street, the quaint main street of downtown Helena. In the battle for economic survival, Helena has the necessary elements that Delta towns like Friars Point don't have: a hospital, an institution of higher education, broadband, viable local banks, and transportation. With these basics, good things can happen here.

The KIPP Charter School is one of those things. KIPP—Knowledge Is Power Program—came to Helena in 2002. The charter school in Helena is one of ninety-nine operating in twenty states. KIPP schools are free, open-enrollment, college-preparatory public schools. The students wear uniforms and attend school year-round. Ninety-five percent of the students are African American and eighty-five percent are eligible for free or reduced lunches. KIPP maintains a core set of operating principles known as the "Five Pillars": High Expectations, Choice & Commitment, More Time, Power to Lead, and Focus on Results. The KIPP School has profoundly changed educational opportunities in Helena. At its first commencement, twenty-three students graduated— and twenty-three kids were slated for college. Governor Beebe, the commencement speaker, noted—with some understatement—that the graduating class "transcends the stereotype of the kids in the Delta." The only criticism of KIPP in these parts—and I believe that it was said tongue-in-cheek—is that their school buses create a traffic jam on Cherry School when school lets out at 4:00.

Helena's access to the Mississippi River is now being exploited for recreational purposes. The Mississippi is famous for its dangers: snags, whirlpools, and eddies, to say nothing of the occasional sand boil. Those problems don't include the challenges posed by tug boats, barges, or chiggers. You know there have to be lots of mosquitoes and chiggers on the river. Take a canoe down the Big Muddy? Who in their right mind would do that?

The Quapaw Canoe Company of Clarksdale, Mississippi, has opened an outpost in Helena. Quapaw Canoe offers trips down the big river. Owner John Ruskey of Clarksdale isn't a native; he's originally from Colorado. After high school, he came with a buddy to float the Mississippi in a wooden raft. They crashed and, clinging to the wreckage, the boys landed on a river island, built a bonfire, and were later rescued by the Coast Guard. He has said that the experience "drove the river deep into my soul." John returned to the river after college and has spent his adult life there. He spends up to 200 days a year on the river.

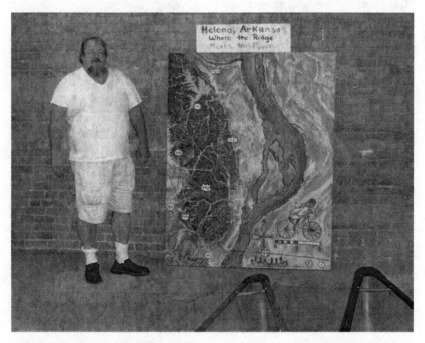

John Fewkes of Quapaw Canoe Company

With the main office of Quapaw Canoe located inland at Clarksdale, Mississippi, operating an outpost at Helena's harbor makes sense. The Helena outpost operates from the first floor of an old warehouse building in downtown Helena. Canoes and equipment are stored on one side. Wood shavings lie on the other side of the cavernous building. These shavings are the byproduct of the KIPP School dugout canoe project. Making a dugout canoe must be complicated: It will take the students over a year to build their canoe.

John Fewkes is Quapaw Canoe's man at its Arkansas outpost. Originally from Chicago, John moved to the Delta in 1994. He hasn't lost any of that hard upper-midwestern twang, so I didn't even bother to ask if he was native. I did ask if he liked the Delta. He replied, "I must because I could move back to Chicago anytime I want to. I don't, so I must like it here." When he's not working with the canoe company, John is a poet and a painter. He finds time to work with Habitat for Humanity. And he helps the county with their gardening projects.

Quapaw Canoe offers two basic trips from downtown Helena. The first trip starts upriver from Helena. John drives his customers ten miles or so into the St. Francis National Forest and drops them and their canoes off at one of two drop-off points. The first is located at the confluence of the Mississippi and St. Francis Rivers. The second drop-off point is two miles up the St. Francis River. The second drop-off point allows rookies to get their canoeing bearings on the easier St. Francis before entering the big water. From either place, it's a pretty easy day trip back to Helena. This upriver route also allows canoeists to explore Buck Island, a 1,500-acre island which at low water can be five miles long and a mile and a half wide. From Buck Creek, it's a short distance directly back into the Helena harbor.

The alternative trip is down river. You can canoe down river as far as you like. You rent a canoe at the outpost and walk it a few blocks to the Helena harbor's public access point. Or John will give you a lift in his truck. Most people canoe to Friars Point in a few hours. Some folks go as far as Greenville or even Vicksburg, which is a multi-day experience. For all of these trips, unless you are expert, you'll need a guide. (On overnight trips your guide may double as a cook. John Ruskey is reportedly the Julia Child of the Dutch oven.) Given the dangers of river canoeing, you'd have to be nuts not to have a guide with significant Mississippi River experience to undertake this adventure.

Canoeing the Mississippi is similar to canoeing the Ocoee near Ducktown, Tennessee, only because both activities use a river and a canoe. Outside of those two things, it's completely different. Located along a U.S. highway, the Ocoee has shallow, narrow, fast-running water. The Mississippi is deep, wide, slow moving, and not near any road whatsoever. The Mississippi's water is brown, not clear like the Ocoee's. It doesn't froth but moves quietly. The impediments to travel on the Mississippi aren't rocks in the river bed; they are confusing currents, floating trees, and barge traffic.

Remoteness provides much of the appeal of Mississippi River canoeing. Of seeing the river in a primal sense, John Fewkes said:

> Other than a few spots, you see the river as the Indians and the French explorers saw it. It's like being back in a pre-industrial time. If you camp, you are not near any artificial light. You see shooting stars every night. Mars looks red. You hear the river otters and the shriek of the shriek owls at night which scares the crap out of most people. At some point almost everyone has a spiritual or religious experience. We call it "receiving the Spirit of the River." Last week, Charlie Musselwhite's group canoed down the St. Francis and he told me the Spirit of the River came into the boat the first hour of the trip.

(For those of you who may not know, Charlie Musselwhite is a well-known blues musician from Chicago and recently one of the headliners of Helena's annual King Biscuit Blues Festival, one of the oldest and largest blues festivals in the world.)

John explained the Mississippi canoe experience as he gave me a tour of Helena in his pickup truck. Driving to one of the Civil War battery positions, he saw a car headed his way, stopped his truck in the middle of the city street, rolled down the window, and proceeded to talk with the driver:

> John: "Hey, man—whacha doin'?" (Remember John's from Chicago so it's said with that hard Midwestern twang)

> Friend: "Jes gwan' from Point A to Point B. I'm headed to Elaine to pick some greens. You know 'bout 'dem." (Elaine is pronounced E-lane.)

> John: "Yeah, I heard the greens out there were ready for pickin'."

John explained later that a farmer near Elaine, a town about twenty-five miles away, planted greens on some land near the highway. The greens were available to anyone who wanted to come by and pick them—literally free food for the taking. As we drove back from another part of the Civil War battlefield, he pointed to a tall, good-looking woman standing on the street and said laughingly, "See that woman over there—it's really a guy." Not something I thought I'd see; I guess the Delta's a little more cosmopolitan than I'd imagined.

After saying farewell to John Fewkes, I walked Cherry Street and had my choice of going to Messina's Liquor Store, Gist Music, or Bubba's Blues Corner. I eschewed Messina's even though the owner's family has been here for generations. It was a little early in the day to be hanging around a liquor store. Unfortunately Gist Music was closed. Mr. Gist being eighty-four, he opens the store only a few hours each day.

I headed down to Bubba's. Once inside, I met the owner, Bubba Sullivan, an old hippie redneck with a big white mustache. Many years ago, Bubba farmed near Elaine and often complained that there was no place to find blues records. So Bubba decided to do something about it and opened his record store in 1986. About that same time, he and some others started the King Biscuit Blues Festival. He's been the festival's announcer ever since. As the festival's master of ceremonies and owner of the Blues Corner, he meets musicians as they pass through.

Bubba knew Levon Helm, who was from nearby Turkey Scratch, since high school. Levon left the area when he was sixteen and made his name as a musician with Bob Dylan, the Band, and later in his own right. He became a movie star; his best-known role was as Loretta Lynn's father in *Coal Miner's Daughter*. Levon was promoted prominently both inside the store and on the store window. You can pass a lot of time at the Blues Corner looking at CDs, vinyl, and old posters, and talking with Bubba because Bubba has a story about most of the musicians on his walls. My favorite Bubba story is about Robert Plant, the lead singer of Led Zeppelin. Robert has fallen in love with the Delta and become friends with Bubba. Bubba says Robert loves the Delta so much that if his next child is a girl, she'll be named Lula Moon Lake Palmer, after two places in the Delta.

Bubba at his Blues Corner store

After leaving Bubba's, I continued walking down Cherry Street toward my car. As I neared it, an old, white-haired man approached me with posters in his hands. He walked up and asked in a strong English accent if I was "from around here." Laughing, I replied, "No sir, I'm from Little Rock, but I know you're not." He smiled and said I was wrong. He introduced himself as Neville Jones, an engineer who had come to the area from England some thirty years before to run the Helena Chemical plant—and had never left. Mr. Jones handed me a poster for the upcoming Warfield Concert series. The Warfield series is a totally free concert series which brings cultural events to Helena throughout the year. As he explained, a ticket to see one of the acts, the Russian National Ballet, could cost $50 to $100 in a large city. I could come to Helena, spend the night, and see the free concert for not much more. Or I could bring a busload of friends, have a nice dinner, and see a free concert. In a decidedly un-Delta accent, this former Englishman said goodbye. As he walked away, he turned and over his shoulder said that he hoped to see a busload of people from Little Rock this year.

Duck Gumbo

Just past Crowley's Ridge, the discriminating traveler notices subtle changes. The land doesn't change—it's still flat and open—but now there's no cotton. It looks like those pictures of Vietnam: rice paddies with humped irrigation ditches snaking throughout the fields. You're in the Grand Prairie.

The prairie's existence in Arkansas remains an enigma. The prairie has a thin layer of topsoil. Below that is a thick layer of clay, which is all but impenetrable to both water and roots. This clay substratum allowed only grasses and wildflowers to thrive on the Grand Prairie. Since the thin prairie soil was not good for cotton growing, the Grand Prairie's development lagged behind the Delta's.

All that changed in the early twentieth century when it was found that the layer of impenetrable clay aided rice growing. Over the next forty years, most of the Grand Prairie became rice land and Arkansas became the country's largest producer of rice. Until drying facilities were developed, harvested rice was left to dry in the fields. Since the Grand Prairie is part of the Mississippi Flyway, this crop became a great attraction to migratory fowl making their annual trek southward. As a direct result of the rice crop, Arkansas' Grand Prairie gained the reputation for the finest duck hunting anywhere in the world.

Hunting is a constitutionally protected individual right in Arkansas, added recently to the state constitution as a result of a statewide referendum. Exclusive jurisdiction over hunting matters rests with the Arkansas Game and Fish Commission, a constitutionally protected state agency. The Game and Fish Commission's jurisdiction is carefully detailed in Amendment 35 to the Arkansas Constitution; the amendment also passed in a statewide election. Appointment to the commission is perhaps the highest, most sought-after patronage position in state government.

Duck season is but one of many hunting seasons in the hunting-happy South. The U.S. Fish and Wildlife Service estimates that twenty-six percent of Arkansas' population hunts and/or fishes. Besides duck hunting, there's trout fishing on the White or Little Red Rivers, turkey and wild boar hunting, and, of course, deer hunting. During the first weekend of deer season, construction projects and other non-essential activities cease because 100,000 hunters head to the deer woods.

Duck hunting is different. It's like golf: Many of its devotees take it up at an early age, become hooked, and enjoy it for a lifetime. The rich spend lavishly on guns and equipment and hunt on private preserves. The not-so-rich participate by hunting public lands or relying upon the grace of others for a place to shoot.

Since the sport involves migratory fowl, federal regulations limit the season. Arkansas' season generally starts just before Thanksgiving and goes to the middle of January. There are mandatory breaks during the season when hunting is not allowed. One break generally comes in late December, so the weary hunters can return home for holiday celebrations and remind their families what they look like. Migratory fowl experts contend, however, that the breaks are for the benefit of the ducks.

The duck hunting season starts with a social event called Wings over the Prairie. The festival occurs over Thanksgiving weekend, culminating on Saturday with the Duck Gumbo Cook-Off and the World's Championship Duck Calling Contest. These competitions occur in Stuttgart, Arkansas, which during duck season is the center of the universe. (The correct pronunciation of Stuttgart: the first syllable rhymes with *rut*, unlike the German city for which it is named. In Germany, the first syllable rhymes with *hoot*.)

Stuttgart has a surprisingly impressive skyline for a town of about 10,000. From a distance you think you're coming to a small metropolitan area with tall buildings. But as you get closer, the sense of tall buildings disappears and is replaced by an awareness of monstrously tall rice dryers.

Stuttgart's skyline

Stuttgart is relatively large and prosperous for eastern Arkansas. Relatively prosperous, but not prosperous like the Brentwood suburb of Nashville or Buckhead in Atlanta: There's no high-end shopping, no Starbucks. It's prosperous relative to the Delta. There is a semblance of a middle class in Stuttgart that you don't see that much in the Delta— nothing fancy, just a small-town middle class that makes its money from the soil.

Stuttgart is the county seat of the northern part of Arkansas County. Arkansas County actually has two county seats: Stuttgart in the north and DeWitt in the south. DeWitt is smaller, but there's competition between the two towns. If you want to have some fun, stop in at Mack's Prairie Wings, the local purveyor of all things duck, and ask whether it's true that the duck hunting is better down near DeWitt. Stand back and watch heated discussions begin.

After their morning hunt the Saturday after Thanksgiving, duck hunters head to Stuttgart's main street. Those with families take the kids on a tilt-a-whirl ride, look at the off-road vehicle exhibition, and eat foot-long corndogs at the festival. Those without children head to the Duck Gumbo Cook-Off, which is held every year in a very large tent near the rice mills.

As my son Will and I approached the tent on foot, we could hear a low hum from inside the tent contrasting with the small-town quiet. The low drone of voices increased as we walked closer to the tent.

We arrived at the tent's mouth. No signs indicated where we were supposed to enter. Evidently we should have known that. We picked a spot and tried to walk in, but we were stopped immediately by a big man in a uniform. He politely asked to see my wristband. I explained to the man that I didn't need one, as I didn't plan to drink. He said he didn't care whether I drank, but that if I wanted in, I needed to fork over twenty bucks. He told me to wear the wristband to prove I'd paid. So I asked the gumbo guard where a person could get a wristband. He grunted and pointed over to a table—no signs, just a table.

I asked the lady behind the table for a wristband. She handed me one, and I asked her what I should do if I wanted to buy a beer. She pointed and smiled, directing me to a long line under a Budweiser sign, where I could buy "drink teekets." So I was out twenty bucks, and if I wanted a beer, I was going to have to stand in a long line for drink tickets, and then try to find the beer stand. It was barely past noon, but these "gumboers" are hardy stock.

Inside the tent the gumbo contestants had constructed rows of little two-story kiosks. They dispensed gumbo from the lower level and threw Mardi Gras beads to the crowd below from the upper level. The stands were decorated with straw and camo to look like actual duck blinds—with a little Bourbon Street atmosphere thrown in.

Inside the tent, the noise was overwhelming. At the far end of the tent, a rock band was playing, operating on the principal that the louder they played the better they sounded. You had to scream directly into your companion's ear to be heard. After a few minutes of standing around screaming and drinking, it was time to go check out the gumbo.

Gumbo is a Cajun dish—a really hearty soup—with seafood, vegetables, rice, and a little sausage thrown in. In Stuttgart, the after-Thanksgiving variation doesn't rely on seafood. Instead, the residue of unfortunate winged visitors simmers in the broth. Also, duck gumbo relies more heavily on sausage than traditional Cajun gumbo does. I believe this is to hide the duck taste, but no one admits to that.

So there you are—a couple hours walking around sampling gumbo, listening to music, and, of course, drinking beer. And a quaint custom, known as "stickering." Each cooking team obtains rolls of gummed stickers that identify their teams. As civilians pass by, cooking team members "sticker" the innocents. It's fun because the men get "stickered" by women and vice versa. They don't waste time with bothering to ask if you want one, they just slap a sticker on your derriere as you pass by.

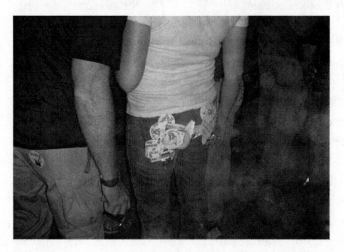

Stickering

After filling up on gumbo and being covered with stickers, Will and I headed back out to the quiet of the parking lot. From there we drove the few blocks to Main Street to attend the World's Championship Duck Calling Contest. Since Main Street was blocked off for the festivities, we parked on a side street and walked about as far as we drove.

Duck-calling contest

A small stage sits just off Main Street in downtown Stuttgart. On the Saturday after Thanksgiving, the best duck callers in the country stand on that stage waiting for their moment to shine. There are no chumps here. Each of the sixty-six participants has won either a sanctioned state or regional duck-calling contest to qualify for this world championship event.

More than 60,000 people attend the festival, the oldest of its kind in the nation, but the centerpiece of the festival is the duck-calling contest. The first duck-calling contest, held in 1936, had seventeen contestants. The first-place prize was a hunting coat valued at $6.60. Today, six divisions of callers compete, including women, junior, and intermediate, and the prize package is worth more than $15,000.

One of the great things about this competition is it dispels the notion that America has become so homogenized that you can't tell where someone is from by the way they talk. Each contestant introduces himself. The boys from Georgia and South Carolina are authentic with their true southern drawls, distinct from the locals' accents. Then there are midwestern twangs. And you don't have to ask who's from Minnesota or South Dakota.

It was easy to spot out-of-towners because the locals didn't look up at every flock of geese or ducks winging above them. Everyone was dressed in camouflage clothing, but the locals' "camo" reflects hard use. On the other hand, visitor outfits looked like they'd recently been hanging on a rack in Mack's Prairie Wings, the local "Premier Waterfowl Outfitter."

For some reason, the competition was delayed. The crowd milled around, visiting with one another, eating hot dogs and other food from the carnival down the street. I asked my son if he thought a crowd in a major metropolitan area would wait quietly for an hour without any explanation about what was delaying the show. His nonverbal response made clear two things: My question was obviously stupid, but not as stupid as the decision to leave the gumbo cook-off.

Festivities began with the introduction of Queen Mallard, the beauty contest winner who will compete in the Miss Arkansas contest later in the year. Abby Richards, a junior psychology major from the University of Arkansas at Fayetteville, was the reigning Queen Mallard. When she was introduced, Abby—attired in her camouflage pants, camo jacket, and tiara—stepped up and waved to the crowd.

The master of ceremonies, trying to kill some time during the delay, asked the crowd if they wanted Abby to do a little calling. After a rousing ovation, Queen Mallard pulled her duck caller from her jacket and warmed up briefly. She then made a quarter turn from the audience and cupped her hands over a call, squatting low to the ground, she began calling, "Qwaaack, wacck, wacck, wacck." For approximately sixty seconds, the attractive Queen called like a flock was circling overhead and she might convince a mallard to land. The crowd gave her a great ovation. Everyone was ready for the championship.

With sixty-six competitors, I wasn't sure how long the competition would take. If each contestant took six minutes to judge, the competition would take six and a half hours. That's longer than a NASCAR race. The process seemed fairly standard. The judges sat behind a partition where they couldn't see the contestants and could judge solely on sound.

Each contestant walked onto the stage when his or her number was called. Each contestant was allowed a brief warm-up. Once warmed-up, they began the routine, which lasted about ninety seconds. The calls were supposedly different, but it would take someone with a better-trained ear to describe the differences. Will said they all sounded alike to him. With three down and sixty-three to go, the contest was processing contestants in a fairly expeditious manner, but a decision was still hours away. We decided to abdicate the selection to the judges and made our way toward Little Rock, some sixty miles down the road.

The scene stayed the same—flat land stretching as far as the eye could see.

Meeting the Governor

Though it has a large landmass, Arkansas is a small state. With a population of less than three million people, its citizens tend to know (or know about) one another. Some people contend that Bill Clinton met more than half the entire state's population before getting his promotion to Washington.

I have lived three blocks from the Arkansas Governor's Mansion for almost thirty years and have met every one of its inhabitants during that time. They are my neighbors. The route I take to walk my dog follows the western edge of the mansion's property. One spring day, I saw the governor sitting on a bench, looking back toward the mansion. I said hi, and he introduced his dog, a German shepherd named Mosel.

Mike Beebe had been governor for about a year, and this was the first time I'd seen him out in the mansion's grounds. As our dogs sniffed each other through the fence, I asked how things were going, just as I would have with any neighbor. He said that it had been one of those days. He'd been to areas of the state hit by recent tornadoes to see damage firsthand. He talked about how difficult it was to comfort people who had lost all they owned. Later that day, he attended the funeral of a Pine Bluff soldier who'd been killed in Iraq. He reported that the funeral was even more difficult.

I told him I'd heard he'd been in Pine Bluff because my mother attended the same funeral. She'd told me she was very proud of the governor for attending. He was gracious in hearing my mother's compliment, but it was clear that he didn't think he'd done anything to earn it. He said that when he ran for governor he recognized that he would get to do a lot of nice and fun things as the head of the state government. He had been prepared to work hard on the business of operating the state government. But no one had ever prepared him for the duties that he had discharged today. I didn't know what to say, except that I hoped days like today would be rare. As I walked away, I reflected on how much like a small town Arkansas still is.

Downtown Amagon, Governor Mike Beebe's hometown

Knowing Governor Beebe's story, his take on being governor that day was interesting. His is a true American success story. As they say in the Delta, he's a "poor boy who dun good." Mike Beebe was born in Amagon, Arkansas, a small community just outside the Delta town of Newport. He never knew his father; his mother was a waitress at the local coffee shop. He and his mother lived in Detroit, St. Louis, Chicago,

Houston, and Alamogordo, New Mexico. They returned to Arkansas and he graduated from Newport High School. After college and law school, Beebe moved to Searcy, Arkansas, where he practiced law for almost thirty years. He was a state senator for twenty of those years.

Mike Beebe

Several months later, I had my next meeting with the governor on a cold rainy winter day. Visibility was bad—but made worse by the rooster tails of water that the cars ahead kicked up. As the Arkansas State Capitol rose in the foreground, I dreaded my long walk to the building through the cold rain. At least I had an umbrella. As I turned my car into the huge state-owned parking lot, I began to think that there would be no visitor spaces and I would have to spend time driving around just finding a place to park. But luck was with me, and I spotted an open spot which allowed one hour of public parking. Getting out of the car, I readied myself for the wet walk to the capitol building.

The parking lot attendant motioned me over. I didn't want to spend any more time in the rain than necessary, but to ensure my car would not be towed, I headed over to him. He was friendly, asking me what my business was. I knew he worked for the secretary of state, not the governor, so I really didn't think it was any of his business. I simply said I had a meeting.

He pressed further, and I disclosed the meeting was in the governor's office. He then asked if I was meeting with the governor's chief of staff, Morrill Harriman, or "the big guy himself." If he hadn't been so friendly, I would have taken offense at the intrusive questions into my business. I simply confirmed that my meeting was with "the big guy." He smiled again and said, "If you're going to try to get money from him—good luck 'cause you're gonna need it."

I laughed and thanked him for the advice. I asked him to make sure my car wasn't towed if I took longer than my allotted hour. He smiled and told me not to worry.

Arkansas' capitol building is a handsome, smaller version of the national capitol. It was built at the turn of the twentieth century on a hill that was the site of the old state penitentiary. I climbed the steps through the rain and made it to shelter. Shaking off the rainwater and passing security, I found the governor's office and walked in with my dripping umbrella a few minutes early. My plan was to collect my thoughts in the waiting area. No time for that. I was ushered immediately into the governor's office.

Governor Beebe stood to greet me. I've been in his presence before, but I'm always surprised how physically imposing he is. My guess is he's six-two or three, with lots of hair, a big smile—all the attributes of a modern-day politician. As we shook hands, I remembered a friend telling me that you can't get elected governor of Arkansas if your name is more than three syllables long, unless your name is Rockefeller. I checked later, and he's right.

I asked the governor to discuss why Arkansas had had such extraordinary governors over the past thirty-five years. Dale Bumpers and David Pryor had been very distinguished senators, and Bill Clinton and Mike Huckabee both ran for president—one successfully. His reply:

> Arkansas is a populist state. It is a tradition that our voters, because of the size and demographics of our state, have inculcated a tradition in the political arena where they have to know their governor or their major leader. And whether they know them or not, they want to at least feel that they want to know them.
>
> This causes the kind of retail politics that exists where if you are not personable and good at it, you don't get elected. There are always exceptions, but somebody who is not articulate and is not a people person, or cannot connect on a more personal level with the voters, tends not to win in Arkansas.
>
> It is not a media-driven electorate market, like Texas, where you have Houston and Dallas and Austin and San Antonio and El Paso, and nobody ever expects to meet the damn governor. So everything is driven off of something other than the kind of personal skill that relates to somebody on a more individual level.
>
> And so Arkansas tends to elect people who are first of all articulate, and second, personable. People in New York or Washington or across

the rest of the country say, "Dang, what's going on in Arkansas? You've got a Dale Bumpers, look how well he speaks, and David Pryor, he's not as articulate as Bumpers, but look how personable he is and how people relate to him. And this Clinton guy, gosh, we didn't know people were that smart in the South, much less in Arkansas. And how he can take a message and wrap it up. And this Mike Huckabee guy, you can put him on a stage and he can talk and he's funny and he's witty. And Jim Guy Tucker, he looked good and he knew how to talk to people."

Over and over and over again, my answer to people is that's the way it has always been in Arkansas; and to your point, that's what Arkansans are used to. That's who they elect to statewide office, to the U.S. Senate, to the governor's office. That's who they want to elect because those are the attributes they expect a person to have, or they are not going to vote for you. They are going to vote for somebody else and it doesn't matter what party you are in. It is a personality and personal-trait driven electorate; and if they like you and think you are honest, then you have a better chance of getting elected.

We talked for almost an hour. I returned to my car. The rain had subsided, and I sought out my friend at the parking lot. As he saw me walk up, he broke into his big grin and asked whether I got any money. I laughed and said no. Even though he was laughing, his reply was sincere:

I told you he'd be tough to get money from. What people don't realize is that he's a good man. He's one of us. I know things are tough right now, but he's out there fighting for us. I know it's hard to get jobs into Arkansas, but if anybody can get them, he will. Now they may not be real good jobs; they may only pay $7.50 an hour. But if you're not too proud to work for $7.50 an hour, and believe me there are a number of people who are, he'll help you.

I asked the attendant his name, and he replied, "Rick."

I said, "Well, Rick, I know you don't work for the governor, but are you trying to get a job as his campaign manager?"

He said, "No sir, I'm sure he could get someone better than me."

"I'm not so sure," I replied.

As I drove away, I thought about disgraced former Illinois governor Rod Blagojevich and whether he could be elected governor of Arkansas. Nope: too many syllables in his name.

Water, Water Everywhere

Hot Springs, Arkansas, a small city of about 35,000 people, is about as far west as this Journey goes. Williamsburg and the Atlantic coast are over 1,000 miles away. Indian country, the Oklahoma border, is less than 100 miles away. We're in the center of America now. The U.S. Census Bureau places America's population center in southwestern Missouri, a few hundred miles to the north of Hot Springs.

Remember Concord, North Carolina, and its sister city Kannapolis, the small towns which are now suburbs of Charlotte? Both places had to restrict their growth because of the lack of water. Hot Springs is the opposite of these two places, hydrologically speaking. Where Concord and Kannapolis have to curtail water usage, Hot Springs has ample water supplies for the foreseeable future. The city has two lakes for its water and two additional lakes in reserve. Yes, Hot Springs has lots of water, more than enough for essential drinking and industrial uses and plenty for boating, fishing, and swimming. Restricting water usage for things like lawn watering or car washing is incomprehensible to the residents of Hot Springs. Besides the public water supplies, water just bubbles up from the ground and people bottle it.

The hot springs have always drawn people to this place. For hundreds of years people have come to "take the waters." As the story goes, these pilgrims made Hot Springs neutral ground. The Native Americans agreed to leave their weapons when they came to bathe in

221

the thermal waters. Gangsters from New York and Chicago made similar agreements. They came to gamble and relax in the bathhouses, not kill each other. Major league spring training began here in 1886 when the Chicago White Stockings, the forerunner of the Cubs, thought it would be helpful if their baseball players kept themselves in shape in the mild Arkansas winters. The players weren't averse to spring training because they could take the baths between trips to the local horse track or downtown casinos. Old-timers still talk about seeing Babe Ruth hit a ball out of Whittington Park Field and into the tourist-filled alligator farm next door. Until the late 1960s, Hot Springs was a gambling mecca. In the time before Las Vegas, Atlantic City, and the Mississippi River casino boats, gambling in Hot Springs was illegal, but wide open.

At the beginning of the Ouachita Mountain range, the mountains around Hot Springs aren't that tall. The area resembles the Carolina Piedmont. Between Hot Springs Mountain and West Mountain, hot water flows from numerous springs. The Native American tribes called this place "the valley of the vapors" because the escaping hot water created clouds. It's estimated that the area springs produce almost a million gallons of water a day. It comes to the surface at a temperature of 143 degrees Fahrenheit.

From the mid-1500s, the springs were claimed by the French and occupied by Native Americans. The French sold the land to the United States as part of the Louisiana Purchase in 1803. While Arkansas was still a territory, the lands around the springs were declared a federal reservation to protect the water and have remained federal property ever since. This federal action gives the Hot Springs National Park the distinction of being America's oldest and smallest national park.

My host for this Hot Springs water expedition was James Breckinridge Speed. For an Arkie, Breck has an interesting lineage. His ancestors came from Kentucky. Joshua Fry Speed was Abraham Lincoln's best friend. Joshua's brother, James, served as Lincoln's attorney general during the war. James was an ardent abolitionist. The Breckinridge in his name comes from another famous Kentucky family whose family tree included America's youngest vice president, John C. Breckinridge. Vice president under President James Buchanan, Breckinridge was the highest-ranking United States official to become a Rebel. Even though Kentucky did not secede, Breckinridge became a general in the Confederate army and later a cabinet member—secretary of war—in the Confederate States of America.

Breck Speed of Mountain Valley Spring Water Company

Breck is the president of Mountain Valley Spring Water Company, the oldest continuously operated, single-source spring water operation in America. The company's pretty headquarters building is located on Central Avenue, the main street of downtown Hot Springs.

Breck says that none of his family history helped when he decided to quit practicing law in Little Rock and start selling water for a living. With a truck and one employee, he began delivering water around Little Rock in the late 1980s. It soon became apparent that his business needed to grow. He did so by building a bottling plant, buying spring water from nearby Montgomery County, and bottling that water under the name of

Clear Mountain Spring Water. In the early 1990s, still expanding, he tried to buy a small Mountain Valley distributorship. He was rebuffed and told that he would never be able to buy a Mountain Valley distributorship. As these things often happen, he didn't just buy a distributorship, he bought the entire company.

Bottling water is not a new business in Hot Springs. There were dozens of bottling plants in Hot Springs in early and mid-twentieth century. Most of these businesses folded when chlorinating municipal water sources made public waters consistently safe to drink. But the plants remain standing. The buildings have either been repurposed or allowed to decay. Near a patch of mobile homes, the ruins of a bottling plant have been overtaken by the forest. Before I could see the building, I knew we were walking near a spring because, even during a dry summer, the ground was wet.

Mountain Valley Spring Water is the only area business still bottling water for profit, but that doesn't mean you have to buy from them to get local spring water. There are eight "jug" fountains around town. Six fountains dispense hot spring water and two provide cold spring water. The fountains are designed to allow people to collect water in bulk. Most jug people are locals. But many outsiders make regular trips from as far as Monroe, Louisiana, to get hot water directly from the springs. They are discriminating consumers preferring the taste of one spring to another. They come with a truckload or carload of empty jugs, fill them up, and head back home. The water's free. Federal regulations prohibit anyone from charging for it.

A few miles outside of Hot Springs lie the major assets of Mountain Valley Spring Water, the spring and the 2,000-acre buffer of land above it. For almost 140 years, Mountain Valley Spring Water has been bottled from that single spring. This plant bottles premium water. Most people would be surprised to find out that about a third of today's bottled water is tap water, but premium waters are mineral-rich spring water.

Mountain Valley water competes with the likes of San Pellegrino and Vichy. Europeans buy premium water for what's in it, meaning minerals like calcium, iron, and manganese. Americans generally buy bottled water for what is not in it—biological or environmental contaminants.

Mountain Valley appeals to both groups. Mountain Valley is naturally high pH water and picks up a number of minerals in its 3,500-year journey from rainwater back through the rocks under the Ouachita Mountains. So Europeans like it. Because of the natural filtering over this extended recharging period, it is pristine and not subjected to any pollutants. If you'd like, Breck will provide you with a "product" analysis showing everything that's in his water.

Jug people in Hot Springs

The first time I drank a bottle of Mountain Valley water was forty years ago. I picked up what I thought was a soft drink from a tub of soft drinks being iced down in an old country grocery store. I took the green glass bottle from the icy water thinking it was a lemon-lime drink. I paid the clerk thirty cents, which I thought was a high price for soda pop. I used a bottle opener to take the cap off the top of the bottle and took a long slug. I spit it out when I realized it wasn't soda pop and before I realized it was just water. I distinctly remember thinking, "Who in their right mind would pay thirty cents for a bottle of water?" Now I'm paying $28 for a case of twenty-four half-liter glass bottles of water at the company store on Central Avenue. There's plenty more where it came from.

I'm Only 75

Lake Chicot, the largest oxbow lake in North America, is located in the southeastern corner of Arkansas just before you get to the Greenville Bridge which crosses the Mississippi River. An oxbow lake forms when a river bend gets separated from the river. In this case, Lake Chicot used to be a big bend in the Mississippi River, but around 600 years ago, the river cut a new channel. Now the former river bed is a lake almost three-quarters of a mile wide and twenty-two miles long. It's huge. When you see it from a plane, Lake Chicot looks like a big "C" of water which contrasts against the surrounding checkerboard of farmland.

Just past Lake Chicot, the Mississippi River Bridge comes into view. It's a new bridge and much higher than the old one; it may well be the highest point from Crowley's Ridge some one hundred miles upriver to Yazoo City which is at least seventy-five miles southeast. During the great flood of 1927, the Mississippi River was one hundred miles wide at this place.

Driving the highway, you forget how impoverished the Delta really is. Once you arrive in a town, the poverty hits you. After Memphis, Greenville is the largest place in the Delta. The 2010 census counted 41,633 residents, but its population has since decreased. Decrepit convenience stores and motels litter Greenville's outskirts. Rather than maintaining or fixing a building, developers seem to simply move down the highway and build a new one. A shiny new Holiday Inn Express contrasts with the nearby rusting and deteriorating buildings.

Greenville is the undisputed center of the "tamale trail." Twelve of the forty-four stops on the Mississippi Tamale Trail are located around here. Tamales, along with fried catfish, are true Delta cuisine. Tamales are cornmeal dough, filled with pork, beef, or perhaps turkey, and some spices. The meat is browned or boiled. Then everything, cornmeal and meat, is wrapped up in corn husks and simmered in bundles of six or so. Tamale-makers keep their spices and spicing techniques secret. Some just spice the meat; others spice everything, even the water the tamales simmer in. Tamales are sold at convenience stores, gas stations, mobile homes, and small shops throughout the Delta. For more on these wonderful treats, see the Southern Foodways Alliance's website on the Tamale Trail, www.tamaletrail.com. As they say around here: Tamales "shore are good eatin.'"

Downtown Greenville's main street is nice. (Not typical for the Delta.) Getting to downtown from the highway, however, requires going down streets with severely deteriorating residences and unkempt lawns. But Washington Street, the main street, is wide, clean, and well-maintained. Most of the store fronts are maintained, and one in particular, S. Goodman's, appears to be doing very well. I went into Goodman's and found that they had plenty of merchandise to sell, mostly clothing. It's hard to believe that it competes with the Wal-Mart on the highway. But it does—and good for it.

At the other end of Washington Street stands Jim's Cafe. Jim's has been around awhile. I stood outside the door debating whether to go inside. It was after 2:00 and I was afraid they wouldn't be serving this late. I had intended to eat tamales whenever my Journey intersected the Tamale Trail. But I took a chance on Jim's because I had made a bet with myself that the waitress would call me honey or hon. That doesn't sound like much of a reason, I know, but when you're traveling alone, you find you often make wagers with yourself. Anyway, Jim's wasn't closed: It stays open until 3:00 p.m. But Jim didn't have much business. There was a table in the back with three old men talking, a table of two young people who left soon after I sat down, two waitresses, and me. Plenty of room in a restaurant that could seat upwards of eighty to a hundred people.

Jim's Cafe in Greenville

With plenty of seating options, I took a table where I could keep track of the conversation at the other tables. The talk was mostly about politics, and clearly they didn't approve of President Obama's recent actions. I fully expected to hear a racial reference. I was pleasantly surprised when I didn't. A few people came in to get carry-out food. The waitresses greeted everyone who entered with friendly inquiries about family members.

One man, evidently the owner, announced that when he took over the business in 1959, things were different: "That's back when we did some business around here. We didn't close early; we had a big dinner crowd. We were open seven days a week and only closed on Christmas Day. Now, shoot, we close at three and lunch really ain't all that much. Now, those were good times." His dining partner replied, "I'm not as old as you. I'm only seventy-five. I don't remember those kind of good times."

I got up to leave and left $15.00 on the table for an $8.00 lunch. When I had sat down, the waitress had come by the table with a menu and asked, "What can I get you to drink, hon?" She won the bet.

Nitta Yuma

The Delta can be seen as a collection of small dying villages as America consolidates into metropolitan areas. If you look at maps from the 1930s, there were a lot of small towns in the Mississippi Delta. Most of them are gone now. In the Mississippi Delta, each new major north-south road was built on higher ground farther from the river. Highway 1, the great river road, literally bumps up against the river's levees at times. Some fifteen miles farther east, U.S. Highway 61 was built. Later still, Interstate 55 came and was built farther east still.

As the major roads migrated eastward and agriculture became mechanized, the vitality of the river valley deteriorated, and no other economic opportunities developed. People left to find work. It's evident that many more people once lived in these little Delta towns by the number of abandoned and deteriorating commercial buildings. But out in the country you see little evidence that a lot of people used to live here.

Fifteen miles north of Greenville is Scott, Mississippi. Today Scott is an unincorporated community in Bolivar County. It's barely a wide spot on Highway 1. Scott is the former headquarters of the Delta & Pine Land Company, one of the country's first agribusinesses. During the 1930s, D&PL operated the largest, most successful cotton plantation in the United States.

This plantation formed in the early twentieth century when the textile manufacturers of the Fine Cotton Spinners and Doublers Association, Ltd., in Manchester, England, wanted a dependable source of raw material.

These Englishmen created D&PL which bought approximately 36,000 acres in Bolivar County, Mississippi. It cleared the virgin land and grew the first crop in 1913. Even though the company lost $500,000 during the flood of 1927, the plantation ultimately proved to be a good investment.

When Jonathan Daniels was here in 1936, the company's president noted:

> In our operations at Scott, we have planted approximately 11,000 acres of cotton. The production of this crop gives employment to about 900 families consisting of around 4,000 human beings. With a successful cotton picker and by the use of tractors and other equipment designed for labor saving, we could operate this property with probably 75 or 100 laborers.

He was right. By 1945, 6,300 acres of cotton production required only 612 sharecropper families, involving 1,547 workers. As farming steadily mechanized and farm equipment got larger and better, the number of workers required to plant and pick cotton steadily decreased.

In 1978, the English sold D&PL to a group of Memphis investors. The American owners sold the land to an insurance company and retained the side business of developing new strains of cotton and soybeans. This side business grew. In 1993, D&PL became a public company selling cottonseed and soybean seed in thirteen countries. In 2007, Monsanto Company acquired D&PL for $1.5 billion. D&PL has been an operating division of Monsanto ever since.

Little evidence remains of the thousands of people who worked the D&PL land for so long. There are a couple of brick residences built in the 1950s or 1960s, along with the agricultural buildings necessary to maintain a modern farming operation, but that's about it. Where over 4,000 people used to live and trade, no tenant buildings remain, and no other commercial buildings remain. There's just flat land.

In her book *During Wind and Rain*, Margaret Jones Bolsterli writes about the disappearance of such communities:

> When considering change in the part of the world we are discussing here, it is good to remember that farm houses, villages, and even towns can disappear without a trace in a very few years because most buildings are built of wood. In Europe, the skeletons of villages unoccupied for years

are still there in roofless stone buildings and cobbled streets. By contrast, in the Delta within a few months after a house goes vacant, nature begins retaking its space: weeds eight feet tall fill the yard, vines grow over the house, saplings come up through the porch floor, the roof collapses, and then the whole thing falls down and rots or is eaten by termites. Saplings in the yard become trees and make woods again unless the place gets cleared and planted as part of the field that surrounded it to start with. In a few years, every single trace of human habitation can be erased.

Traveling Highway 61 south toward Vicksburg, I noticed remnants of these small plantation villages, most of which are no longer noted on modern maps. A plantation house sat on the east side of the highway, often obscured by trees or hedges. On the west side, the community contained a few farm buildings and a couple of modest workers' houses. About halfway between Hollandale and Anguilla and just past Panther Burn, I noticed a discrepancy in this pattern: A couple of well-kept, older homes were located on the west side of the highway in a little community called Nitta Yuma. Since Nitta Yuma broke the pattern, I turned off the road to learn more.

Nitta Yuma has two short streets and a dozen houses; most of the recent ones are manufactured housing. The main street is about two city blocks long and ends in a cotton field. As I turned around, I stumbled upon this ruin.

Mrs. Crump's House, in the process of being erased

Nitta Yuma is the name of the surrounding plantation and this was probably the old plantation house. It's been a ruin since 1973 when a storm uprooted a tree which crashed into the house. The house must have been built well to withstand these many years of abandonment. Even though it's now dilapidated and unrecoverable, it still retains a charm as the Delta takes it back.

A Coffee Shop in Vicksburg

The sudden appearance of hills reinforced the impression that I was no longer in the Delta. I hadn't seen a hill or even a hillock since I left Hot Springs. Arriving in Vicksburg, I'd left the Delta behind.

David Cohen, a twentieth-century writer from Greenville, Mississippi, has said the Delta starts at the lobby of the Peabody Hotel and ends in Vicksburg. Vicksburg and Natchez, its neighbor to the south, are different from the Delta because they are river towns born to ship cotton, not grow it. The two towns seem to have a sibling-like attitude toward each other, a relationship that alternates between pride and envy. During the Civil War, Vicksburg was bombarded continuously for fifty days, and its citizens were forced to eat rats during the siege. Even though Vicksburg surrendered, its people never cooperated with the Yankees. In the old Courthouse Museum, the "black list" the Yankee occupiers compiled of suspected Rebels and their sympathizers is displayed proudly. Until recently, Vicksburgers didn't celebrate the Fourth of July because it was on the fourth of July that the city fell.

Today, Vicksburg has a more diverse economy than Natchez. Geographic location plays a part, as Interstate 20 passes a few miles south of downtown. The casino business has taken hold in Vicksburg. With its proximity to interstate travelers and Jackson's relatively large population base, Vicksburg now has six casinos. But Vicksburg is more than a gambling center. It has a working port and an industrial base with fifty manufacturing firms. The Army Corps of Engineers maintains a large presence. It has a major tourist attraction in the National Military Park. And it's close enough to the capital city to attract commuters desiring small-town life.

Eschewing the bypass, I took old Highway 61 straight into downtown Vicksburg. It was dark and I was hungry, so I stopped at the first restaurant where I saw pickup trucks parked out front. I stepped through the front door of Rusty's Riverfront Grill and walked into a group of African Americans waiting for a table. One of them turned and smiled. I said hi and looked past them to a table where two African Americans were eating with three white people. I watched as one of the white people touched one of her African-American dining partners on the arm. At the same time, one of the people in the group in front of me touched me on the arm, smiled, and said, "You'll need to tell the waitress that you're waiting for a table." I thought, *These sure are touching people.* And, *There probably wasn't much interracial touching going on forty years ago.*

The next morning I visited the Highway 61 Coffee Shop. Vernon Anaya, a recent immigrant from Santa Fe, worked as the barista, and Christian, a young resident of Vicksburg, assisted him.

Recently retired, Vernon followed his wife, an Episcopal priest, to Vicksburg. I asked him what he thought of the South. He said that except for rare days, it doesn't get cold very often, which is a plus. Christian added that it had been in the thirties for the last couple of days and that she was sick of winter. She said she couldn't wait until it was ninety-five degrees outside and she could go looking for a swimming pool.

Vernon told me that Vicksburg reminded him of the Santa Fe of his youth. He said when he walks down Main Street, people speak. He said in Santa Fe today he wouldn't know anyone at the square because they're mostly tourists. A gentle man, he told me one surprise about the Delta was the harsh—even mean—way bosses talk to workers. Not a racial thing, he said, because the white workers are not treated any better. In New Mexico, you wouldn't talk to any worker that way regardless of color because the discussion would escalate into a fight.

Vernon told me about the art gallery upstairs above his shop—and recommended I visit it to see the regional art and meet Leslie Silver, the proprietress.

Vernon Anaya and Christian, his assistant

The daughter of an artist, Leslie was born in Birmingham, Alabama, and moved to Vicksburg after marrying her husband. The art studio started from a chance encounter in 1971 when Leslie visited Los Angeles with her husband. While touring an art gallery, she engaged the owner in a conversation. The gallery owner, intrigued at meeting someone from Mississippi, invited Leslie and her husband to dinner. During dinner, the gallery owner inquired about local Mississippi art galleries and was surprised to learn there were no art galleries in or near Vicksburg, the closest being in New Orleans.

The gallery owner mentioned that, on the West Coast, people often gave art as wedding gifts instead of silver and china. Leslie's husband ordered $500 worth of prints for his jewelry and bridal shop. The shipment of art was later delivered to their home while Leslie was hosting a birthday party for her young daughter, and the mothers of the young partygoers helped Leslie unpack the art—and purchased three or four pieces before the art even made it the store. The serendipitous delivery is largely responsible for the gallery's existence: Leslie could see that art could sell in Vicksburg.

Leslie Silver and Lucille Hume

Now Leslie carries works of dozens of artists in her upstairs gallery. Her walls are crammed with works of well-known and not-so-well-known southern artists. Leslie displays the works of artists who work with bottle caps and other household materials alongside that of those who work with brushes. Leslie's annual show draws people from all over the country. This year, the works of fifty artists will be shown.

As Emily Resner wrote in the *Jackson Free Press* some time ago:

> In 1971, Leslie Silver started the Attic Gallery. Thirty-something years later, the funkiness quotient has led to a quintessential, artistic celebration of Southern culture. Not the nostalgic south, the real south.

From the Attic Gallery, I went to lunch at the Main Street Market. I had to wait for a table. As I sat down, the waitress brought me a menu and told me to be sure to try the pickles. She called them "sweet butter pickles," and added, "We make 'em—you can't buy 'em anywhere." Before I knew it, she set down an extra helping. Then there was the pie—

specifically, Chocolate Chunky Pecan Pie. A couple of tables over I watched an elderly gentleman finish off his lunch and then order a slice, tempting me to do the same. I thought I would eat light at dinner.

As I ate, I watched "Miz" Bullard, the hostess, go from table to table saying hey to everyone in the establishment. She knew everyone there. Well, almost everyone since she hadn't met me yet. About the time I finished off the last remnants of the Chocolate Chunky Pecan Pie, Betty spotted me, introduced herself, and we chatted. Betty's husband was a long-time Vicksburg lawyer who became a judge. She told me that he had his fatal heart attack while on the bench. He had been Vicksburg's mayor during the late 1960s and early '70s, when Interstate 20 was constructed.

Besides acting as hostess for her daughter's restaurant, Betty is a developer working to revitalize downtown Vicksburg. She got started because she owned a building across the street from a decrepit boardinghouse. Because of the blight across the street, no one would rent the building from her. After much negotiation with the landlord, she purchased the rundown property and began restoring it. She asked if I'd like to see it, and so we took off, walking the few blocks it took to get there.

She had removed the asbestos shingles from the main façade and had replaced the front porch. She showed how the interior had been returned to its original floor plan with the removal of non-original walls. She also took me to the roof to see a great view of the river. The old abandoned house that had once been a rundown apartment house had become a wonderful bed and breakfast. In 2006, Betty received a Heritage Award from the Mississippi Heritage Trust for her rehabilitation of the 1850s George Washington Ball House; Ball was a grandnephew of George Washington.

I asked if I could get a room if I came to Leslie Silver's annual show. In a perfect Mississippi drawl, Miz Bullard said they were usually fully booked at that time. But with a twinkle in her eye, she said she might be able to squeeze me in—if I gave her enough notice, of course.

Mississippi Praying

Like Little Rock, Jackson is a small, livable city of about 185,000 people. Jackson has sprawled to the north, and the metropolitan area is about two to three times that number. At the intersection of I-55 and I-520, shiny new multi-story buildings house old-line law firms, banks, and other white-collar enterprises. Ten miles north in Canton, a Nissan plant employs 4,000 people. Most Jackson-area commuters spend less than twenty-five minutes getting to work, and that's only during the worst of the rush-hour traffic.

Of all the southern states, Mississippi perhaps embodied racial hatred most. It was home to the "Mississippi hate stare"—a stare of unalloyed hate a person of one race gave another. In his book, *I Ain't Comin' Back*, Dolphus Weary relates a joke about a black man returning to Mississippi:

> I was driving down to Mississippi and I got down to Tennessee. I got outta my car and started prayin' "Lord, you know I'm scared. I'm getting' ready to go to Mississippi and I'm afraid Lord, please go with me. Please give me a sign that you're goin' with me."
>
> And the Lord said, "Man, even I don't go into Mississippi."

Remember Vernon Anaya, the coffee barista in Vicksburg? He told me that his wife, an Episcopalian priest, worked with a group from Jackson called Mission Mississippi. Mission Mississippi works with churches throughout the state to promote racial healing. I decided to contact them. They hold weekly prayer breakfasts and invited me to attend one.

At 6:15 a.m., I was in my car and on the way to Antioch House, the late nineteenth-century house just outside of the downtown business district that serves as the meeting house for Perkins Ministries. Good thing it was summertime because even the sun doesn't get up this early in the winter. With virtually no traffic on the road, I arrived a few minutes early and found a dozen or so people congregating around a kitchen table at the back of the house.

The prayer breakfast follows a script. Breakfast starts at 6:45. If you're not there by 6:45, you join the program in progress because they want to make sure the meeting ends in time for everyone to get to work. The first fifteen to twenty minutes are spent talking and sharing a light breakfast of doughnuts, juice, fruit, and coffee. Thank goodness they had coffee. A devotional came next. This day John Perkins spoke for five to ten minutes. He said that at the age of eighty-five, he was in his bonus time and he had more money than he could spend. Speaking without notes, he had all the qualities of a great speaker—a simple message punctuated by changes in cadence and volume. His soft Mississippi accent lulled you into listening closely. Then when John started speaking loudly, the effect was dramatic. He spoke loudly that day about transferring your treasures on earth since you can't take them with you.

John is something of a celebrity. The rock group Switchfoot recorded the song "The Sound (John M. Perkins' Blues)." As the writer said about his song:

> John Perkins' story needs to be heard. This song was inspired by a man who sang a louder song than hatred. In a world where we are defined by our differences, Mr. Perkins' life of service and compassion is a tangible demonstration of what it means to live a life of love. Love is the loudest song we could sing. Louder than racism. Louder than fear. Louder than hatred. John Perkins said it right: Love is the final fight.

John is the last of the pioneer generation, the last generation who fought *de jure* segregation in Mississippi, a fight that wasn't easy or safe. Just after World War II, John's older brother, Clyde, a decorated war veteran, was shot and killed by the town sheriff—under mysterious circumstances. Afraid that John might meet the same fate his brother had, the family sent John to California, where he married and started a family.

John returned to Mississippi in 1960 to start a ministry. Initially he did not join the movement for civil rights. Jerry Mitchell describes John's purpose during those early days: "His mission was bringing black Mississippians to Jesus, not to the voting booth." John's mission soon changed, and he began letting his church building be used for civil rights meetings. His resolve only increased when the insurance company canceled his property insurance for holding those meetings.

By 1970, in the midst of an economic boycott of white merchants, John was arrested while trying to bail a friend out of jail. At the police station, he was beaten badly; a pistol was placed against his head and fired. There was a click but no explosion. The officers stuck a fork up his nose and then stuck it down his mouth. When someone else brought money for his bail, he was allowed to leave.

Eventually his health deteriorated from the stress of activism. He suffered with stomach ulcers and later a heart attack, and in 1982, he returned to southern California to begin a new ministry. While he was content in southern California, he returned to Mississippi to assist his son who had remained there to follow in his father's footsteps. When his son died in 1998, John took over the ministry. He has continued developing the ministry since then, seeing himself as a missionary on a mission of racial reconciliation.

After John spoke, the group, now about two dozen people, broke into groups of three for prayer. I was grouped with two ladies, Barbara Beavers and Earlene Morgan. Barbara is a middle-aged woman who moved to Mississippi from Ohio some thirty years before. She's now the director of the Center for Pregnancy Choices, a pro-life counseling center. Earlene is an elderly woman with twinkling bright eyes. As we talked, she surprised me by indicating that she was older than John Perkins.

Ms. Morgan, the leader of our little group, asked me if I had any prayer concerns. I said I didn't, and she indicated that was fine. She asked Barbara the same question. We three then clasped hands, bowed our heads, and closed our eyes. Ms. Morgan began to pray, praying for the needs of others.

She prayed for me. So far as I know, it was the first time anyone ever publicly supplicated on my behalf. It was a strange thing to hear. In her kind, soft voice, she asked the Lord to give me strength as I traveled to strange places, meeting strangers while doing the research for my book because she knew how hard doing those two things must be. I wondered how this elderly African-American woman, who probably had very little travel experience in her own life, identified what I had come to know as the most draining aspect of the Journey.

I can't really say how long we held hands and prayed. At one point, I opened my eyes and noticed how her dark skin contrasted against my white skin. A strange thought occurred to me: This had been the longest direct physical contact that I'd ever had with a black person. I'm not sure what that means, but I realized at that moment that I was very conscious of race.

After the small prayer groups, the whole group congregated in the hallway in a circle. Three or four people from the Perkins Foundation were called into the center of the circle, and hands from the others were placed on their shoulders—the laying on of the hands. This time another person began praying. The prayer lasted for at least five minutes and closer to ten minutes, a long time to stand with head bowed and eyes closed. Less than halfway through the prayer, I opened my eyes and began watching the group. They stood motionless with their eyes closed as the prayer leader went through the litany of concerns. I noticed how quickly and unhaltingly the prayer progressed. No notes, but no time wasted searching for words or phrases to express thoughts, and no delay in changing from one concern to another. Once this prayer was complete, people said goodbye and left for work.

After the prayer breakfast, I met Neddie Winters, the chief executive officer of Mission Mississippi. Neddie grew up in the Delta town of Clarksdale and went to college at Alcorn State in Lorman. He lived most of his formative years under *de jure* segregation. As he became a young adult, racial segregation went from being the strong public policy of Mississippi to an illegal—outlawed—policy. He lived the change.

Neddie told about lying to get a summertime job. The story reveals that while there may have been a change in the law, it didn't change attitudes. In Clarksdale, the station master of the bus station, a good

Christian man, was very proud of helping two or three local boys go to college by hiring them during the summer school vacation. The man bragged about helping these local youths, all white, get a college education. Neddie came back from Alcorn State University one summer and applied for a job at the bus station. The good Christian man wasn't going to hire him for summer help because he didn't want temporary help and was afraid that Neddie would leave at the end of the summer. Once Neddie assured him that he couldn't afford to go back to college, the man hired him. Of course Neddie was lying. Well maybe not completely. If he hadn't worked that summer, he might not have been able to afford college. But with the wages from a summer job, there was no way he was staying in Clarksdale when the school year started. Even now, over forty years later, Neddie can't believe that the man, who was so proud of his role in providing summer employment opportunities to white college boys, never gave a thought to extending help to a deserving black student. It wasn't hateful; it was simply the attitude: Neddie and others like him didn't need to go to college.

John Perkins on right

Neddie Winters of Mission, Mississippi

After *de jure* segregation fell and the law required desegregation, Neddie's generation saw the first concrete benefits of desegregation— the first black fireman hired, the first black police chief, the first black

Rotary president, and so on. It was easier and safer than the challenges that John Perkins' generation faced, but much more complicated. Neddie's generation competed directly with whites in the workplace; the law required it. The next generation faced the problem of *de facto* discrimination—judgments about a person's ability, based on race—by authority figures like the bus station manager. Those judgments proved to be daunting obstacles, particularly because they didn't involve direct hatred, just ignorance.

I asked Neddie, who was the chief executive officer of Mission Mississippi, what racial reconciliation was, and, in particular, in light of the history of Mississippi race relations, what type of friendly relations were they trying to establish? He said, with a smile, that Mission Mississippi works only with Christians, not with heathens. He said racism hinders the gospel and that you can't be a Christian and a racist. With "Grace is greater than race" as their motto, they try to create a climate in which it's safe for black and white Mississippians to create and build relationships. As Neddie says, "I can't pray for you if I don't know you," adding, "How can I pray for your children if I don't know their names?"

Jerry Mitchell represents the next generation. He's a reporter working for Jackson's daily paper, the *Clarion Ledger*, a newspaper so thoroughly racist in its past that it ran the following headline after Martin Luther King's famous "I Have a Dream" speech: "Washington is Clean Again with Negro Trash Removed." Black residents of Jackson referred to it for years as the "Klan Ledger."

Largely because of Jerry Mitchell's work over the past two decades, the *Clarion Ledger* is no longer known by that nickname. Jerry works to bring cold cases from Mississippi's bad old days to justice. As a result of Jerry's efforts, the man who murdered Medgar Evers, Byron De La Beckwith, was put behind bars, many years after his crime. Jerry's work has also helped jail others including Ku Klux Klan leader Sam Bowers; Bobby Frank Cherry, who killed four little girls in the bombing of a Birmingham church; and Edgar Ray Killen, one of the organizers of the killing of three civil rights workers, the subject of the film *Mississippi Burning*.

Jerry Mitchell of the Clarion Ledger

Jerry is at least a generation younger than Neddie or John. He's not a native of Mississippi, having grown up in Texarkana, a town which straddles the Arkansas-Texas state line. He didn't know about Mississippi's civil rights history when he moved to Jackson in 1986. Soon after arriving in Jackson, he attended the press premiere of *Mississippi Burning*, the 1988 movie about the killing of civil rights workers James Chaney, Andrew Goodman, and Michael Schwerner outside of Philadelphia, Mississippi, in the summer of 1964. He stayed after the movie and met former newsmen and FBI agents, who gave him the true account of the incident. As he said, "The thing that horrified me most of all was that there were twenty guys involved in the killing of those kids and not one had been prosecuted for murder."

For his two decades of investigative reporting, he's been called "the South's Simon Wiesenthal" and has won more than thirty national awards, one for a story on the reconciliation of John Perkins with a former

Ku Klux Klan member. He's also won a MacArthur Foundation Genius Grant, a designation he says would shock his college professors.

To interview Byron De La Beckwith, Jerry had to pass a racial purity test. Where was he from? Who were his parents? Whoever gave him the test wanted to make sure that De La Beckwith was not meeting with an African American, or as bad, a mongrel—someone with African-American blood. It wasn't a hard test for Jerry to pass. He's one of the whitest, fairest-skinned men you've ever met.

Leaving Jackson later, I thought about the day. I'm uncomfortable with public displays of religion and question mightily when people, particularly religious people, tell me what God wants me or anyone else to do. But here, in the center of Mississippi, not many years ago, good Christians ran a thoroughly racist government that excluded African Americans from participating. Presumably they read the same Bible as their maids and yard boys, and the gospel they read gave them sufficient comfort to exclude black people from having basic civil rights. How then does a racist system run entirely by Christians change? Does praying help? I pondered that question as I crossed the Pearl River.

Wide Spot on Highway 28

The modern route from Jackson to Natchez doesn't go through Union Church, Mississippi, like it did in the 1930s. Interstate 55 passes thirty miles east and takes you twenty miles south of Union Church where it intersects with the new four-lane highway to Natchez. The old route, Mississippi State Highway 28, winds through the gently rolling hills and piney woods of rural Copiah County. Unlike the Delta, where I had seen no new construction, these piney woods have an occasional construction site and a few newly constructed brick houses, nothing large or showy, just basic three-bedroom, two-bath houses. There was plenty of time to look at the scenery because there's not much traffic on Highway 28 anymore.

Near the Copiah/Jefferson County line, road construction reduced traffic to one lane. A Mississippi Highway Department flag man stopped the westbound traffic to allow the eastbound traffic to proceed. I was the third vehicle in line, behind a great big eighteen-wheel truck. A quick glance in my rearview mirror confirmed that that no one had joined us during the few minutes we'd been stopped.

I glanced over to the left side of the highway and noticed a gravel driveway leading to a couple of old cars and two deteriorating buildings. Upon further inspection, I saw a couple of kitchen appliances and tires decorating the front yard or, should I say, weed lot. Besides the trash in the front yard, I noticed movement near one of the parked cars—it was a horse, tethered to a tree. The beast moved to graze in a different spot, even though the short leash didn't give it much of a grazing area. In contrast to its surroundings, the horse seemed well cared for. As I waited for the flag man to let us pass, I wondered what kind of people lived there. Was the horse used in their business and, if so, what kind of business was it? If not, was having it just a perk of country living or had a little girl persuaded her father to let her have a pony? This little reverie was disturbed by the truck in front of me taking off. Another quick check backward and I saw that I was no longer last in line. During the ten-minute delay, two other vehicles had joined our little line.

Horse tethered in front of car off Highway 28

A few miles after waving to the flag man, I rounded a small curve in the road and came to the intersection of Highway 550 and the community of Union Church, Mississippi. Calling Union Church a community is a stretch. Two derelict commercial buildings, which have been abandoned for some time, and a small post office building make up Union Church.

There's also a very pretty church and a very conspicuous graveyard in the bend of the road. A large vacant lot with a big sign advertising Coca-Cola and Varnado's Grocery sits at the junction of the highways.

Varnado's was Union Church. According to the postmistress, Kelly Brown, Varnado's was a general store, the place to go for all kinds of merchandise and food. She learned over the years to check Varnado's before going thirty miles to the Wal-Mart in Hazlehurst because Varnado's often had just what she needed. Old men met for coffee there around a pot-bellied stove. A Civil War–era ammunition wagon had been dragged into the store many years before and used to display merchandise. Stuffed rattlesnakes and deer heads decorated the walls.

A Natchez nursing home brought its residents to Varnado's on day trips. Ms. Brown said the old people would line up at the cold cut section to get head cheese. Head cheese isn't cheese at all but head meat from a cow or a pig, boiled and jellied and shaped into a sausage. I'm sure they reminisced about the old days, but what brought them back year after year was the head cheese.

Sadly, I was too late to experience Varnado's. A few years ago, after over 150 years of continuous operation, Varnado's burned. One morning a fire started in the bathroom. Within a few minutes, the building was an inferno, burning to the ground before anything could be saved. Locals wanted the Varnado family to rebuild, but Mr. Varnado, who was ill, died soon after the fire. After that, there was no talk of rebuilding. I asked where the old men drank their coffee these days. She replied, "At home, I guess, because there's no place around here."

Not a Soul in Sight

In Tidewater Virginia, I traveled the Colonial Parkway. I passed near the Blue Ridge Parkway a couple of times while traveling through the mountains of western North Carolina. I spent a great afternoon traveling from Florence, Alabama, to Nashville, Tennessee, on the Natchez Trace Parkway.

Now taking a slight detour into Natchez, I picked the Trace back up again. It was just as remote in Mississippi as I remembered it being in Tennessee. Not a soul in sight, and after ten miles of traveling, I hadn't seen a car coming or going. While the cell phone companies have done a good job of providing cellular phone coverage for the most of the country, they missed an area between Port Gibson and Natchez.

With no traffic, the tendency is to speed. But if you can resist the temptation, cruising the Parkway around fifty miles per hour is quite relaxing. If you pull over and turn off your engine, there are no sounds.

I stood outside my car reflecting on the quiet as three dogs trotted down the road. I was first concerned for their safety. But as I watched them move along, I realized they were wild—much like the road they were traveling.

The Rose Lady
Comes to Camellia Land

Founded in 1716, Natchez is older than Vicksburg, which wasn't settled by Europeans for another ninety-five years. Natchez is prettier, largely due to its treatment during the Civil War. Residents from both cities claim that Natchez surrendered after one shot. It's a point of pride in Natchez. Only one Natchez house was destroyed during the Yankee occupation because the locals tried to get along with the invaders. The sole loss supposedly occurred because the homeowners offended a Yankee officer during a social event.

The population of Natchez is around 18,000. It's relatively remote—sixty-two miles from Interstate 20 and seventy miles from I-55. Natchez's major industry is tourism. The city boasts over 500 antebellum buildings. These structures date from the French, Spanish, and American eras. In 2003 the National Trust for Historic Preservation recognized Natchez as one of America's Distinctive Destinations. It has been suggested, by Natchezians mainly, that Vicksburgers try mightily to attract tourist dollars for simple commercial purposes. In Natchez, they contend that their heritage tourism is more successful because it's done with a higher purpose. Besides the old houses, there are garden tours, the Great Mississippi Balloon Race, and so many other events that one resident said, "This may look like a sleepy little town, but there's always something going on here."

The first person I met in Natchez was an immigrant from the west, California this time. Karen Dardick was born and raised in Manhattan, educated at Northwestern University near Chicago, and spent several years in Los Angeles where she worked as a writer. The Dardicks are the vanguard of the small but great eastern migration to Mississippi from southern California. Her migration story begins with lunch at the Huntington Tea Room in Los Angeles. She met a couple who had moved to Natchez the year before; they assured Karen and her husband that Natchez was nice and, as the song says, "the living is easy." Their description of life in the Mississippi River town fell on receptive ears. Karen and her husband had long been concerned about the quality of life in California. They owned a modern, glass-walled house on a hill, which had appreciated dramatically in monetary value but was less livable as the Los Angeles congestion increased.

Intrigued by the South, Karen began an Internet search of available properties and couldn't believe the price difference between Mississippi and southern California homes. Karen and her husband heard it could get hot in the summer so they decided to visit Natchez in July. They met a real estate agent in the heat of a Mississippi summer and went house hunting. Since the heat didn't seem too bad, Karen wanted to make an offer on the first house they saw. The price seemed incredibly low. Unlike a typical southern California agent, her Natchez real estate agent objected to writing up an offer, saying, "You haven't seen enough houses yet." After looking at more houses the next day, they wrote an offer on the first property. It was accepted, and the Dardicks began their move to Mississippi.

Three years later, Karen has no regrets. Two pleasant surprises are extremely low real property taxes and the number of smiling faces they encounter on a daily basis. Natchez reminds her in some ways of New York City when she was growing up: Women dress up, and there is an old-style civility reminiscent of an earlier time. That's not to say that there haven't been adjustments. Karen's a vegetarian and the local cuisine leaves much to be desired. No catfish, barbecue, or tamales for her; she travels some eighty miles to Baton Rouge for vegetables and other select items.

But there was a learning curve to living in the South. For instance, Karen and her husband have had to learn about drying basements: Sump pumps are unknown in California. They learned about letting your water faucets drip on cold winter nights so your pipes won't freeze. Fortunately, freezing nights in southern Mississippi are rare.

A good immigrant, Karen is a positive influence on Natchez. A national gardening writer for several years, her enthusiasm for gardening is contagious. Largely through her efforts, the Symphony of Gardens tour has become an annual spring event. One of the tour gardens, the Van Court Townhouse garden, is owned by some other southern California ex-pats. Ron and Lani Riches have integrated into Natchez society after buying the deteriorating Monmouth Plantation in 1978 and transforming it into a small luxury inn. There is a Reuben Harper Sanctuary in Monmouth, built to honor Reuben "Buzz" Harper for his help in assisting with antique selections in the various renovation projects. I was scheduled to meet Buzz at his house, Ravennaside. That's the next story.

The Salon at Ravennaside

S*alon* is a French word meaning "large room," but it also means a gathering of people to meet, discuss ideas, or watch artistic perform- ances. Ravennaside is a 10,000-square-foot Colonial Revival house built in Natchez in 1902 on three acres of land. As I attended a formal lunch- eon at Ravennaside, the word *salon* kept coming to me. The first meaning was apparent given the mansion's magnificent public rooms. The second meaning became apparent during the second or third course of the five-course lunch.

I called my host in the morning to confirm the time for lunch. I told him I was casually dressed but would be happy to change, if I needed to be more formal. He replied that he liked to dress formally and would be wearing a coat and tie, but that his other guests would be casually dressed so that I could come as I wished.

I found myself a little intimidated arriving at the front gate and walking up the front steps to a beautiful front porch. A butler ushered me into a parlor where I waited for my host, Mr. Reuben "Buzz" Harper. Buzz might be described as colorful. The writer of an article in *Southern Living* about Natchez described him well:

> ...a distinguished gentlemen gliding in gracefully with a cane. His three-piece suit will be buttoned, fingers weighted by bejeweled rings and white hair pulled tight into a pony-tail.

Ravennaside in Natchez

As I said, colorful. Even though Buzz wore a coat and tie for lunch, to me he was a homeboy because he hails from the Arkansas Delta. Buzz grew up in Newport, the county seat of Jackson County, Arkansas, where Governor Mike Beebe went to high school. He mentioned graduating from the University of Arkansas in 1957. Doing some quick calculations, I realized that Buzz was a lot older than he looked. Later Buzz told me he had moved to Natchez from New Orleans, after selling his house in the Garden District to the actor Nicholas Cage.

A meeting being held in another parlor soon broke up. Buzz introduced me to his business associates, Mike Recotta from New Orleans and Bill Probst from Atlanta. His butler offered me a drink, and I soon relaxed in the old-style southern hospitality and enjoyed the conversation. Ms. Lonita Byrne, a friend of Buzz's who had recently moved back to Natchez from Vicksburg, joined us.

Before lunch, Buzz gave us a quick tour of the first floor. He noted that Ravennaside's parquet floors were somewhat unique for Natchez. Most of the finer houses in town were older and had broad plank flooring.

The mantel in the front parlor was not of the appropriate period for the house. Buzz said the original owner had bought it in New York City. It was finer than the other mantels which had been milled locally for the house. He said that he had been offered a lot of money for the mantel. Such offers raised the trader blood in him, but the mantel belonged to the house and wasn't for sale.

Soon we repaired to the dining room for lunch. After the soup and salad courses came a wonderfully encrusted catfish covered with shrimp Creole sauce and served over rice. I don't want to sound like a society columnist, but I must note that my coin silver knife rested on a little silver bridge. I had never seen a little silver bridge before, but I found it to be a pretty handy piece of tableware. I could rest my knife and not worry about soiling the starched tablecloth. Strawberry shortcake with raspberries was served for dessert. A good rule of thumb: When straw-berry shortcake is offered, it's un-American not to indulge.

Buzz kept the conversation moving. He moved from the opening grace to the history of his fine house. He made his guests comfortable and drew us into the discussion. During lunch, the group learned that Bill Probst's brother was a character actor in Hollywood who played Tom Cruise's father in the film *Risky Business* and that Lonita's husband was a former mayor of Natchez. Buzz spoke of his ninety-year-old mother, who had lived most of her life in Newport. He recalled her wise counsel, "Everyone has trials in life. No matter how good things might appear on the outside everyone has hardships they have to endure."

The talk covered architecture, interior decorating, politics, movies, and religion. During the political discussion—which can be risky, as I had discovered in Chattanooga—Buzz declared that Hillary Clinton's election as senator from New York was every bit the accomplishment of a newcomer moving into Natchez and being elected mayor. After some discussion, the group concluded that becoming mayor of Natchez was harder than being elected senator of New York State. A newcomer really stands no chance of being elected mayor of Natchez.

The coffee arrived two hours after our lunch began. After coffee, our group trooped into the kitchen to shake hands with the cook and Charles, the butler.

As I was leaving, I thanked Buzz for a wonderful time and asked if I could take his picture on the front porch. He initially declined, but when I explained I was not a very good photographer, he broke into a large smile and said graciously, "In that case, take as many pictures as you like."

Buzz at Ravennaside

McDonald's Comes to St. Francisville

Louisiana was the eighth state on the Journey. They call things by different names here. The local governmental unit known as a county in the other forty-nine states is a parish in Louisiana. Most people say it's the French-Canadian influence. Except that the French-Canadians, known as Cajuns, settled the land on the west side of the Mississippi River, and this was still on the east side of the river. The parishes east of the river—the "Florida Parishes"—have a different history.

The Florida Parishes began as part of West Florida, which was owned up until 1763 by the French, who later gave it to the British. The Brits owned West Florida for twenty years, until the end of the American Revolution, when they gave it to Spain. Most of that time, these lands were wild and unknown. The Spanish government decided to develop West Florida by offering Americans generous land grants if they would take up residence. Tories looking for a fresh start after the American Revolution and leaders of the failed Whiskey Rebellion took the Spaniards up on their offer.

Americans of English descent settled on West Feliciana's best land nearer the Mississippi River. The Scotch and Irish Americans from Tennessee, Kentucky, north Georgia, and north Alabama settled the less productive land of East Feliciana later. These immigration patterns created distinctions still evident today. West Feliciana has more Episcopalians and Tidewater-style plantation houses, while East Feliciana Parish has courthouse squares and is largely Baptist. While these cultural distinctions have blurred in the past two centuries, you'll still find a lot more rednecks in East Feliciana Parish than in West Feliciana Parish even today.

Spain owned the area until 1810 when, after the Battle of Baton Rouge, self-rule took the form of the short-lived Republic of West Florida. After running the Spanish out, the Republic of West Florida, including southern parts of Alabama, Mississippi, and that part of Louisiana east of the Mississippi River, existed for about ninety days. The freedom fighters passed a constitution patterned after the United States Constitution, and named St. Francisville the capital of this short-lived republic. Its only chief executive officer was Fulwar Skipwith, a Virginia Cavalier instrumental in negotiating the Louisiana Purchase, who then moved to the area a few years afterward. Fulwar Skipwith, possessor of one of the all-time-great names for a politician, was a distant cousin of Thomas Jefferson.

St. Francisville, the parish seat of West Feliciana Parish, is a quiet little town of 1,500 people. Located on a bluff overlooking the Mississippi River and just a few miles from Highway 61, St. Francisville is thought by some to be the oldest town in the Florida Parishes. (Highway 61 is the same highway I traveled through the Mississippi Delta, where it is known as the "Blues Highway.")

Forty years ago, it looked as if St. Francisville was doomed. With Baton Rouge some thirty miles away, St. Francisville was a tiny backwoods Louisiana town off the main highway in the middle of nowhere. But St. Francisville hung on economically with money from tourists attracted to the large live oaks, Spanish moss, and lovely plantation homes.

In the intervening decades things have changed. The city of Baton Rouge has sprawled, eventually reaching the southern part of West Feliciana Parish. As growth crept closer, more houses were built and more people came. If you build enough houses anywhere in America, a McDonald's soon follows. It's a sign of progress. A few years ago, the golden arches came to St. Francisville—though not to downtown St. Francisville. The downtown isn't on the highway. McDonald's, all about the traffic count, is located just outside of St. Francisville on Highway 61.

Residents talk about when McDonald's came. It was a huge status deal having their own McDonald's and not having to drive to Baton

Rouge for a Big Mac. A new McDonald's was only the beginning. More people came—hungry people who wanted their food and wanted it fast. Other fast food providers arrived: Church's Chicken, Sonic, and Subway. So many high-calorie choices, so little time. Once the restaurants arrived, roads had to be widened. Highway 61 is now five lanes, with convenience stores and franchised fast food restaurants. The U.S. 61 right-of-way by St. Francisville's downtown looks like the rest of America.

Growth is enticing to an area that's been impoverished since the boll weevil tore through here over 140 years ago. But not all growth is good, especially for an area that embraced and developed "heritage tourism" some time ago. The director of the West Feliciana Parish Community Development Foundation stated that growth was coming and that his organization was preparing for it. He said if a boom is not managed properly, it could ruin "the rural, small-town feel of St. Francisville." The Community Development Foundation worked on a growth plan, the West Feliciana Parish Comprehensive Plan, to implement a vision of growth gleaned from community workshops. "How do you balance Mayberry and growth in the 21st century?" the planners asked.

The Community Development Foundation also encouraged the Planning and Zoning Board, the West Feliciana Parish Police Jury (the local legislative board), and the St. Francisville Town Council to amend ordinances to prohibit the location of big-box retailers in the parish. As board member Michael Hennessey stated:

> Big-box retail is neither who we are nor who we want to be. Urban sprawl is a natural consequence of this kind of development. We need to safeguard the character of our parish to enable us to be successful in the long run.

There are no big-box stores in downtown St. Francisville, now a historic district. There are retail shops catering to the tourist trade, a few restaurants, a bank, and an auto dealer (one of the smallest ones still operating). There are more bed and breakfast establishments than any other category of businesses in St. Francisville. The in-town B&Bs, along with the ones located in converted plantation houses outside of town, constitute the backbone of modern St. Francisville's economy—tourism.

Among the B&Bs in the downtown historic district sits St. Francisville's only factory, Grandmother's Buttons. But Grandmother's Buttons is more than a factory.

Susan Davis began Grandmother's Buttons in 1985 to provide supplemental income for her farm family. While visiting her ninety-five-year-old grandmother, who had a large button collection, Susan got the idea to convert the old buttons into earrings. Her grandmother agreed and donated her thirty boxes of buttons to the new venture.

Grandmother's Buttons factory and headquarters

In 1994, the Davises purchased the 1905 building that once housed the Bank of St. Francisville. The next year they opened a retail store in the lobby using the original oak woodwork as a backdrop for the cases of jewelry made from buttons. A few months later, the bank vault became a tiny museum of antique buttons. Upstairs is the factory where local ladies convert antique buttons into jewelry. Today Grandmother's

Buttons supplies jewelry to over a thousand shops and boutiques throughout the United States.

St. Francisville is doing well with Grandmother's Buttons and the B&Bs—giving the feel of Mayberry as you walk its streets. But sprawl is edging ever closer. How successful the people of St. Francisville will be in balancing the competing pressures is the subject for another visit.

Crossing the River by Ferryboat

St. Francisville is on high ground, and the Mississippi River is but a few miles away. Leaving St. Francisville, you immediately descend toward the river.

After a couple of curves, the landing for the St. Francisville/New Roads ferryboat comes into view. This boat carries traffic from Louisiana Highway 10 across the Mississippi River. The ferry leaves on the hour and half hour during daylight hours seven days a week. I timed it perfectly. Cars just off the boat heading toward St. Francisville met me. Six cars headed west to get on the boat were lined up.

The ferry ride is a great bargain of the Journey: A buck gets you across. And that's actually the round-trip fare, as there's no charge for going the other way. The next ferry upriver, the Dorena/Hickman Ferry, is some 500 miles away, transporting travelers between Kentucky and Missouri just south of the confluence of the Ohio and Mississippi Rivers. It charges $14 each way.

As you drive onto the ferry, one deckhand extracts the toll from drivers, while another deckhand directs the cars to a spot on the boat. After the cars are loaded, they signal some farm vehicles, which had been parked on the side of the road, to follow the cars on board. Once the combines and tractors are situated, you depart.

The lady in the car next to me was obviously a regular; she stayed in her car and talked on her cell phone the whole time. I immediately got out of my car, headed to the side of the boat, and looked up- and down-river as we departed. The river looks just like it does at Helena—a huge river with no visible signs of development on its bluffs and no buildings in sight. The river banks are still wild. The same can't be said of the river, where traffic is heavy.

We moved slowly into the channel so a barge could pass going upriver. We fell in behind it and crossed its wake. The captain timed our crossing, ducking between two barges heading downriver. Even with all that river traffic, we reached the New Roads side of the river in no time.

Riding a tug boat's wake

The St. Francisville/New Roads ferry won't operate much longer. It will be replaced by the John James Audubon Bridge. While the bridge will be a more efficient east-west connector and a boon to economic development, it's a shame to see the ferry become obsolete.

A few miles south of the ferry landing is New Roads, Louisiana, one of the oldest communities in the Mississippi Valley. Today, New Roads has a population of 5,000 people. Founded by the French in the 1720s, it's the parish seat of Point Coupée Parish. Point Coupée means "the place of the cut-off." In 1699, the explorer Pierre d'Iberville took a short-cut on his explorations up the river by fording a narrow stream over a neck of land, the "point coupee." New Roads was founded at the place of the cut-off.

St. Francisville is English, but New Roads is French. In St. Francisville, you have the Davises, Bennetts, and Walshes. In downtown New Roads, you shop at Langlois' grocery or get an insurance quote from the L. Bouanchaud Insurance Agency. The local legislators were Representative Donald Cazayoux Jr. and Senator Robert Marionneaux.

New Roads boasts of the oldest Mardi Gras celebration in Louisiana outside of New Orleans. Unlike the one in New Orleans, the New Roads parade is open to citizen participation. People in New Roads are also quick to point out that their celebration is more family-oriented than the Crescent City's.

Acres of sugar cane, cotton, and pecans surround the little town. Point Coupée Parish is the leading pecan-producing parish in the state and home to the H. J. Bergeron Pecan Shelling Plant, the oldest pecan-shelling plant in the United States. The Bergerons welcome visitors to tour their facility and view the hundred-year-old pecan trees in their orchard, some of which rise 125 feet. I bought two bags of Elliot pecans, which Mr. Bergeron assured me were the best he had. I munched on pecans while traveling through Louisiana farmland—but for less than twenty miles because the Cajun Highway takes you quickly into downtown Baton Rouge.

Baton Rouge, Huey Long,
and the Movie Industry

Baton Rouge lies on the east bank of the Mississippi River, so coming from New Roads, I crossed the river again. The river widens at every crossing. It's now a monster.

Baton Rouge got its name from a boundary line. The Indians marked the boundary between their hunting grounds on this bluff by stripping a red cypress tree of its bark. As the French explorers progressed up river, they noticed the tree and called the bluff "le baton rouge" or "the red stick." The name stuck. Baton Rouge is the state capital. Its capitol building, at thirty-four stories, is the tallest in the country. During the Great Depression, Governor Huey Long directed, "Build it quick and build it big." The Art Deco–style building was the tallest building in the South when it was completed in 1932, a few years before Jonathan Daniels visited Baton Rouge.

Very few politicians have made as long-lasting an imprint on a city as Huey made on Baton Rouge. His presence is felt all around here. In addition to the capitol, he conceived of LSU's football stadium. Huey had the stadium built—even though the legislature didn't appropriate enough money to build one—using money meant for dormitory rooms to build a stadium with dorm rooms under the stands. Generations of LSU scholars lived underneath Tiger Stadium. Inventive and a man of many talents, Huey also wrote a few fight songs for the Tigers, and some are still sung on Saturday afternoons in the fall.

Though officially Tiger Stadium, the stadium has been known for some years throughout the Southeastern Conference as "death valley." The nickname was originally "deaf valley" because fans here are really loud. In 1988, the crowd's reaction to a touchdown in the waning seconds of a game against Auburn registered at the local geological survey office as an earthquake. The game became known as the "earthquake game."

Entrance to Mike's lair

I wasn't there on a game day so it was quiet around the stadium. So quiet that Mike, the LSU mascot, napped in the luxurious digs that Athletic Department donors have graciously built for him. Mike is a live Bengal tiger. Six Mikes have served since 1936. The present Mike, Mike VI, has been on the job since 2007. Being the LSU mascot is a good gig. Four of the five Mikes have lived to be at least seventeen, which is almost twice the normal life expectancy of a big cat. It's not surprising—Mike's habitat has 15,000 square feet of walking-around area, a viewing wall where fans can see him, a live oak tree, and a couple of water features. Mike has it goin' on.

Huey Long was a radical populist. His one term as governor was marked by huge public projects: 9,700 miles of new roads, 111 toll-free bridges, the new state capitol building, and the football stadium. He instituted free schools and distributed free school textbooks statewide. Elected to the U.S. Senate in November 1930, Huey didn't take his Senate seat until 1932 because he had a few things he wanted to finish as governor; he just left the Senate position vacant until then.

Even after moving to Washington, he still controlled the machinery of state government back home. From this power base, he created the Share Our Wealth Program, his plan for America's recovery, which was considerably more liberal than Roosevelt's New Deal programs. Huey's slogan, originally coined by the late nineteenth-century populist William Jennings Bryan, was "Every man a king, but no one wears a crown."

Long declared that the primary cause of the 1930s economic crisis was an unequal distribution of wealth and political power:

> God told you what the trouble was. The philosophers told you what the trouble was; and when you have a country where one man owns more than 100,000 people, or a million people, and when you have a country where there are four men, as in America, that have got more control over things than all the 120 million people together, you know what the trouble is…

> Now, my friends, we have got to hit the root with the ax. Centralized power in the hands of a few, with centralized credit in the hands of a few, is the trouble.

His program of recovery called for direct redistribution of wealth. The major planks in his proposal for America's recovery were radical even for those times. He proposed the following:

> capping personal fortunes
> limiting annual income
> limiting inheritance
> guaranteeing income at 1/3 of the national average

providing free college education and vocational training
old-age pensions for those over 60
30-hour work weeks
four weeks' vacation for every worker

Long denied that his plan was socialistic. He credited the Bible and the Declaration of Independence as his source materials. He claimed that his plan was necessary to thwart a communist or socialist takeover of the country. Once he told his fellow senators that a mob was coming for them and he wasn't sure whether he'd stay with the Senate or lead the mob.

By 1935, he was making plans to run against Franklin Roosevelt for president of the United States. A few months later, while attending a special session of the Louisiana legislature, Huey Long was assassinated. The official version of events made a young Baton Rouge doctor the assassin, though more recent evidence indicates that Huey wasn't shot by the young doctor. The bullets taken from his body don't match the doctor's gun, but were the same caliber of bullets that his bodyguards carried. Whether he was killed by accident or on the orders of his local or national political enemies remains unknown. Huey Long and Robert F. Kennedy are the only two U.S. Senators to be assassinated while in office.

Huey Long's resting place at the capitol

269

Huey Long was buried on the capitol grounds. On the day I visited, a spray of fresh flowers adorned his grave—his son Palmer honoring Huey's birthday.

Birthday card from Huey's son

Louisiana politics have changed, and a politician with Huey's views couldn't get elected dogcatcher in modern Louisiana. There are no modern Cajun Keynesians like Huey in Louisiana politics today. Rather than making direct investments into large public projects like roads and schools, modern Louisiana tax policy provides tax rebates to create economic activity. One example is the movie industry. If you make a movie in Louisiana and spend at least $300,000 in the state, you get a thirty percent tax credit from the state of Louisiana for every dollar spent there. TV shows also qualify. You also can get an extra five percent on wages if you hire locals rather than bringing in out-of-state laborers. The State of Louisiana will repurchase the credits for eighty-five cents on the dollar—or you can sell them in the open market to a Louisiana taxpayer if you can get a better deal.

So suppose a movie group spends, say, twenty-five million dollars making an alien invasion movie called *Battle: Los Angeles*. If they spend their money in Louisiana, they will get a basic Louisiana tax credit of $7,500,000 ($25,000,000 x 30% = $7,500,000). If the state repurchases the tax credit at eighty-five percent, the movie guys receive a check from the state for $6,375,000. This payment incentivizes the movie guys to spend their money in Louisiana rather than Los Angeles, New York, or New Mexico. Yes, New Mexico also gives a generous state tax credit to moviemakers. And I think Ohio and Michigan are also in the movie tax credit game.

The state auditor found that in 2010 the tax credit program cost the State of Louisiana almost $170 million in tax revenues. However, Louisiana's film industry produced an economic impact of a billion dollars to the Louisiana economy—that's a lot of apartments and cars rented for movie people, meals consumed, sets constructed, locations rented. Louisiana is now third only to California and New York in domestic movie production, and the impact of a billion dollars keeps a lot of people employed.

With other states competing to subsidize movies, it's not just tax breaks that bring movie people here. The geography, weather, and the cooperation of the locals are also important considerations. In this endeavor, the people and governments in Louisiana shine. They are happy to help these image makers expedite their activities. For example, Bossier City shut down a portion of its interstate for five weeks so that movie makers could replicate Los Angeles–like freeway scenes. Louisiana film people contend that Louisiana is so diverse that it can provide any set a movie maker might want except an outdoor snow-skiing scene.

Huey wouldn't approve of direct government subsidies to rich people. Huey would say that these movies don't help "the boys at the fork of the creek" or create permanent improvements to Louisiana like a road or bridge would. Huey's misgivings notwithstanding, film tax credits have produced results for Louisiana and Baton Rouge.

On to Opelousas

Taking the Acadiana Trail due west from Baton Rouge, the next stop is Opelousas (pronounced "OPP a luses"). Opelousas is the capital of the Cajun Prairie and self-proclaimed world zydeco capital. Arriving at the city center of Opelousas late Friday afternoon, I asked the nice ladies at the tourist information center if there would be "any zydeco dancing around here this evening." They laughed and gave me a simple sheet of paper listing local events.

I took the paper and quickly scanned it. Having done my homework, I asked specifically about Richard's (pronounced "Reechard's) in nearby Lawtell. The tourist information ladies told me the club had changed its name to the Zydeco Hall of Fame—a little pretentious, I thought. I also asked about Fred's in Mamou and Opelousas' own Slim's Y-Ki-Ki Club. Surprisingly, the ladies were unsure if any of them would be open. They told me that Chris Ardoin had played the week before.

I considered their responses a little strange. I'm sure Chris Ardoin was good and all, but it was Friday and I assumed all nightclubs would be open on Friday night, especially in fun-loving Cajun land. If they weren't going to be open, I wondered how they could expect me to—as they say in the local vernacular—"pass a good time."

I set out with the directions to Slim's Y-Ki-Ki Club, which was indeed closed. I then headed toward the Zydeco Hall of Fame, figuring surely it would be open. Strike two. So it was on to Mamou, a small town of 3,500, to search for the famous Fred's Lounge. Fred's was mentioned prominently in a 1990 *National Geographic* magazine article. Later, Peter Jennings, Charles Kuralt, and all three major television networks visited and did stories about Fred's. It is even listed as an "American must see" in a French tourist brochure. I found only an empty parking lot in front of Fred's, which was closed.

Happenin's in Opelousas

So I headed back toward Opelousas. This is rice country and looks a lot like the area around Stuttgart, Arkansas. I noticed that lots of rice fields were flooded, which I thought curious since it was winter.

Re-entering the outskirts of the little town of Eunice, I saw a sign announcing that Zaunbrecher's Boiling Hut would be open from five to eight. Next to the hut, I saw six or so men doing something under a tent. There were no cars in the parking lot, just a few pickup trucks. I wheeled into a parking space by the little building. As I got out of my car, I was greeted by a young man with a beer in his hand. I told him I was passing through and wondered what they were doing. He explained to me through his thick accent that they were "bawling" (boiling) crawfish, also known as mudbugs, to sell later that evening.

273

Crawfish field near Opelousas

He said crawfish season started around Super Bowl weekend and would continue through early May when the water in the fields became so warm that the crawfish would no longer be desirable. He explained that within the hour cars would line up to the highway to buy complete meals: bags of boiled crawfish, ears of corn, and potatoes. The price this week was $3.99 a pound for the boiled crawfish; the corn and potatoes are thrown in for free. $3.99 is the early season price, he told me. It would drop as the season progressed and might end as low as $.79 a pound.

My guide's name was John Zaunbrecher Jr., a student at McNeese State University in Lake Charles. His family farms rice and soybeans in the area. In the winter, they flood their fields to raise crawfish, as many other local farmers do. It was these flooded fields that I had noticed earlier. John returns home on weekends to help his older cousin, Byron, with the "bawling." To explain the process to me, John first needed another beer.

Byron Zaunbrecher and boiled crawfish

Every Friday and Saturday, the Zaunbrechers harvest crawfish from the flooded fields and bring them directly to the boiling hut. Once they arrive, the crawfish—which look like small lobsters and have pinchers that can draw blood—are readied for the boiling pot. After boiling, the crawfish are seasoned and packaged.

The younger Zaunbrecher, who, I discovered later, raised the grand champion lamb at the 2007 Acadia Parish Junior Livestock Show, demonstrated for me the correct way to peel a crawfish. First, you hold it upside down, taking the body in one hand and the first tail joint with the other. You push in slightly, then pull to remove the tail. You throw away the body. The tail is peeled and eaten like a shrimp. The meat of a freshly boiled crawfish is tender and quite delicious. Some people talk about sucking the head, but thankfully we didn't go there.

As workers brought him more beer, John told me that in a few weeks they would be "chasin' cheekens." The chicken chasing is part of the local Mardi Gras celebration. Mardi Gras isn't celebrated with float parades down crowded city streets like it is in New Orleans. As he said, "It ain't about masks and beads; we go on a run to chase cheekens." Last year John and his friends started at 7 a.m.; they covered about twenty miles and he got two chickens. What my young friend described, I later discovered, was the Courir de Mardi Gras, a Mardi Gras "run." Each small town on the Cajun Prairie has one. It's an old tradition where a group of revelers go on horseback and on foot from house to house begging the owners for ingredients for a gumbo.

The Courir is a somewhat formal affair with a captain leading the revelers. In a concession to modernists, they allow trucks and trailers to carry some of the celebrators. The captain's followers are known as the Mardi Gras. When they arrive at a house, the captain requests permission from the property owner to come onto the property. Once permission is given, the Mardi Gras group sings and dances for the property owner until he offers them ingredients for the gumbo. Owners often throw a live chicken into the air and the Mardi Gras group chases it, competing with one another for the honor of catching the chicken. This scene repeats from property to property lasting most of the day. The Courir ends with a parade down Eunice's main drag in the late afternoon.

The Courir is a party for everyone. Signs prohibiting the consumption of alcoholic beverages are posted. But John said the prohibition is not too strictly enforced. John admitted that, after eight hours of beer drinking and chicken chasing, he is usually in bed around six o'clock on Fat Tuesday evening, and after a good night's sleep, is ready for mass on Ash Wednesday.

I asked if he cuts class to participate in the run. John gave me a look of disbelief and replied quickly, "No sir. There ain't no school that week on the Monday, Tuesday, or Wednesday. We out."

Travel Notes:
What's a Coon Ass?

A Cajun is defined as "a Louisianan who descends from French-speaking Acadians." Cajun history begins with the Great Derangement, or as the Acadians say, *"Le Grand Dérangement."* After the French and Indian War, the British expelled thousands of French Catholic settlers from the maritime provinces of eastern Canada and the coastal region of northern Maine, which was then known as Acadia. Many of these Frenchmen traveled the Mississippi River looking for a place to land. They resettled in the western regions of French Louisiana, alongside enslaved Africans, freed slaves from the Caribbean, and the native Coushatta Indians. *Acadians* was shortened in English to *'Cadians* and later to *Cajuns. Cajun* was once considered a derogatory term, but as it gained acceptance in polite society, the derogatory reference was replaced with the much less polite *coon ass.*

The origin of *coon ass* remains obscure, but some believe it arose during the First World War when Cajun soldiers were used as interpreters. The dialect of these Americans differed significantly from the French, as spoken by Europeans. The French called the Cajun interpreters *conasse* because they didn't understand many words the Europeans used. *Conasse* is French slang meaning a stupid man or woman or a man who does stupid things. Thus using the term *stupid* before *coon ass* would be considered redundant.

The offensive nature of the term has judicial support. In the case of *Roach v. Dresser Industries,* 494 F. Supp 215 (W.D. La, 1980), the federal court ruled that a lawsuit could proceed where Calvin J. Roach, a Cajun from Mire, Louisiana, objected to being called a coon ass by his supervisor. He claimed that his outspoken refusal to be called a coon ass led to his termination. The court held that Cajuns are a federally recognized group subject to protection under the Civil Rights Act, and Roach had a right to be protected from objectionable references to his heritage in the workplace.

Cajun vs. Coon Ass

Now against this backdrop—where I knew that it might be inappropriate to call a Cajun a coon ass—I asked Byron Zaunbrecher if he were Cajun. He said, "Hell no! I'm a coon ass and proud of it." He did not seem to appreciate my question. Since I was his guest and he was much bigger than me, I let the matter drop. But I was still curious.

As best I can tell from my research, the Zaunbrechers aren't Cajun. They came to Louisiana in the 1880s with a group of immigrants from Germany. An ancestor, Nicholas Zaunbrecher, is credited with being the first person to sell rice commercially in Louisiana. This branch of the Zaunbrecher clan farms a couple thousand acres of rice and soybeans as their main business. Raising and selling crawfish is a sideline, similar to rice farmers in Arkansas flooding their fields in winter to attract ducks so they can profit from hunters. So why does a person of German descent proudly refer to himself as a coon ass?

The term *coon ass* now has taken on a meaning like *redneck* or *cracker*. While a decade before, any of those terms would be considered derogatory, the words now denote a regional pride. This would be consistent with a secondary meaning of the term *coon ass*, which has at its root the Caribbean Indian word *cunaso*, which means someone who lives simply, on and with the land. The inhabitants of the Cajun Prairie live simply and close to the land. More importantly, they like to have a good time. You often will hear around here, "*Laissez les bons temps rouler!*"—"Let the good times roll!"

As I drove back to Opelousas, I saw a pickup truck with a bumper sticker that said, "Coon Ass and Proud." Made me think I should delay my search for zydeco music so I could find some more boiled crawfish.

Zydeco Dancing

I t's nighttime and I'm in a strange town. I ask the clerk at my hotel about Slim's Y-Ki-Ki Club. "You should've been here last week because Chris Ardoin played," she said. "I'm not sure they will be open tonight if no one is playing."

She recommended a restaurant which was on the way to Slim's. She advised that I'd have plenty of time to eat because things wouldn't get cranking until at least 10 p.m. I questioned whether it was safe for a middle-aged white guy to hang out there. She smiled broadly and said, "Oh, it'll be okay. Now most of them will be black, but they're not the kind of people you have to worry about." So after dinner and full of crawfish, I arrived at the Y-Ki-Ki Club about 10 p.m. There wasn't a car in the parking lot.

Returning to the hotel, I reported the lack of zydeco to the clerk, who said, "Well, I was afraid of that, after last weekend with Chris Ardoin. You really should have been there." I turned to head back to my room when she said, "Why don't you go to the track?" Opelousas is the home to Evangeline Downs, a thoroughbred racetrack. I was thinking that I didn't come all this way to watch horse racing. She explained that in the off-season, bands played at the track. I still wasn't sure that I wanted to hear some second-rate band underneath a racetrack grandstand. "Let me see who's playing," she said as she turned away, picked up a phone, and made a call. Turning back around to me, she announced, "You're in luck; T. Broussard is playing at Mojo's."

Determined to find live zydeco music, I headed to the track. Evangeline Downs has a racino and is open during the off-season. To attract gamblers, they offer live music on the weekends. I walked in hoping Mojo's wouldn't be crowded, and it wasn't. T. Broussard and the Zydeco Steppers were in the corner of a large room with lots of big TVs hanging from the ceiling, broadcasting horse racing from Delta Downs, a small track in western Louisiana.

T. and his band were playing to a sparse crowd. Most of the crowd watched; only a few dozen people danced. Within the hour, I was one of only a small handful of observers. Everyone else was dancing or taking a rest before returning to the floor, having lots of fun. I was learning what the phrase "passing a good time" means.

Broussard and the Zydeco Steppers is a typical zydeco band. T. is the lead singer and accordion player. The Steppers back up T. with drums, bass guitar, keyboard, and a scrub or rub board, also known as the *frottoir*. The frottoir is worn like a vest and scratched with spoons or bottle tops. Each song begins with the accordion intro.; the frottoir then follows. The beginning of each song becomes repetitive if you are listening to recorded zydeco music. Live zydeco is completely different. T. gave a quick verbal introduction as he started the accordion intro. The crowd responded to his words, and the accordion intro. got them moving.

Zydeco isn't Cajun music; it's Creole music. *Creole* originally referred to those born in the colonies—natives to the territory, as opposed to new immigrants—and wasn't a reference to an individual's ethnicity. Later the meaning changed to describe mixed race individuals. The racial composition of the Creoles in the Cajun Prairie is more mixed than in other places in the South. Blood of African-American slaves, Native Americans, and Haitians are mixed with that of Cajuns and Europeans to create the Louisiana Creoles. These blood lines affect the music. Creole music is a melting pot of African slave songs, blues, and Cajun influences. Zydeco is a relatively recent genre of Creole music. It first arose in the early twentieth century from what was known as "LaLa music," music played at rural house parties. It was a vernacular music played with only an accordion and a washboard. Later rhythm & blues and jazz influences were incorporated in the LaLa music to form modern zydeco.

The term *zydeco* comes from the French phrase *les haricots* (pronounced lay-ZAH-rec-coe) *sont pas sales*, which translates into "the snap beans are not salty," a phrase arising from a time when Creoles seasoned their food with salted meat. During bad times, salted meat was too expensive to use, so their food was bland. A similar phrase is used by a hunting lodge operator in Arkansas—"Times were so bad that we had to buy mustard"—a reference in a hunting lodge business to guests bringing and leaving behind squeeze bottles of mustard. If things get so bad that a hunting lodge operator has run through all the left-behind bottles of mustard, well, things are real bad. So, too, if the snap beans aren't salty, times aren't good.

Like Cajun music, zydeco is dance music. The lyrics are secondary to how the tune moves your feet. Zydeco is couples dancing with a general eight-count step. Zydeco dancing differs from Cajun dancing primarily because the dancers do not travel around the floor but stay relatively in the same place.

It's happy, upbeat music, and the crowd had come to dance. The musicians recognized many in the crowd. The players smiled at the dancers, took requests, and bantered with them between songs. There were half a dozen white couples in one corner. Aside from the white couples, the couples were all different hues, all dancing with one another. The ages ranged widely. Young women danced with elderly men, and middle-aged women danced with young men.

I stood at the bar watching and struck up a conversation with a young man next to me, who told me that his grandma "zydeco-ed" until the year before she died at the age of 106. He said his grandmother, his father, his uncle, and sisters all zydeco. As for him, he confessed that he needed a few drinks to loosen up his dancing shoes. He pointed to his girlfriend on the dance floor and told me, "I love to watch women zydeco. You can see all their curves."

Then he pointed out a man in a three-piece suit, pocket-square, and brightly shined wingtip shoes. My new friend said, "See that man? He's eighty-six and he still zydecos." I replied that not many eighty-six-year-olds would even be up this late, let alone dancing. He said that his grandmother always told him, "The mind doesn't wear out; it just gets hard."

We watched as the eighty-six-year-old got up from his table and walked across the floor to a young lady. I guess from his perspective they were all young, but she was less than half his age. He took her by the hand, and she followed him onto the floor. Just as they began dancing, the band took a break. He bowed from the waist to her, and they went their separate ways.

One of the female dancers complained while leaving the dance floor that the band hadn't been playing long enough to deserve a break. I replied that T. probably needed to rest his voice. She told me about another club in town where the band plays four hours straight before taking a break. She said that if the Zydeco Steppers were serious about getting the crowd going, they needed to play longer.

As I left at about 11:30, Mr. Eighty-Six was sitting at his table. I have a new hero. I wish I had gotten his autograph, or at least his name.

Boudin, Sugar Cane Farming, and More Crawfish

Just when you think America has become a homogenized collection of subdivisions and franchised retail operations radiating from interstate exits, just when it seems that the Journey is reduced to traveling from one McDonald's location to another, glimpses of regional differences peek out. One example of regional identity occurs on I-59, outside of Opelousas, where a tire center advertises familiar national tire brands. Above the tire store sign looms a billboard advertising the local boudin and cracklin king.

Now I'll bet you can drive from New York to Florida to Michigan and not see a similar sign or find many people who even know what boudin (pronounced "boo-dan") is. Boudin is a pork rice sausage and is often served with cracklins—fried pigskin or, as they are known in other parts of the South, pork rinds. Boudin stands are ubiquitous in Cajun country. Expatriates often return to the motherland solely to retrieve real Cajun boudin.

A few miles south of I-10 is the heart of Cajun land—St. Martin Parish. Reportedly, on a percentage basis, more people speak French in St. Martin Parish than anywhere else in America. Almost thirty percent of the population speaks French at home. Here's a little interesting geographic tidbit: As a result of an 1868 surveying error, St. Martin parish is split into two noncontiguous parts. The lower part is separated by a portion of Iberia Parish stuck in between. Luckily, the lower part of St. Martin Parish is rural. But you still have to wonder how the garbage service works.

A boudin legend

It's also sugar cane country.

Sugar cane farming differs from farming other row crops. First, it's planted vegetatively, that is, with whole stalks rather than seed. Second, sugar cane is a true grass and grows again after being cut. A planting makes more than one crop, generally three to five crops.

Sugar cane farming in Louisiana was started in 1751 in New Orleans by Jesuit priests. Today, approximately 15,000 people are directly involved in growing and processing this crop. According to the American Sugar Cane League, nearly 415,000 acres of land produce sugar cane throughout twenty-three Louisiana parishes. Two parishes, St. Martin and Iberia, are the heart of Louisiana's sugar cane industry. Sugar cane farmers from St. Martin Parish process a million tons of cane each year.

Just south of New Iberia, the parish seat of Iberia Parish, is the little town of Jeanerette. Jeanerette has 6,000 residents and a couple of sugar mills. Jeanerette is where I met Jesse Breaux, sugar cane farmer. I tried to meet Jesse late Saturday afternoon. Jesse informed me that he worked Saturdays. If he knocked off work a little early on Saturday afternoon, it was so that he and his wife could take his in-laws to church. He mentioned that they probably would have dinner after church at the Yellow Bowl, a local restaurant. Jesse said that if I had time and wanted a bowl of the best étouffée in the area, I should check out the Yellow Bowl.

Jesse Breaux, sugar cane farmer

Since Saturday was out, I met Jesse at his farm's workshop on a rainy Sunday morning. Like most sugar cane farmers, Jesse grew up on a cane plantation. Also like most sugar cane farmers, Jesse is a sharecropper. His rent is one-fifth to one-sixth of the crop, which he gives the landowner for use of the land. Jessie pays all production expenses. He has eleven employees and, by all accounts, has been a successful sugar cane farmer for over thirty years.

A college graduate, Jesse began working after college for another farmer. In the mid-1980s, after a decade of working for someone else, he bought his own operation. Through the intervening years he acquired more land leases, and he now rents 2,400 acres from sixty-four owners. Jessie is particularly proud of one leasehold interest. It's the one that Jessie's grandfather once farmed until, according to family legend, he was given twenty-four hours to leave after a dispute with the landowner.

Even with his success over the years, Jesse's continued economic viability is precarious. It's the same with all sugar cane farmers. He has no ability to control the price of his product because the buyers are larger, more powerful economic entities. He has no control over costs of production, like diesel fuel. And he can't compete equally with foreign growers due largely to differences in wage and environmental regulations with South American and Central American countries. Despite these disadvantages, Jessie has done well over the past three decades doing what his father and his grandfather did—growing cane sugar.

His main protector is the federal government. His economic existence is tied directly to the farm bill, which is supposed to protect him and other sugar growers. The farm bill requires the U.S. Department of Agriculture to estimate domestic sugar consumption and divide the market by assigning quotas to U.S. growers and foreign countries. The government offers non-recourse loans to processors, who agree to pay growers for deliveries of sugar cane at USDA-set minimum payment levels. These loans provide direct price support for sugar cane farmers. While having price supports sounds good in theory, it does have its downside. Prices don't change until the government allows it. These price changes occur in increments of a fraction of a penny and often are unrelated to increases in production costs. Jesse told me that the price he gets for his sugar has been essentially unchanged for years.

So Jesse spends most of his days in humid southern Louisiana, where he continues to pay his employees a living wage while watching the price of diesel and other production costs increase. He also monitors changes in technology that create substitutes for cane sugar, such as high fructose corn syrup. He sells his product to Nestlé's, Hershey, or some other large corporate sugar consumer. Before making any capital investments, he must assess the likelihood that Congress will change the farm bill and put him out of business. After he does all that, he works six days a week, sometimes seven and, if he's caught up, he takes his mother-in-law to church on Saturdays and dinner on Saturday night at the Yellow Bowl. The man is a glutton for punishment.

Which brings me back to the Yellow Bowl, a locally known restaurant which sits in a non-descript building on Highway 182 between New Iberia and Franklin. Originally the Yellow Bowl was a bus stop for the Greyhound Bus Line, when Highway 182 was the Old Spanish Highway, the main highway between New Orleans and San Diego, California. Later it became a roadhouse and dance hall. After World War II, the Yellow Bowl fell on hard times until 1953 when it was purchased by Tony and Margaret Roberts of Breaux Bridge. The Yellow Bowl is now operated by Tony and Margaret's daughter, Coleen Roberts Hulin, and her husband, T. K. A local music legend, T. K. had some success in the '60s. After finally settling down, he now plays the area and was advertised to be playing the Cypress Bayou Casino. T. K. was slated to play between 9 and 10 p.m., and I wanted to attend.

Since Jesse said the Yellow Bowl was the best place for crawfish étouffée, I was pretty well set on what to order. On the Journey, I came to realize that étouffée was French for "bathing in cream and butter." Looking at the menu, I discovered that the Yellow Bowl offered a crawfish platter. I could get crawfish prepared a half dozen ways: fried, au gratin, étoufféed, stewed, en bisque, and in a ball. A crawfish feast. Now it's hard to say which I liked best. Jesse said the étouffée was the best. Margaret wanted to make sure I had the crawfish bisque, but I have to admit to being partial to the crawfish ball. If you like crawfish and hush puppies, this dish offers the best of both worlds. All of it was very good.

When I was offered dessert of bread pudding or an ice cream friazo, a local treat, it was not difficult to beg off as I still intended to go see the proprietor of the Yellow Bowl play music at the casino down the road. You may recall that this is precisely the same position I found myself in Opelousas—looking for zydeco music and being directed to a casino. I guess casinos have become the modern-day equivalent to roadhouses. Live music emanates mostly from gambling houses these days.

Margaret's other daughter, Stephanie Claudel, was holding down the fort at the restaurant that night. She asked me if I wanted to meet her mom. I figured I had plenty of time to see T. K. play. Margaret, an octogenarian, was a great delight. A true Acadian, she spoke with a lovely lilt in her speech—I think it's called a patois—which was sometimes hard to follow because her inflection rested on different words and syllables. It kept me on my toes.

Stephanie Claudel and Margaret Roberts

Margaret and her late husband, Tony, were both born and raised about thirty miles away in St. Martin Parish. Margaret said that as newlyweds they decided to buy the restaurant and move to Jeanerette. Her parents were concerned about her moving so far away and, more importantly, to a strange place. Her mother expressed one major concern: so far as she knew, no one spoke French in Jeanerette. How would they get along? It was a time when, outside of St. Martin Parish, Cajun was not cool. Her mother was right. No one in Jeanerette spoke French in public. But Margaret added that after she and Tony had lived there for a few years, a few residents would sidle up to her and surreptitiously speak French.

Margaret said she spoke French better than her husband did. However, Margaret's Cajun ancestors had substituted a number of non-French words over the years for their experiences in America so that she had come to use a lot of non-French words. Tony had learned Creole French, a different dialect from Cajun French. Since many Creoles emigrated from Haiti, the dialect is more like the French spoken in Europe. Once when entertaining a visitor from Paris, Margaret had trouble communicating with the guest—who didn't understand many of the words she used. To her husband's delight, the Frenchman preferred talking with Tony. It seemed that in communicating with a modern Parisian, Creole French was a closer match than Cajun French.

Margaret was so delightful that I missed seeing T. K. perform. When I left them, I thought I should have invited Margaret to go to the casino. At the very least, I should have asked her if she knew Mr. Eighty-Six up in Opelousas. As my friend at Mojo's had noted, "The mind doesn't wear out; it just gets hard."

The Road to New Orleans

Before heading to New Orleans, I decided to swing by Avery Island. The island is home to approximately 2,000 people and is still entirely owned, I think, by the McIlhenny family. The island is one of five salt domes rising above the Gulf and is, quite literally, a mountain of salt surrounded by swamps and marshes. The salt is mined from a shaft 530 feet deep.

Live oaks on Avery Island

It costs a dollar to get on the island—which only entitles you the opportunity to pay more money if you want to see how Tabasco sauce is made or, if you prefer, tour the 250-acre Jungle Garden. Since they don't offer tourists trips into the salt mines, I chose the Jungle Garden.

Unlike the nearby mainland, Avery Island has rolling hills, with huge live oaks, the Spanish moss hanging from their great limbs. The Jungle Garden of Avery Island boasts the world's most complete collection of camellias—no fewer than 750 to 1,000 varieties on the island—and thousands of azaleas.

The Jungle Garden began when Mr. McIlhenny, the island's owner, began Bird City. In the late nineteenth century, plume hunters had nearly wiped out the egret population supplying feathers for ladies' hats. In the spring of 1892, Mr. McIlhenny captured and caged eight young egrets to watch them grow, mate, and nest. At the beginning of the next migratory season, he released the birds. They migrated to South America where they spent the winter. In the spring, they returned to nest on Avery Island. Today, 20,000 nests are located on Avery Island for the annual return of some 20,000 egret families.

Egrets at Bird City

On the far side of the Gardens is Bayou Petit Anse, a good-sized waterway. Just off the Bayou are the lagoons, where the alligators hang out, relaxing in the water and on the bridges.

In addition to studying and saving the egret, Mr. McIlhenny studied alligators and wrote a book titled *Alligator's Life History* in 1935. It's on sale at the Garden's Gift Center, a must-have for your basic herpetology library. Most of the photos are of very large alligators. One shows a forlorn man near a typical alligator's nest and on the next page, another shows a worker opening the nest so the photographer can take a picture of the eggs in the nest. The second doesn't show the man's face, but I'm sure he's no more comfortable than in the first photo.

Baby alligator sunning itself

It's difficult to comprehend how much work it takes to maintain a park-like quality on 250 acres. Every area is manicured. It's a lot like Central Park, except, of course, for the presence of alligators and the absence of people. I shared the island with fewer than a half dozen tourists. And no noise: It's a very quiet place, and you can wander in any direction with only alligators and birds as your company. And bugs, there are lots of bugs.

As I wandered around the Garden, I thought about the Journey being half over. Washington DC was at least 1,200 miles away. I was about as far away from Washington, literally and figuratively, as I was going to be on the Journey. The Piedmont and mountains of North Carolina and Tennessee were a distant memory. Here in the land of alligators and moss, the humidity rivals the Delta's, but no one would confuse it with the Delta. I had been on flat land for a long time, with just a few rolling hills interspersed. From here, I would be traveling toward DC, rather than away from it. I wondered if I would see any real hills before Atlanta.

I bought a Coke and Mr. McIlhenny's book on alligators and took off for New Orleans on U.S. Highway 90. Out in Cajun Country, U.S. 90 is a new four-lane, divided highway without the limited access of an interstate. Driving these divided highways is easier travel than driving on interstates because there are fewer trucks. Since the highway is relatively new, it bypasses the big cities on the route. *Cities* may be too strong a term because they're large towns, really. Morgan City and Houma passed quickly. I did stop at Houma to see its downtown area, which was completely deserted on a Sunday afternoon. I took a wrong turn and traveled a residential side street of modest houses. A young white kid wearing urban wear and a skullcap walked down the road. He looked up, smiled, and flashed me a peace sign, a nice touch.

Curiously, out in the country, the highway was nicer. Closer to New Orleans, the highway is no longer divided. It has turn lanes and traffic lights and is much more crowded. Signs point to the new interstate connector, I-310, which takes traffic across the Mississippi River to metropolitan New Orleans. This was the fifth time crossing the river and somehow the least impressive. The new bridge is so high that the Mississippi is not visible. Only trees and the distant city skyline are visible from the bridge. In only a few minutes of traveling an eight-lane interstate highway, the relaxed pace of Cajun country was gone.

Once the Levees Break

et's face it: New Orleans is a strange place. New Orleans reminds me of my crazy uncle, the husband of my dad's twin sister. A dentist by profession, he moved his family to the Georgia barrier islands and opened an office. His office hours were arranged to fit his golf and party schedule. He didn't mind working, but he wanted to have some fun along the way. New Orleans is like that.

It's appropriate that you can get a good cup of gumbo virtually anywhere here. Gumbo is a hearty soup which incorporates French, Spanish, Native American, Caribbean, and African-American cooking influences (along with a hint of Italian in some places). These same ingredients make New Orleans' culture unique among American cities. Founded by the French in 1718 on high ground between the Mississippi River and the Indian trade routes, New Orleans was until the early twentieth century the main southern port of entry into the United States. The Spanish owned it for a while but gave it back to the French, just in time for it to become the centerpiece of Thomas Jefferson's Louisiana Purchase in 1803. Just after Jefferson took title to New Orleans, unrest in the Caribbean sent thousands of refugees from Haiti to Cuba and then to New Orleans. The refugees were pretty evenly divided among whites, slaves, and a new group, "free people of color." All of them spoke French. These arrivals from the Caribbean in 1809 doubled the city's French-speaking population. They also caused New Orleans to become

America's "blackest city," darker than Charleston's fifty-three percent. But unlike Charleston, New Orleans' "colored" population had many hues. These hues affect the city's culture still.

Many natives talk like my new friend from Jeanerette, Margaret Roberts. However, a lot of them sound like New Yorkers. Most first timers to New Orleans are surprised to hear New Orleaners sound like they're from Brooklyn. Visitors believe that New Orleaners either talk with a southern drawl like you hear in Mississippi or sound like a Cajun. Not true—many speak Yat, a hard, flat, Yankee-sounding dialect.

Half of the metropolitan area is below sea level, which has always been a concern for these city dwellers. In late August 2005, their worst fears were realized. After taking a direct hit from Hurricane Katrina, the levee system, built in response to a 1965 hurricane, failed. Over eighty percent of the city flooded. Some places had fifteen feet of water. Two-thirds of the flooding was directly attributed to the levee failures. The worst flooding occurred in the Lower Ninth Ward, a lower-income neighborhood. There, the floodwaters came from three different directions; but the worst of the floodwaters came from the breaches of the Industrial Canal. The floodwaters from the canal came with such ferocity that they carried a barge from the canal and deposited it in the neighborhood.

The news coverage—with pictures of people stranded on the roofs of their houses, the dire circumstances of those who retreated to the Superdome and the Convention Center, and the nearly 1,000 deaths from the flooding—showed that Katrina was one of the major events of the new century.

Lots of things have changed in Katrina's aftermath, but New Orleans is rebounding. The metropolitan population, which fell by almost half after the storm, is now close to pre-Katrina levels. The school system—which was largely dysfunctional before the storm—has become a laboratory for modern educational theories. Seventy percent of its public school students now go to charter schools, the nation's largest percentage. With the large infusion of federal dollars for rebuilding the levees and other infrastructure repairs, New Orleans weathered the great recession better than a lot of places. In fact, it was the fastest-growing large city between 2010 and 2011.

One reason for New Orleans' rebirth is its culture: a 2007 *New York Times* article, "36 hours in New Orleans," said it best:

> What other city, after being half-drowned and left to starve, foiled by bureaucracy and attacked by the auto-immune disease of rampant crime, could stagger to its feet to welcome visitors with a platter of oysters on the half shell and a rousing brass band? What place barely two years after Hurricane Katrina could provide street car rides and impromptu parades, riverboat calliopes and sidewalk tap dancers?

New Orleans' rebound is fueled in large part by tourists attracted to the fun. In the past few years, New Orleans has hosted America's largest athletic events: the BCS Championships, the NCAA Final Four, and the Super Bowl. But special events aren't the main driver of New Orleans' tourist trade: no, the tourist trade revolves around festivals and parades. There are celebrations year around. These celebrations are not just simply tourist events; the locals operate under the principle of "the more, the merrier." It's been said that a real New Orleaner has five costumes in his or her closet, and they wear each one regularly.

The year begins with Mardi Gras. Technically, Mardi Gras is one day, the culmination of Carnival season. But, many outsiders incorrectly refer to all events during the entire carnival season as Mardi Gras. The carnival season begins on January 6, the twelfth night after Christmas. Pretty tidy, the Christmas holidays end and Carnival season begins. Throughout Carnival season, groups throw costume and king cake parties. It's only at the tail end of the carnival season that parades happen, generally starting about three weeks before Fat Tuesday. Carnival season ends forty-seven days before Easter, on Fat Tuesday. New Orleaners generally refer only to Fat Tuesday as "Mardi Gras," which is celebrated with the one-day street celebration.

Each parade is sponsored by a private organization called a "krewe." Each parade has a theme. The krewes create complicated mechanized floats to carry revelers down the parade route. The krewe members are generally the revelers on the floats. Most parades start with the krewe captain at the head of the parade in a convertible or special float. He is followed by the king and queen of the parade. The title float is next and, after the title float, other floats carrying krewe members and guests follow. If one adds those who participate in the parade but are not on the floats, such as motorcycle squadrons, bands, and clowns, the number of paraders in a parade can exceed 3,000 people. There are over seventy parades in the New Orleans area during Carnival season.

As they parade, krewe members throw cheap plastic beads and large coin-like doubloons to the people who line the streets. Now, the practice of bead-throwing never made much sense to me until I watched a bunch of children yell at the floats, "Throw me some beads, mister!" And they scramble in excitement to catch them.

Remember young Zaunbrecher back in Eunice, Louisiana? He celebrates Mardi Gras differently on the Cajun Prairie. His Mardi Gras celebration involves riding horses and chasing chickens. In the city, celebrants line up on concrete sidewalks and watch people parade down the street on mechanized floats.

Once Ash Wednesday and Lent arrive, there is a short break before St. Patrick's Day celebrations begin in early March. On St. Patrick's Day, another parade occurs with beads, doubloons, and other trinkets being tossed to bystanders, who yell, "Throw me some beads, mister!" See a pattern forming?

After St. Paddy's Day, the pattern breaks with the Tennessee Williams Literary Festival. There's no parade, but the festival brings authors, actors, and musicians to New Orleans for five days. While most of the action occurs indoors, on Sunday afternoon, the festival holds a "Stella" shouting contest outdoors at Jackson Square. Contestants dress up and recreate the famous scene from A Streetcar Named Desire. Female participants get to yell, "Stanley!" No beads are thrown.

April and early May are filled with two music festivals. The first one, French Quarter Festival, started out thirty years ago as a block party. It now has grown to four days of 150 performances across twenty-one stages. Last year, the free celebration drew over a half million people.

As good as the French Quarter festival is—and it is good—the celebration pales in comparison to the New Orleans Jazz & Heritage Festival at the horse-racing track, the Fair Grounds. During the two weeks of Jazz Fest, plenty of music, food, and crafts are available at the Fair Grounds. The first time I went, I was told that it was a festival of jazz. Since New Orleans is the birthplace of jazz, that pronouncement made sense, but the festival covers more than jazz and encompasses all genres of regional music. There are twelve stages; the large ones are for the big-time acts that come to play. Others are devoted to regional music: blues, zydeco, Cajun, gospel, and, of course, jazz; all have stages. There is so much music that you need a program to follow. Each stage has a grid of who is playing each day of the festival. These grids are called "the cubes." The release of the cubes before the festival is a big pre-event; attendees start planning who they want to see.

There are plenty of food and beverage vendors and craft vendors at Jazz Fest. Since the festival is so popular, there are no vacancies for crafts-men and rarely a vacancy for food vendors. When vacancies occur, vendors are selected for a specific food category. The last time I went, I was on the bus to the racetrack, The Jazz Fest Express, when I heard someone behind me ask if there would be food other than alligator and crawfish. When her companion replied that she hoped so, otherwise they would both go hungry, I wanted to turn around and tell them about boudin and cracklins. But I refrained because I knew they could get a cheeseburger if they wanted to look hard enough.

New Orleans' weather is pretty tropical. I've seen people mow lawns just before Christmas. The organizers advise:

> The springtime weather in New Orleans can range from pleasantly warm to uncomfortably hot, so you'll want to dress in cool, unrestrictive cloth-ing. Lightweight cotton is never a bad idea. There are a few shady trees scattered here and there throughout the Fair Grounds, but the infield is, for the most part, wide open to the sun. Therefore, most people consider sunglasses to be essential, not to mention sunscreen or sunblock. A hat with a wide brim or visor is also a good idea. Wear comfortable shoes, as you may be doing a lot of walking. You'll want to keep hydrated, too: there are beverages available throughout the Heritage Fair, and cold drinking water can be found in the Grandstand, which is also a good source of shade and air conditioning, not to mention many of the Festival's hidden treasures. Also, several stages on the infield and in Heritage Square are under tents that offer relief from the sun.

Pretty optimistic. I've been to Jazz Fest a few times and I've missed the pleasantly warm weather. Late April and early May are downright hot and sticky.

I arrived in New Orleans a week after Jazz Fest. In the aftermath of a big festival, things were quiet. There were few tourists and the weather was spectacular. Normally I try to stay in the Lower Garden District, the first neighborhood upriver from the French Quarter, but this time I decided I would stay in a new neighborhood. Besides being accessible to the French Quarter by streetcar, the lower Garden District is the neighborhood with the best-named streets: Clio, Erata, Thalia, Felicity, Calliope, Prytania, and Terpsicore.

I stayed in a bed and breakfast in Faubourg-Marigny, a small neighborhood just downriver from the Vieux Carre, the French Quarter. A New York analogy: The French Quarter is like Greenwich Village, while the hipsters of Faubourg-Marigny act like those in East Village. It's only a few blocks from the French Quarter, but the innkeeper warned me that New Orleans is still a dangerous place. He told me that once I got to the Quarter, I would be fine. On my way out, the innkeeper repeated his warning that anytime I was east of Esplanade, the divide between the Quarter and Faubourg-Maringny, I should be vigilant. He told me that under no circumstances should I wander in the other direction toward St. Claude Avenue or go east of Franklin Street.

Even though it's a fun place to visit and the public schools are improving, New Orleans has some real problems. The poverty rates, and more ominously, child poverty rates, have returned to pre-Katrina levels after moderating somewhat in the aftermath of the storm. Crime is still on visitors' minds.

Official corruption still runs rampant. Here's the short list of relatively recent activities. Ray Nagin, who was New Orleans' mayor during the storm, was indicted on charges that he took bribes. His former city tech chief already has pled guilty to taking kickbacks from a city vendor. Five city policemen were indicted in the shooting death of a man in the aftermath of the storm. Aaron Broussard, president of neighboring Jefferson Parish, was sentenced to forty-six months in jail for public corruption. His relatively light sentence occurred because the judge ruled that the series of regular payments from a city vendor constituted but a "single" bribe.

How can you tell how New Orleans is doing? Do you look at the positives? The French Quarter is back. The Jazz Fest is larger than ever.

Schools are recovering. Or do you look at the negatives, that crime, corruption, and grinding poverty have returned? Do you look at the neighborhoods with moderate damage to see how they have rebounded? Or do you judge by looking at the progress of a really devastated neighborhood such as Holy Cross neighborhood, a formerly wonderful lower-income neighborhood in the Lower Ninth. It is less than three miles from Faubourg-Marigny, just across from the now famous Industrial Canal. The flooding there was so great that the highest point in Holy Cross had three feet of floodwater. So great was the destruction that it took months before curfew was lifted. It was the last neighborhood in the city to be released from curfew.

How has it done since? It's estimated that the population of the Lower Ninth is somewhere between twenty-five and forty percent of its pre-Katrina population. In 2012, Nathaniel Rich wrote an article, "Jungleland," for the *New York Times Magazine*, describing the present situation in the Lower Ninth:

> To visualize how the Lower Ninth looked in September—before the city's most recent campaign to reclaim the neighborhood—you have to understand that it no longer resembled an urban, or even suburban environment. Where once there stood orderly rows of single-family homes with driveways and front yards, there was jungle. The vegetation had all sprouted since Katrina. Trees that did not exist before the storm are now 30 feet high....For six and a half years, the neighborhood has undergone a reverse colonization—nature reclaiming civilization. Residents have fought with hatchets and weed trimmers to rebuff the colonizers: Southern cut grass, giant ragweed, Chinese tallow tree. But the effort has been largely futile. The lots require constant vigilance. A lot left untended for three months will be thick with knee-high weeds; after five months, saplings begin to rise. By last August, the sixth anniversary of Katrina, it was clear that nature had triumphed.

I contemplated the question of how New Orleans was doing as I walked Canal Street. I've always enjoyed walking Canal Street, the ancient neutral grounds and the border between the Vieux Carre and the Central Business District. It's a big city street with lots of activity. It has recovered nicely. In recent years, high-end hotels have replaced retail in the Canal Street commercial buildings. No signs of the storm's devastation interrupted my walk. Little surprise because the damage was storm damage: wind and rain damage, broken windows and downed power lines—things like that. Those problems were fixed soon after the storm. I'm not minimizing the damage around downtown, but it was nothing like what hit the Lower Ninth. Mr. Rich writes:

> The closest analogy to what happened in the Lower Ninth...is a volcanic eruption on the order of Mount St. Helens. The next closest is the tsunami that hit Japan's northeast coast a year ago....Katrina was not merely destructive; it brought about a catastrophic reimagining of the landscape.

I soon determined that answering the question was beyond the scope of my short visit. Even though the Lower Ninth is part of a large urban area, it now fights the same natural forces that many other areas along the Mississippi have fought for years. Friars Point, Hillhouse, and Sherard have fought this fight for generations. And then there is the lonely house at Nitta Yuma. It doesn't give one much hope for the Lower Ninth. Not unless they build a casino there. I grieved a moment for the losses in Holy Cross and throughout the Lower Ninth.

Later I walked into the Ritz-Carlton bar to check out their mint juleps and found, much to my surprise, they don't serve them. A few minutes later, I saw two men in tuxedos carry drinks into the bar and sit down. I was beginning to think about another analogy of how New Orleans is similar to New York, but stopped when I saw one of the men pull a can of chewing tobacco from his inside pocket and take a dip. Not something you'd see in a high-end hotel in the Big Apple. This is still the South.

Mississippi Gulf Coast

Ten miles east of New Orleans, there is no city, just wild marshlands, a narrow strip of lowland with a road running through the middle of it. The Gulf of Mexico is on the right, Lake Pontchartrain on the left. No old buildings sit on this land; Katrina blew them away. New vacation houses, simple structures built on stilts covered with plastic siding, stick up out of the ground at regular intervals. The stilts rise a couple of stories before the living space commences.

Soon I come to the Rigolets—French for trench—a small strait connecting the Gulf of Mexico with Lake Pontchartrain. In the days of sailing ships, it was New Orleans' shipping lane. No longer though, because the trench is too small for many of today's ships. I wasn't on the interstate but on Chef Menteur Highway, which before I-10 was the main highway east from New Orleans. Now it mostly carries local traffic. Chef Menteur literally translates as "chief liar." There's some controversy over whether the chief liar was a Frenchman or an Indian.

The Chef Menteur Highway crosses the Rigolets at Chef Menteur Pass by way of a drawbridge, which was in the up position as I arrived. Cars sat in line, waiting for a boat to pass underneath. From the old highway, I watched the traffic whiz eastward unimpeded on the new higher interstate bridge. Soon the drawbridge lowered, and the other drivers and I crossed the pass.

A few miles later, signs indicated that the State of Mississippi owned the marshland. Mississippi law must require positioning a casino near every roadway into Mississippi. After the casino, Waveland and Bay St. Louis, the two major towns in Hancock County, come into view. Hancock County was ground zero for Hurricane Katrina. The eye of the monster storm made landfall just to the west of these small communities. As hurricane watchers know, just east of the storm's eye is the worst place to be. Fifty-seven people from Hancock County lost their lives in the storm. The twenty-eight-foot storm surge took most of Waveland away. The waves at the Hancock County shoreline measured fifty-five feet high during the worst of Katrina.

According to Charles Gray, executive director of the Hancock County Historical Society, Bay St. Louis is the highest point on the Gulf of Mexico coastline. Katrina's storm surge caused the first-ever recorded flooding of Bay St. Louis. Nearly half the houses in Bay St. Louis, along with homes up to ten miles inland, were swept away by the historic surge of water.

Few people in Bay St. Louis had flood insurance. One resident said that the local insurance agents told people it had never flooded in Bay St. Louis, so buying flood insurance was a waste of money. Another man who'd lost his house said he'd been told the same thing and later discovered that flood coverage was available for $386 a year.

Even today, signs of the storm are everywhere. The Hancock Bank building sits overlooking the Gulf at the most prominent point of the Bay. It has been completely restored, but the buildings to its east are empty, while to the west there are now vacant lots with concrete slabs where buildings once stood. Behind the bank building is an impressive courthouse, which suffered substantial damage but is almost put back together. Behind the courthouse, the Hancock County Historical Society occupies the Kate Lobrano historic house, which made it through the storm intact. Other than the local coffee shop, the Historical Society had the only activity the day I was there. In fact, the Historical Society was a beehive of activity in this quiet town of fewer than 6,000 people.

These people take their history seriously. I entered the building to hear a spirited discussion among three men about a plantation that had ceased operation at the end of the nineteenth century and the family who owned it. A few other researchers ignored the conversation and busily studied historic records. I introduced myself to Charles Gray, the society's executive director. While I was visiting with Mr. Gray, at least two people came in to discuss nineteenth-century matters with him.

Being the third-oldest city on the Gulf of Mexico, Bay St. Louis is rich in history. This small town contains four separate historic districts. The Historical Society had inventoried all 728 buildings listed on the National Register of Historic Places before the storm swept many of them away. Mr. Gray lost his own historic house during the storm as had one of the people who was discussing the long-closed plantation. They understandably remained stunned at the vagaries of the storm which had taken away their houses. But there was no self-pity. All had picked up and moved on.

Everyone agreed that rebuilding the Highway 90 Bridge was the most significant event since the storm. The bridge crosses the bay and connects Bay St. Louis with the rest of the Mississippi Gulf Coast, Pass Christian, Gulfport, and Biloxi. Without the bridge, the five-minute drive to Pass Christian and the rest of the Mississippi Gulf Coast is nearly an hour. Each day without the bridge cost Bay St. Louis an estimated $100,000. Despite predictions that a new bridge across Bay St. Louis would take several years to design and build, the new bridge reopened in May 2007, less than fifteen months after the design work began. The new 2.1-mile bridge towers eighty-five feet above the bay. There's a great view.

Even though the bridge traffic to Pass Christian has returned, downtown Bay St. Louis doesn't seem very vibrant. Will normalcy ever return? Some things can be rebuilt; others are lost forever. A new house gets built, the bridge to Pass Christian gets replaced, the bank and courthouse reopen, but does life ever return to normal? Does the sense of loss ever go away? Will the locals quit referring to events as pre-Katrina and post-Katrina? Maybe in a generation, but not yet.

The density of development increases as you travel east. Historically, Bay St. Louis developed as the beach for the wealthy from New Orleans. Pass Christian, on the other side of the bay, became the playground for the plantation society of Alabama and Mississippi. Plantation owners built big cottages and owned large tracts of beachfront property. The Gulf Coast cottages were so large that Pass Christian was often referred to as the "Newport of the South." When Katrina blew those cottages away, it created large gaps in the beachfront. Katrina's winds and her thirty-foot tidal surge destroyed over 300 buildings listed on the National Register of Historic Places.

Pass Christian segues into Long Beach, which turns into Gulfport, which transitions into Biloxi. In Long Beach, single-family dwellings become small condominium projects; in Gulfport, the condo projects become larger. Biloxi is no longer a sleepy little fishing village. It's denser than the rest of the coast with the Beau Rivage Casino and Hotel. Rising above Biloxi's sand beach, it's the tallest building in Mississippi. Biloxi may not be Vegas, but then again Las Vegas doesn't have the Gulf and the beaches Biloxi has.

The oldest golf course in Mississippi, the Great Southern Golf Club, established in 1908, lies on the boundary of Gulfport and Biloxi. When Jonathan Daniels visited, the Great Southern was one of the best golf courses in the South and a stop on the PGA tour. A few years after his visit, the Great Southern was the site of a duel where Sam Snead defeated Byron Nelson in a nineteen-hole playoff to determine the winner of the PGA event held there, the Gulfport Invitational.

Today, the Great Southern Golf Club is not doing well. It's not because of the train track that runs through the middle of the course; those tracks have always been there. It's not the location either. Designed by Donald Ross, one of the great golf architects, the course is perched on the Gulf of Mexico. If it weren't for the southern heat and humidity, the salt breeze and endless view of blue water would remind you of a Scottish links course.

The Great Southern Golf Club may ultimately be a casualty of Katrina. The original colonial-style clubhouse collapsed when hit by Katrina's thirty-foot wall of floodwater. Two holes nearest the Gulf were completely washed away. Many of the trees were either knocked down by the force of the wind or died from the effects of the saltwater.

But Great Southern keeps on. It reopened some six months after the storm on temporary greens and with temporary facilities. It was so damaged that the owners reduced greens fees by half. With reduced income, repairs haven't come easily or quickly. What remains is a tired, struggling golf course like you see in small towns across the South. The clubhouse remains housed in a small manufactured housing facility. As I arrived late one afternoon, the operator announced that the clubhouse was closing so that he could go close the back nine. Closing part of a golf course when hours of sunlight remain was a new one to me. He said he closes access to the front nine holes with a chain and then returns to finish cleaning the carts.

Tom Atkins, a retiree who looked to be in his 70s, told me that he worked at the course two days a week, twelve hours a day. As we talked, we were interrupted by a man saying that he had just retired to the area and wanted to know about joining the club. Tom told him the Great Southern was a great golf course and the best bargain on the coast.

The potential new member left, and Tom and I resumed our conversation. He related his Katrina story. Tom had been working at another golf course near the airport, a few miles farther inland, when Katrina hit. He worked the day of the storm. He started to leave the golf course as the storm arrived, but heard that the roads were flooded already. He and two other workers piled into his car on the golf course's parking lot. The situation deteriorated quickly, and they drove to the highest point on the golf course. The storm surge and winds buffeted the car. Water rose up past his car's hubcaps. In all his years on the coast, he'd never seen a storm that bad. The storm eventually passed, and he and the others drove back to the wrecked clubhouse.

Farther inland, Katrina's waters flooded his home. After it dried, mold grew and created respiratory problems for him. He could not afford the required repairs so he let the house go. He now lives with his daughter in Picayune, Mississippi, some sixty miles away. I noted that it was quite a commute after putting in a twelve-hour day. Tom replied that he doesn't commute on the days he works but stays over, sleeping in the back of the clubhouse. He said that not only was it too far to drive, but that high gas prices make commuting each day untenable.

There wasn't much else to say on the matter to a seventy-year-old who sleeps on some days in the back of a small manufactured commercial building to make ends meet.

I asked Tom about the future of the Great Southern. He wasn't optimistic. The owners were like him—without much money. They had suffered through the damage and the decreased revenue, and now they had some tough decisions to make. One idea was building a casino on the Gulf side of the property while retaining nine holes on the back of the property. Tom said it was a shame to lose such a fine course, but Great Southern couldn't compete with the new courses with connections to the casinos. He said with the present shape of its facilities, Great Southern couldn't attract that crowd, that the marketplace had changed in Biloxi for golf course operators.

I mused that a lot of re-development had occurred since Katrina. Tom disagreed, saying that unless you were a developer with a lot of money, you couldn't do anything in the area. Normal folks just couldn't afford it. Most of the small business people he knew were leaving the area. Only outsiders started new businesses.

Tom invited me to ride in the golf cart as he locked up. I told him I wanted to walk around the course for a bit and enjoy the breeze. As I walked I thought about Tom sleeping in the back of the mobile home pro shop so that he and Great Southern could compete for tourist dollars for a few more months. I thought maybe they wouldn't make it because the gamblers wouldn't want an old golf course. They would want some-thing new and manicured.

Travel Notes:
Beauvoir

Beauvoir, the retirement home of Jefferson Davis, the only president of the Confederate States of America, was built in 1852. Davis purchased Beauvoir some years after the Yankees charged him with treason but let him go without a trial. After his death, his wife sold the property to the Mississippi division of the Sons of Confederate Veterans on the condition that the property would be used as a home for Confederate veterans or as a memorial.

Its architectural style is known as the "Louisiana raised cottage." The house is elevated on massive ten-foot brick foundation piers that form an above-ground basement. This construction style has allowed Beauvoir to withstand nearly three dozen hurricanes during its existence. This last one almost got her. Even though the house sustained extensive damage from Katrina's storm surge, pictures still remained on its walls after the storm. On June 3, 2008, after a $4.1 million rehabilitation, Beauvoir reopened. It was Jefferson Davis' 200th birthday.

The gift shop, like the Great Southern Golf Club, is in a manufactured housing building with a soda pop machine out front—not an auspicious place to begin a tour. But after all the Katrina-related destruction I'd seen in the last couple hundred miles, I wasn't judging.

Withholding judgment ended once I got inside. The modest gift shop is festooned with Confederate flags and other items of "southern heritage." Other merchandise—green frog figures, gray Confederate hats, postcards, t-shirts, and, of course, the obligatory Dixie license plate— "American by Birth—Southern by the Grace of God"—is on the shelves. They are harmless enough remembrances of a bygone era.

I really had not thought much about the southern heritage items until I came to the book section. The first one that caught my attention was titled *Was Jefferson Davis Right?* I picked up three more books—*The Constitution of the Confederate States of America, The Southerner's Instruction Book,* and *Andersonville: A Southern Perspective.* Then I discovered the bargain bin. I picked up a t-shirt on sale for twenty-five percent off. It was the 200th Birthday Commemorative t-shirt. The back of the shirt had a picture of Jefferson Davis. The front of the shirt displayed an emblem with ole Jeff's picture and the inscription "The right man—in the right place."

I thought, *Stop. Stop y'all. That's enough.*

I'm southern enough. I have distant cousins who are big in the Sons of Confederate Veterans. My great-great-grandfather was Captain James L. Lemon, a member of the 18th Regiment, Georgia Volunteer Infantry. He fought at Seven Pines, Seven Days, Second Manassas, Sharpsburg, Fredericksburg, Chancellorsville, and Gettysburg. He was shot in the head during the battle for Knoxville and taken prisoner for the remainder of the war. I have a copy of the letter he wrote from the Yankee POW camp asking his wife for food and clothing if there were any to spare. My family remembers and honors his service much the same as we do my grandfather's service in World War I and my dad's and uncle's service in World War II and Korea.

Only recently did I learn that the Sons of Confederate Veterans had awarded my ancestor a Confederate Medal of Honor in 1995. In his wartime journal, Captain Lemon acknowledged that his side lost. He lamented that one of the worst things he would have to do in order to get paroled was take an oath of allegiance to the Union. It was a requirement to get home. As distasteful as that act was, he honored it. After he returned to Georgia, he never went north of the Mason-Dixon Line and never knowingly talked to a Yankee again. The last entry of his journal says it best:

> June 12 1865 Ft. Delaware—I have done the unspeakable but I am now paroled & today set out for home. My duty to my country is done, mine to my family remains.

And he became a loyal American. I know that lots of people consider remembering the Civil War to be celebrating their heritage. I don't get it. We were Rebels and we lost. If we'd lost the Revolution seventy years earlier, the English would not have been near as kind to us as the Yankees were after the Civil War. If the Colonials had lost the battle at Kings

Mountain in North Carolina, the British commander no doubt would have killed all of the traitors he could find. So it was right neighborly of the Yankees not to try Robert E. Lee, Jeff Davis, or my ancestor after the war and hang them. We ought to remember that.

I think the least southerners can do is not throw up the fact that we didn't want to be part of this great country. In the twenty-first century, the idea that Jeff Davis was the right man at the right time strikes me as un-American. I wish the folks at Beauvoir would consider that.

But Beauvoir has its charms. *Beauvoir* means "beautiful view" in French; the view of the Gulf from Beauvoir's front porch is better than beautiful.

Mobile

Sometimes you have to wonder whether it's the town or you. Sometimes the wind is at your back; sometimes not. Sometimes things just seem to jibe; other times they don't. I arrived in downtown Mobile late one morning without anything planned. None of the feelers I sent before coming had borne fruit. Without any appointments, I walked around downtown taking in the ambiance. Mobile has the same grittiness, but not the big-city feel, of New Orleans. Situated on a bay, it doesn't have the views of the Gulf of Mexico like Bay St. Louis or Biloxi, but it sure has the humidity. Thinking that hunger might be affecting how I was feeling, I repaired to the closest seafood place on my list, Wintzell's Oyster House on historic Dauphin Street. Wintzell's is one of the oldest oyster bars in Mobile; it recently became a regional chain. Their motto is "Oysters any way you want them: fried...stewed...& nude."

I was a little early so I was able to get a seat near the big open windows where I could look out on Dauphin Street. Since I don't live near a coast, I order seafood at every opportunity when I'm on or near a coast. The rule works well on short trips, but after five or six days of seafood (and near-seafood), a cheeseburger was beginning to look good. The crawfish dishes in Jeanerette, Louisiana and the meal at Mary Malone's in Biloxi were wonderful. Maybe I was a little tired of seafood. I probably would have ordered something non-fishy like chicken, but before the waiter came, I began thinking how weird tourists at the Acme

Oyster Bar in the French Quarter look eating non-seafood dishes. What's the point of being in an oyster bar if you're not eating oysters? I'm not strong on rules. But there are certain immutable laws in life: gravity, supply and demand, and the brown water next to the bank of the Mississippi River runs faster than the brown water in the middle of the river. (I learned that last one in Helena). After some mental gymnastics, I ordered a basket of fried oysters. I decided I wasn't going to look weird in front of a bunch of perfect strangers.

Wintzell's is a great place to eat by yourself. The original owner, J. Oliver Wintzell, was apparently a character. His shtick included covering the walls with homespun sayings—so waiting for the food to come was no problem. (The menu cautions not to expect fast food because nothing is "prebattered.") You can walk around the restaurant reading the wisdom: "An office clock is rarely stolen—everyone is watching it" and "Actions interpret thought" and "A person should be judged by his questions rather than by his answers." My favorite was "The worst place to live is just beyond your income." The oyster basket came along soon enough.

After a good lunch, all was right with the world, and I was off to see the Mobile Museum in the old city hall. I found a parking place right in front of the museum. The museum is not near other commercial buildings and there didn't seem to be much of a demand for parking. The meter allowed one hour of parking. I guess I could have found a parking lot a few blocks away and wouldn't have had to worry about getting a parking ticket. I figured that outside a tourist attraction, the City of Mobile wouldn't be all that strict about checking the meters. I put my quarters in the meter, buying the maximum amount of parking, an hour's worth, and headed into a wonderful pre–Civil War building.

Mobile has a lot of history. It was founded in 1702 as the capital of Louisiana and didn't become part of the United States until the War of 1812. As a major port, it grew dramatically during World War II, building Liberty ships. Mobile is also the home of Hank Aaron and Satchel Paige, two of America's greatest baseball players. Mobile had so much history I couldn't absorb it in one hour; it took one hour and seven minutes, by my count. A meter maid must have been waiting for my time to expire.

She was nowhere to be seen, but I knew she'd been around. Getting that parking ticket just a few minutes after an hour was emblematic of my visit to Mobile.

Mobile didn't strike me as a friendly place. Unlike the other places along the Gulf Coast and throughout Alabama, it didn't feel comfortable to me. I later related my feelings about Mobile to people in Montgomery and Birmingham. Their responses were fairly consistent. Everyone smiled and asked if I had used an intermediary to give an introduction before contacting someone in Mobile. When I said that I hadn't, they smiled more broadly and explained that Mobilians are insular even with other Alabamans. Without a proper introduction, they might not be very inviting to a stranger.

Nice people probably, but there is something about Mobile that's a little standoffish.

Hank, Biscuits, and Green Roofs

Montgomery is the capital of the Black Belt, Alabama's cotton-growing area. In his 1901 autobiography *Up from Slavery*, Booker T. Washington wrote of the Black Belt:

> The term was first used to designate a part of the country which was distinguished by the colour of the soil. The part of the country possessing this thick, dark, and naturally rich soil was, of course, the part of the South where the slaves were most profitable, and consequently, they were taken there in the largest numbers. Later and especially since the war, the term seems to be used wholly in a political sense, that is, to designate the counties where the black people outnumber the white.

The city's history centers largely on this racial divide. It was the first capital of the Confederate States of America. Later it became a central theater in the battle for African-American civil rights, with the Montgomery Bus Boycott and as the terminus of the Selma-to-Montgomery freedom marches.

Montgomery is also the capital of Alabama and a small-sized southern city very much like Little Rock and Jackson. Montgomery is big enough to have some art, theater, and other niceties of larger cities. But it's still small enough that people on the street look at passersby to see if they might know them. It's also friendly enough that they smile and acknowledge strangers.

I arrived in Montgomery on the day of Michael Jackson's memorial service. Throughout the day, cable channel commentators breathlessly described every aspect of the fallen King of Pop's life. They speculated on whether he had overdosed, who had given him the injection, and the overall strangeness of his life. The news networks later showed crowds gathering all over the world to pay tribute to Jackson.

Montgomery is the hometown of Hank Williams, the great country and western singer. My hotel was only two doors down from the Hank Williams Museum. The parallels between these two musicians are eerie. One of Hank's biographers, Paul Hemphill, describes him in *Lovesick Blues*:

> Hank Williams had come to us from out of nowhere—sprouting like a wild dandelion in the dank forests of south Alabama, some primordial beast who had been let loose on the land, a specimen heretofore undiscovered—and by this summer of '49 nobody seemed to know exactly what to make of him. Only two months after his debut on the Opry with "Lovesick Blues," a startling performance raucously received at old Ryman Auditorium in downtown Nashville,…he had suddenly become the best of the best in the best of all times. Born sickly, half-educated, an alcoholic by his teen years, untutored musically, unlucky in love at every turn, he had somehow emerged as a tortured genius, a raw poet, the "hillbilly Shakespeare," a Vincent van Gogh of the southern outback. The more traumatic his personal life got, the better he became as a songwriter. To some, it was like looking at a bad wreck. If he wasn't America's greatest songwriter then certainly he was its most enigmatic.

Three and a half years later, he was dead.

On January 1, 1953, Williams was the King of Country music, whose personal life could only be described as an unholy mess—divorce, alcohol, drugs, paternity issues. Hank was due to play in Canton, Ohio, but he was unable to fly because of the weather. He hired a driver to take him and his Cadillac from Knoxville, Tennessee, to Ohio. Before leaving, Hank received a shot of vitamin B-12 and morphine to perk him up. Once on the road, he went to sleep. When his driver tried to wake him somewhere in Ohio, Hank was unresponsive. He rushed Hank to a hospital, where he was pronounced dead. He was twenty-nine years old.

Despite all evidence to the contrary, Cecil Jackson, founder of the Hank Williams Memorial Foundation, contended in an interview that the star died of a heart attack in the Cadillac that night. "I feel that Hank was a 75-year-old man at age 29," Jackson said. "He was wore out." Three days after Williams' death, a memorial service was held at the Municipal Coliseum in Montgomery. The coliseum's capacity was 2,500. Ten times that number showed up. Twenty thousand stood outside and listened to the service over loudspeakers.

Tourists still visit Hank's grave to commune and drink whiskey at midnight. Ever the intrepid traveler, I found Oakwood Cemetery, where Hank is buried next to his mother and his first wife, Audrey. It's on a hill with a fine view of the surrounding area. The grave site is not hard to find because the Williams monuments are huge. Hank's monument has a marble cowboy hat with the inscription "Luke the Drifter," a name Hank used early in his career as he traveled the country singing gospel songs. A list of his hit songs is also inscribed on the monument.

Hank Williams' final resting place

A few years ago, Hank Jr. provided Astroturf at the grave site because the number of visitors had worn out the grass. Hank Jr. also placed a sign on the monuments, which reads,

Please do not desecrate this sacred spot
Many thanks
Hank Williams Jr.

I sat on the bench looking at Hank's tomb, my feet touching the Astroturf. I didn't have any Jack Daniels to toast the man many southerners consider the greatest songwriter who ever lived. My thoughts turned to a lost musician from Gary, Indiana. I wondered if Michael Jackson would ever be taken back to Gary. Would people sixty years after his death still go to his grave, leave gifts, and commune with his spirit? He is now buried in Hollywood, and it may be that before long no one will care where he is laid.

I returned downtown to find Riverwalk Stadium and see some minor league baseball—the Montgomery Biscuits were in town. The stadium was not too far from my hotel, and on the nice July night, I walked. My path took me by an old warehouse, recently rehabilitated. Now, it's home to Dreamland Café, one of Alabama's most celebrated barbecue joints.

John "Big Daddy" Bishop opened the original Dreamland Café in Tuscaloosa in 1958. Big Daddy was a hard-working brick mason. The story goes that one night he got on his knees and prayed for another way to make a living. After falling asleep, he dreamed of opening a café. And the rest is Alabama barbecue history. Today, the Dreamland Cafés are a small chain of restaurants across Alabama from Huntsville to Mobile. Dreamland has also expanded into Georgia, and there are two restaurants in the Atlanta area. In 2006, USA Today included Dreamland as one of the top 10 "barbecue joints" in the country. It's been successful for over a half century, with no signs of slowing down.

Barbecue in Alabama is still pork, not beef, although they did have chicken and sausage on the menu. As an old guy from south Arkansas once said, "Ain't no better eatin' than pig." Barbecue has come a long way. In the days of segregation, white people broke the color line to find good barbecue in hole-in-the-wall cafés or from trailers. Here in Montgomery, the capital of the Confederacy, in a rehabbed warehouse, exposed brick walls are covered with photographs of black people—

the owners. The wait staff is made up of clean-cut white yuppies, all dressed in khaki slacks and oxford shirts. Black and white customers sit together. I was contemplating what Jefferson Davis or George Wallace would say when I noticed the kitchen door opening and the cook coming from the kitchen. He was Hispanic. A multicultural South is a good thing, but it's a bit disconcerting in a barbecue place. A few minutes later, I ordered the sausage plate. Call me what you will. That's what I did.

After dinner, it was on to Biscuit baseball, a relatively new form of entertainment in Alabama's capital city. On December 3, 2002, by a 7-1 vote, the Montgomery City Council approved building a twenty-six-million-dollar stadium downtown. The "aginners" were led by Charles Moore Jr. of East Montgomery, who during the meeting referred to the council and mayor as "scoundrels." He advised them, "Let me tell you something about this state: If it's not Auburn or Alabama or Alabama State or Tuskegee football, people won't support it."

The stadium funding was approved by the city, in what can only be described as a progressive vote for this football state. After the election, the Southern League unanimously approved relocating the Orlando Rays to Montgomery.

After the relocation announcement, a Name the Team contest was held and received more than 2,800 entries. The winning entry was "The Montgomery Biscuits." The owners said they became partial to Biscuits because of the many pun possibilities, like "Hey, butter, butter, butter—swing, butter, butter, butter." During the games, biscuits, not t-shirts, are shot from air cannons into the crowd. It's probably the only ballpark in the world that serves biscuits and honey or biscuits and gravy. They also sell their souvenirs at a shop quaintly called the "Biscuit Basket."

Since I wasn't planning to stay long, I bought the $7 lawn ticket, watched a few innings, and took in all the sights of minor league baseball: families with young children, old men religiously keeping box scores of every batter's performance, and teenage boys preening around teenage girls. (Some things are universal.) From my perspective, Mr. Moore was incorrect about Alabamans' support of our national pastime. The Biscuits played the Birmingham Barons that night and the game was well

319

attended. At the Biscuit Basket, I paid $8.50 for a souvenir Monty the Biscuit Mascot, an anthropomorphized buttermilk biscuit complete with feet and a pat of butter for his tongue.

Monty the Biscuit Mascot

After a few innings, I left and walked through the deserted downtown area. I was surprised at the amount of activity on this summer night. Now, downtown Montgomery was no Greenville, South Carolina, the gold standard for vibrant small city downtowns. On the other hand, they don't roll up the sidewalks at five o'clock. The downtown area had a goodly number of people, stores, and restaurants still around after dark. While Montgomery suburbanites might not have been comfortable walking around downtown after dark, I felt safe, which is the best compliment a visitor can give to a town.

Earlier, while driving around downtown, I had noticed a number of green-roofed buildings. The green roofing indicates a Retirement Systems of Alabama building, whose slogan is "The stronger the RSA can make Alabama, the stronger the RSA will be." Before I left Montgomery, I had realized the slogan reflects a strong belief—indeed a mission.

I met Dr. David Bronner, head of the Retirement Systems of Alabama, to discuss the development of the Robert Trent Jones Golf Trail. According to the RSA, "The Robert Trent Jones Golf Trail was built to provide the finest collection of public courses in the world and to run them as a successful business investment." I wanted to discover who thought up the Golf Trail, a truly original idea. A retirement system developing golf courses in the 1980s was kind of like Lewis and Clark leaving St. Louis in 1804 to find the Northwest Passage. It might seem like a good idea, but who knows how it can be done because no one has ever done it before. I remember when I first heard about Alabama's plan to develop a series of golf courses designed by the well-known architect Robert Trent Jones. I distinctly remember thinking, *That's stupid. I bet they'll all be in bankruptcy before Arkansas governor Bill Clinton loses the Democratic presidential primaries.* (Remember, this would be 1991. Not my worst prediction at that time. I also remember telling a young lawyer that the facsimile machine would never catch on.)

No one would confuse Dr. Bronner with a native-born Alabaman. His fair complexion and upper Midwest accent give him away. It's ironic, but someone who has lived in Alabama for forty years and is arguably its greatest change agent since Martin Luther King is an obvious foreigner (that is, non-southerner). He seems to enjoy the outsider status, but that's another story.

Bronner grew up the son of a pool hall owner in Austin, Minnesota, and came to Alabama in 1969, following a professor from Mankato State University. He enrolled at the University of Alabama in what was essentially a combined JD/PhD program. He got his law degree in 1971 and his PhD in 1972. He took over the RSA in 1973.

So here's Bronner's story on the Robert Trent Jones Golf Trail. Throughout the 1970s and early 1980s, Bronner worked to make the RSA financially sound. Once he felt like this goal was achieved, he began traveling the United States, recruiting industry to Alabama. About the time Bronner started these travels, the Professional Golfers' Association selected the best golf course in Alabama, Shoal Creek Country Club, as the venue for its annual championship. So far, so good.

Things went so well that the PGA scheduled a return to Shoal Creek in 1990. Just before that tournament, a reporter for the local newspaper interviewed the founder of Shoal Creek, Hall Thompson. Responding to a question about the propriety of the City of Birmingham contributing $1,500 for a tournament being held at a place which excluded blacks from its membership, Mr. Thompson answered,

> Bringing up this issue will just polarize the community...but it can't pressure us....We have the right to associate or not to associate with whomever we choose. The country club is our home and we pick and choose who we want....I think we said that we don't discriminate in every other area except the blacks.

All hell broke loose, and Alabama was once again in the forefront of the segregation issue. The publicity surrounding the remark was exactly the type of publicity that Bronner didn't want. He was trying to sell Alabama to international businessmen, saying Alabama's "bad old days" of segregation were over and that modern Alabama was a good place to live and do business.

Bronner decided to do something about the situation. If businessmen wanted to exclude people from their country clubs, Bronner wanted to make sure that those excluded had an alternative. Moreover, he felt that a bunch of good, really good, public golf courses would benefit the state's long-term economic interests. They would create tourism, recruit industry, and attract retirees. Think about the slogan: "The stronger the RSA can make Alabama, the stronger the RSA will be."

Bronner announced he would be putting up one hundred million dollars of RSA money to develop a network of world-class public golf courses along the state's main thoroughfares. He sent out requests for proposals to numerous golf course architects, most of whom sent back pro-forma responses. One, a guy by the name of Robert Trent Jones, arguably the most prominent golf course architect in the country, did something radical. He called Bronner on the telephone to discuss the idea. As they say, the rest is history.

One more story about the Trail: After getting Jones on board, Bronner contacted U.S. Steel about some land near Birmingham. Essentially, the deal was that U.S. Steel would donate land near Birmingham for the golf course and the RSA would build and operate the course. Now the donation by U.S. Steel wasn't charity. U.S. Steel retained plenty of land around the donated tract, so it stood to make a lot of money by developing those tracts for upscale housing. Bronner thought the deal was finalized sufficiently to sign documents. When he arrived at what he thought would be a closing, U.S. Steel officials informed him that additional items needed to be discussed and feasibility studies to be undertaken. In short, they weren't ready to sign documents yet. After hearing out the officials, Bronner ended the meeting in under eight minutes, saying that he felt he was being played (not the verb he used). He also told them they would be hearing an announcement about another place in Alabama developing the first Robert Trent Jones golf course in the next few days.

Bronner knew that the mayor of Mobile previously had offered some land near the "garbage can of the county" as a potential site. After leaving the U.S. Steel meeting, Bronner called the mayor and told him that if the city board would approve the deal quickly, a deal for a golf course near Mobile would be on go. When informed that the city board was meeting the next day, Bronner allowed that tomorrow was quick enough.

As Bronner predicted, in a few days, U.S. Steel officials read about the great new golf development being built outside of Mobile. Those same officials called Bronner saying they had removed the impediments raised a few days before and asked if he was ready to move forward. He said sure. So now the RSA had two places to begin the trail. Soon afterward, he struck deals near Huntsville and Opelika. So within two years of the Shoal Creek controversy, the Robert Trent Jones Golf Trail opened four 54-hole complexes, the equivalent of 12 eighteen-hole courses. Green fees started at less than $50 for a round of golf, and the *Wall Street Journal* wrote that the Trail "may be the biggest bargain in the country."

Since that auspicious opening, the Trail has expanded to 468 holes at eleven sites throughout the state. The Trail's success created a secondary problem because visitors expected upscale lodging when visiting the golf courses. The RSA solved this problem by becoming Alabama's largest hotel developer, building lodges and conference centers at their golf sites. Expanding further, the RSA purchased an old resort, the Grand Hotel, originally built in 1847 in Point Clear, Alabama, and developed hotels in downtown Mobile and Montgomery. Some twenty years later, there is little talk about the racial composition of Shoal Creek's membership roster, but a lot of talk about the golf courses in Alabama—which are open to everyone.

A couple of years ago Dr. Bronner met with officials of Hyundai Motors about locating a plant in Alabama. The head of Hyundai didn't know much about Alabama except that it was home to the Judge Golf Course on the Robert Trent Jones Golf Trail. How had he come to know the Judge Course? It was featured in a video golf game that he played at his home in Japan. Soon Mitsubishi located a plant not more than thirty miles from the Judge Golf Course. Another example of the slogan: "The stronger the RSA can make Alabama, the stronger the RSA will be."

Forty Miles to Tuskegee

It's only forty miles from Montgomery to Tuskegee, but the cultural distance is much greater—from the first capital of the Confederacy to a town nationally known as a center of African-American achievement. Tuskegee is home to Tuskegee University, perhaps the most influential private, historically black university in the country. Founded in 1881, the Tuskegee Institute's first president was Booker T. Washington. Dr. Washington believed that if newly freed slaves were provided with skills, they would become self-sufficient in the rural South. Being self-sufficient would lead to their becoming productive members of their communities and to their acceptance by white Americans. Dr. Washington's theory of education became the Institute's mission.

Later, Tuskegee became famous for the Tuskegee Airmen, the 994 World War II airmen who trained at Tuskegee Army Air Field and saw action overseas. Their service was an experiment of the Army Air Forces. They showed that given equal opportunity and training, African Americans could fly, command, and support combat units as well as white units could. The Tuskegee Airmen overcame segregation and prejudice to become one of the most highly respected fighting groups of World War II. They proved conclusively that African Americans could operate and maintain sophisticated combat aircraft. The Tuskegee Airmen's achievements paved the way for full integration of the U.S. military.

Tuskegee has also become known as the location of the National Center for Bioethics in Research and Health Care. The center located there because of a scandal involving the Tuskegee Study of Untreated Syphilis in the Negro Male, a government study conducted between 1932 and 1972. The Tuskegee Study recruited 399 poor, mostly illiterate syphilitics for research related to the natural progression of the untreated disease. The forty-year study became a scandal when researchers failed to treat patients appropriately when penicillin became known as an effective cure for the disease. Study participants were left untreated so that effects of the disease could be studied further. These ethical lapses brought about major changes in U.S. laws and regulations to protect participants in clinical research studies.

Downtown Tuskegee

Today, Tuskegee is a small town of about 12,000 people and the county seat of Macon County. It is over ninety-five percent African American. The county itself is eighty percent African American, the highest percentage of any county in Alabama. Strangely, I thought of Copperhill, Tennessee, while walking around Tuskegee's town square. The towns are not similar at all. In Copperhill, a river and a state line divide the downtown; it has no town square like Tuskegee. Copperhill is also hilly, not flat like Tuskegee. Copperhill is completely, or at least overwhelmingly, white. In Tuskegee, I did not see one white face. Yet, without exception, people around the Tuskegee town square acknowledged me with a smile and a nod. A starkly different response from the stares I had received in Copperhill.

I drove a few blocks from the town square to the old post office, now the home of the Tuskegee Repertory Theatre, where I met Dyann Robinson, the artistic force behind the theatre. Dyann is a Tuskegee native who is a proud graduate of St. Joseph Catholic School and Tuskegee Institute High School. She began dancing lessons from her second-grade teacher, a nun. Some years later she made her stage debut in Tuskegee as a member of Jessie Gibson's Gibsonian Dance Troupe, which toured African-American schools and colleges in Alabama and Georgia.

Dyann left Alabama in 1960 to study dance at Butler University in Indianapolis, Indiana. She embarked on a career as a professional dancer, first in New York, then traveling the United States and Europe. Even though she always considered herself a ballet dancer, she became a member of the original cast in the Broadway hit musical *Bubbling Brown Sugar*.

So why is a world-class dancer living in Tuskegee? She came back to be with family. What does a world-class dancer do in Tuskegee? Dance. But to dance, Dyann had to start her own dance company. She developed the Repertory Theatre while she worked day jobs for the City of Tuskegee's Department of Cultural Affairs and later as a faculty member of Auburn University's Department of Theatre.

Now she's mainly a dance teacher. As a teacher, she imparts life lessons to her students. One of her lessons is to always do your best because you never know who is watching. Her best example is a personal one. One of Robinson's biggest career breaks occurred because of a college assignment. The modern dance class at Butler University contained a choreography component. Her teacher was given the responsibility of choreographing some dances for a religious event on campus. But rather than do it herself, she picked four Negro spirituals and assigned Dyann, the only African American in the dance department, to choreograph them.

The assignment didn't go over very well with Dyann. She felt it reflected assumptions the teacher had made about her. The worst assumption was not a racial but rather a religious one. She protested to the teacher, "I am a ballet-dancing Catholic. I know you think we're all rockin' Baptists, but I'm a Catholic, and we hardly talk out loud at church. I don't know how you picked these songs, but I've never heard of any of them except for 'Rock of My Soul.'"

Despite her protests, she soldiered on. By coincidence, Agnes De Mille, the famous Broadway choreographer, visited campus and attended the dance performance. The next year in New York, after graduation, Dyann ran into Ms. De Mille at the Ballet Theatre. De Mille remembered Dyann's choreography of the Negro spirituals and asked her to audition for the ballet she was casting. Dyann believes she got the part because she did her best on a job she didn't like and shouldn't have been asked to do. It's a lesson she passes on to her students.

Lobby of Tuskegee's Repertory Theatre

Now, almost twenty years after its founding, the Tuskegee Repertory Theatre thrives. It produces plays with African-American themes. These productions include *Run Johnny Run*, the story of Johnny Ford, the first African-American mayor of Tuskegee; *Revolt in Storyland*, a musical; *Lonely Eagles*, Tuskegee airmen meet Josephine Baker; *Moton, a Moment of Crisis*, the story of the Veterans Administration Hospital for Negroes in Tuskegee; *The Wives of Booker T.*, the story of the three wives of Booker T. Washington; and *Genesis*, a rap opera. Dyann has written or co-written most of the plays.

At the end of our interview, I asked Dyann if I could take her picture. She declined, saying I was welcome to take pictures of the theatre, but she was protective of her likeness. So I took a picture of a prop from *Lonely Eagles*. I know that it is supposed to be the likeness of Josephine Baker, but it makes me think of Dyann.

Fender Bender in Birmingham

Birmingham—pronounced "Buuminham" by the natives—is a major southern city. The metropolitan area contains almost one and a quarter million people. This constitutes almost twenty-five percent of Alabama's total population. Even though the metropolitan area has grown, the city of Birmingham has not. Its population peaked at 340,000 people in 1960 and has fallen since. Today about 225,000 people inhabit the city while over a million people surround the city limits. In response to questions about Birmingham, one person replied, "There's nothing left in downtown Birmingham except blacks, bankers, and lawyers." Another comment along the same line was that the white people downtown will rob you from their offices while the black ones will rob you as you walk down the street. Not a particularly optimistic assessment of one of the South's major cities.

As in many metropolitan areas, the interstate system—I-65, I-59, I-22, and I-20—encloses the central business district. And as in most American cities, the first close-in view of a new city comes as you exit the interstate. In Birmingham, you get dumped onto broad, largely deserted streets. Mid-afternoon, mid-week Birmingham finds few cars, few people, but wide avenues, more than enough to handle the traffic.

I headed initially to Birmingham's Civil Rights Museum. I turned onto a cross street—again it was wide enough for four lanes, but only a few cars were in sight. The vehicle ahead of me stopped in the intersection, waiting to turn left. When the light changed to red, I looked down at the map to get my bearings. I looked up to see the backup lights of the vehicle ahead of me. It had backed into my car. The collision wasn't bad, and there wouldn't have been any damage except that the bumper of the small pick-up truck was higher than my car's bumper. His bumper hit and crushed my headlight and creased the front quarter panel of my car.

The driver got out of his truck quite upset. He saw there was damage to my car, but he implored me not to call the police. At that time, a young woman drove up and told us that she was an off-duty police officer. The other driver must not have heard her say that because he said, "We don't need no po-lice."

She replied evenly: "I am the police."

He repeated, "We don't need no po-lice."

She looked at him and said more emphatically: "I *am* the police."

"You da po-lice?"

"Yes, I'm the police, and I've already called this in."

Then she said, "Both of you wait here until the patrol car gets here."

"She da po-lice?" He walked back to his car shaking his head.

As the off-duty police officer drove off, the truck's passenger got out and talked with the driver. The conversation got heated and I got a little uncomfortable. Soon though, the passenger walked off from the driver saying to his now former companion's back, "So that's how it is, huh? It's all on me, huh?" The passenger, without looking back, headed toward the group of bystanders who had formed across the street.

In a few minutes, a squad car arrived and the policeman got out. He took statements from both of us, ticketed the other driver for driving without proof of insurance, and gave me directions to the nearest auto repair shop to see whether my car was drivable. The officer warned me that I'd better drive straight to the shop because it would close at five and nothing would be open downtown after that. We all then went our separate ways.

This whole episode took about forty minutes and was quite unremarkable except that I was the only white person in the whole scene. The driver, the passenger, the bystanders, the off-duty cop, and the arriving officers were all African American. All were nice and polite. The police officer was professional, businesslike, and even-handed in his treatment of both of us. I was a complete stranger to the city and, except for witnessing the exchange between the other driver and his passenger, I never felt uncomfortable or unsafe. I never felt like I was being treated unfairly or differently.

So why is this—my fender-bender—noteworthy? Research Birmingham's past; read particularly about the bombing of the 16th Street Baptist Church, which gave it the nickname "Bombingham." Review Martin Luther King's "Letter from a Birmingham Jail." See the videos of high-pressure hoses being used on children by city firemen during the civil rights marches. It might not be surprising for a white guy passing through town to be given a little payback if the opportunity presented itself.

It was an unfortunate incident which marred my trip and car. But as I drove away, I really didn't focus on those problems. I thought of the Birmingham pledge, written by a Birmingham attorney and offered to the attendees of a Martin Luther King Jr. Unity Breakfast in Birmingham in 1997. Ten years later, over 115,000 people have signed the pledge. Part of the pledge states,

> I believe that every thought and every act of racial prejudice is harmful;
> if it is my thought or act, then it is harmful to me as well as to others.

At the traffic accident, was being conscious of each participant's race an act of racial prejudice violating the pledge? I don't believe so. I figure that everyone else was aware of it, too. It's not being conscious of the difference but exploiting it that creates the wrong. I don't think the other driver expected to be treated better by a black policeman because of his race, and I didn't fear being treated worse because of mine.

Remember Neddie Winters of Mission Mississippi in Jackson, Mississippi? He and I had touched on this subject. We talked about race awareness in ordinary events while trying not to prejudge interracial situations. An example we discussed is when children get in trouble at school. One of the first questions often asked by a parent or grandparent concerns the race of the other participants. Neither of us had a good answer as to why parents ask that question. Does it reflect a basic prejudice or just an understanding that race complicates those conflicts? I don't know. But Neddie and I agreed that parents of all races become more defensive when participants in the conflict are of different races.

We also agreed that people are much quicker to perceive racial prejudice than to celebrate those everyday occurrences when racial prejudices could occur but don't. In that vein, I applaud Patrolman Johnson of the Birmingham Police Department for following the pledge in his dealings with one traveler on a fine autumn day in Birmingham.

Iced or Hot? Sweet or Un?

Quick now, what's the quintessential southern drink? If you guessed anything other than tea, you lose. Tea is the second-most-popular beverage in the world, trailing water in worldwide consumption. But hot tea in the hot South isn't all that popular a beverage. Around these parts, when you speak of tea, you mean iced tea. And not just iced tea because people argue whether iced tea can be anything other than sweet tea. In the South, it can't. One southern writer put it rather graphically, "Unsweet tea is liquid kudzu, an unwelcome interloper fouling up the culinary landscape." So when you enter a restaurant in the South and want your tea hot or unsweetened, you'd better speak up and make your desires known when you order. Otherwise, sweet tea will be delivered.

In 2004, over 300 McDonald's restaurants in Virginia were surveyed as to the type of iced tea served. The researchers found that sweet tea wasn't available in the northernmost parts of Virginia, while non-sweet tea was rarely available in the southern reaches of the state. By calculating a median line between the southern McDonald's that offered sweet tea and the northern ones offering non-sweet tea, the survey established a "sweet-tea line" in Virginia. Scientific proof that sweet tea marks regional identity even in Virginia, a state considered southern.

A number of theories exist to explain why sweet tea is identified with the South. It's cheap to make, a real plus when the region lagged behind the rest of the country economically. It's non-intoxicating, a necessity for the conservative Christian teetotalers, and it's thirst-quenching for hot summer days. Others contend that the tannins in sweet tea play well with a southerner's diet of fried chicken, fried catfish, and the vinegary barbecue sauces, but analyzing tannins to explain tea-drinking behavior is over my head.

So far so good, but why pre-sweetened? Southerners prize independence and self-reliance. Why do they willingly give up the right to sweeten tea to their individual tastes. And just as important, why does the restaurant owner take the extra step of putting sugar in the tea rather than offloading that chore onto the customer? The answers to these questions have to do with chemistry. Sugar dissolves better in hot liquids. If you let tea chill before sweetening, the sugar doesn't dissolve as well and the drink tends to be gritty. It also takes more sugar to achieve the same level of sweetness.

The second reason for pre-sweetening is important in the history of Milo's Famous Tea. After returning home from World War II, Milo Carlton opened a hamburger stand on Birmingham's north side. Milo's claim to fame was his hamburger. The distinctiveness of Milo's burgers came not from the meat but from the sauce poured over the burger. Milo developed his sauce solely from his customers' comments. As he experimented with the sauce, he listened to customers' comments as to whether the day's batch was too hot or too sweet. After a while, he got it right and his hamburgers became a regional favorite because of the unique sauce.

In the early days of the restaurant, Milo didn't pre-sweeten his tea. He let the customers do it. That is, until his wife, Bea, complained. In post-war Alabama, sugar was expensive and in short supply. Milo couldn't afford enough sugar for his customer's needs and still have enough for his wife to make pastries to sell at the store and for home consumption. So Milo began to sweeten his freshly brewed tea to conserve sugar. As he had done with the sauce, Milo experimented and listened to his customers' responses. Eventually, Milo developed a recipe that customers liked and stuck with it. Over the years, Milo's sweet tea became the overwhelming beverage of choice for those ordering Milo's burgers.

In the late 1970s, Milo's son Ronnie joined the business. Ronnie's first big idea was to franchise Milo's hamburger stands, and the first franchise operation opened in 1983. Milo's grew into a small regional burger chain which today has seventeen locations in central Alabama. As the chain grew, Milo's sweet tea remained the most-sold beverage in the Milo's hamburger stores.

Ronnie's second big idea was to separate the tea business from the hamburger business. He started a stand-alone business. Soon he began distributing gallons of sweet tea to a few local grocery stores. Who'd ever heard of a business making only iced tea? But iced-tea-by-the-gallon grew into a business concept and, better yet, a profit center. From 1989 to 2002, Ronnie sold iced tea in bulk to area grocery stores and Milo's hamburger stands. In 2002, Ronnie sold the restaurant services business to a third party so he could concentrate on selling iced tea.

Milo's Tea Company makes iced tea and that's all. It doesn't do anything else. Milo's products have three ingredients—two, if you drink the unsweetened version. Milo's tea is all natural—no preservatives, no added colorings, and no added flavors. And no high-fructose corn syrup, only pure cane sugar from Chalmette, Louisiana. Milo's imports tea leaves from Argentina and uses regular Bessemer city water. Ronnie challenges anyone to compare the labels of Milo's with any other bottled iced tea to see the difference.

Ronnie's idea is a simple one: Make iced tea that tastes like your grandmother's iced tea and sell it like milk. Today Milo's plastic gallon jugs are sold in grocery stores next to the milk. And with an expiration date like milk—except Milo's Famous Tea has a shelf life of twenty-five days. If you drink iced tea in Birmingham, Alabama, you probably drink Milo's Famous Tea. Grocery stores in Birmingham sell as much Milo's tea as they do milk. Who would have thought someone could make a living selling only iced tea? When I asked him about the profit margins, he just smiled.

Milo's Famous Tea has expanded by partnering with dairy distributors. It's a natural fit because processing milk is similar to, but easier than, producing tea. Through strategic alliances, Milo's Famous Tea is available throughout the South. They now deliver as far west as Arkansas and Louisiana and as far east as the Atlantic coast. Most of the marketing consists of simply giving the product away. Milo's gives schools, churches, and other non-profit organizations gallons of tea for meetings, parties, and other get-togethers. Ronnie believes that other sections of the South will be drinking Milo's Famous Tea soon: "If you like tea, we'll get you as a customer." He has operated on that principal for the past twenty years.

Metropolitan Atlanta

Atlanta and Birmingham are not far apart—less than 150 miles on I-20 from downtown to downtown. Other than the occasional Confederate bumper-stickered pickup truck you could be pretty much anywhere in America, one interstate exit after another with national chains advertising their products from large signs. There's also lots of construction. Expanding the four-lane highway to six lanes to handle the increased traffic is a big job. Luckily, at the edge of the Birmingham metro area, I noticed a small sign for Milo's. With a #2 Milo's burger (onions and Milo's secret sauce) and some iced tea (unsweetened), I had ample provisions to fight the traffic and construction.

As I ate my Milo's burger, I reflected on the Journey since passing through Highlands, North Carolina, the pretty mountain town between Cashiers and Franklin, where I crossed the eastern continental divide. Now after two thousand miles, I was returning to the divide which runs along the east side of Atlanta's metropolitan area. You can easily cross the divide a half dozen times wandering around the metropolitan Atlanta area. Downtown the divide runs along DeKalb (pronounced De Cab) Avenue. Rainfall on the east side of DeKalb winds up in the Atlantic Ocean, while rain on the west side flows to the Gulf of Mexico.

I wasn't especially interested in visiting Atlanta. Back when I had first thought about recreating Mr. Daniels' Journey, I was excited about visiting Greensboro, Spartanburg, Copperhill, Friars Point, and Mobile.

These were places I didn't know anything about. I was less excited about Charlotte, Nashville, and Birmingham, and really not at all about Atlanta. Of all the places on the map, Atlanta was probably the place I was least interested in visiting, perhaps because of my aversion to the crowded freeways of big cities.

If I had a prejudice against Atlanta, it may have been the sheer size of the Atlanta metropolitan area. The metro area comprises twenty-eight counties, a landmass larger than Massachusetts and six other states. It's an area so large that it has its own specific mixture of gasoline. So large that, on my last visit, it had stormed and flooded the southern part of the metro area but it hadn't even rained in the northern part where I was visiting.

Even though the rain held off, traffic was still bad, one person driving eighty-five miles per hour dodging between lanes to get ahead of those going a little slower, another person poking along at forty miles per hour in the left lane. And the brake lights of vehicles ahead of me lighting up constantly for no apparent reason. That's on a good day, when traffic is flowing well. It's awful. I've learned that bad traffic is the one constant about Atlanta. There's no use asking someone how long it will take to travel someplace because they always respond with, "What time of day?" It could be five minutes to forty-five minutes. Bless their hearts; Atlantans have learned to put up with really bad traffic.

Even though Atlanta is the center of the South—its capital, really—Atlanta is not all that southern. If it is southern, it's more southern California than southern Georgia. On a recent trip to visit family, my cousin from Texas complained that he'd been back for a few days and he'd not heard one southern drawl in Atlanta, except from family members. He observed that "a lot of Yankees must live here."

I've been coming to the Atlanta area for as long as I can remember. I have a lot of family there. As the saying goes, my people hail from here. My extended family has been here since before Georgia was a state. I think my ancestors participated in the Georgia Land Lotteries where the north Georgia lands were taken from the Creek and Cherokee Indian tribes and given to white people via a lottery system.

Three grandparents, numerous aunts and uncles, and countless cousins come from the area. Two of my three siblings emigrated back. Urban sprawl

338

has enveloped the small town of Acworth where the old family home sits. The house is famous as one of the two places in town where Sherman and his officers rested while planning their attack on Kennesaw Mountain. I think the Yankees were kinder to Atlanta than they were to Acworth. The only two houses they didn't burn were my grandparents' house and Mrs. McClure's house. The Yankee officers occupied them when their soldiers started the burning. During the Civil War, a *Harper's* magazine drawing depicted Sherman's arrival at my ancestors' house.

Sherman's arrival in Acworth, Georgia

I've got my own history with Atlanta—great memories from every decade since the early 1960s when I first visited the Atlanta Cyclorama. The Atlanta Cyclorama is a large oil painting of the Civil War battle for Atlanta. Since 1921, the painting has been shown in its own specially designed round building where it hangs from the outer wall. Visitors to the Cyclorama stand in the middle of the building on a platform which rotates so that the battle unfolds before you. It made a strong impression on a young boy visiting the big city. I still recall the vivid depictions of dead soldiers lying twisted on the ground.

Cycloramas once were entertainment. But once motion pictures came in vogue, cycloramas became passé, the great paintings sold, junked, or cut up. Few cycloramas remain today; the Battle of Gettysburg is depicted in one. Having been restored, Atlanta's is great.

The Atlanta Cyclorama hangs from the wall from five panels of Belgian linen. The painting was originally 50 feet high, 400 feet long, and weighed more than 9,000 pounds. Today it's only 42 feet by 358 feet. While it's no longer the largest mural in the world, it still retains the title of largest oil painting in the world. It also contains a diorama. The diorama is a three-dimensional extension of the scene at the bottom of the wall.

In the early 1970s, I visited Underground Atlanta. Underground Atlanta is literally a paved-over urban gully created in the 1920s when viaducts elevated the street system over the first floor of Atlanta's downtown multi-story buildings. Atlanta forgot the five-block area of covered-over ground floors as it grew outward during the next forty or fifty years.

Underground Atlanta was a radical attempt at revitalizing a deteriorating downtown by creating a retail and entertainment district in this subterranean urban area. Initially it was a hit and became the hot area of bars and music. As Rod Hudspeth, former columnist for the *Atlanta Journal*, noted:

> Underground was a phenomenon. Short-lived, but a phenomenon just the same. In its heyday, which lasted only a few short years in the early 1970s, it outstripped New Orleans' French Quarter and Chicago's Rush Street for fun and class.

I was there in its heyday. Visiting my grandmother over Thanksgiving, my college roommate and I went bar-hopping in Underground Atlanta. We felt we were entering a real den of iniquity because Underground Atlanta was a dark, dank area of a dozen or so bars with live music in many of them. I remember a blues band playing to a few seated patrons in one bar. In the second establishment, a nattily dressed black man danced by himself to jukebox music. It's the first time I'd ever seen a person dance like James Brown. I remember wondering how he and James could move their feet so fast, drop to their knees, and rebound in time with the music.

There was the souvenir shop owned by the governor, Lester Maddox. Lester, an avowed segregationist, sold t-shirts in his shop that said "Phooey," one of Lester's favorite sayings. Lester was a strict Baptist, so of course he couldn't swear. He had made his reputation as the owner of the Pickrick Restaurant, where he defied the 1964 Civil Rights Law—newly enacted—by refusing to serve African Americans. Within three years of his defiance of the new federal law, he was installed by Georgia's General Assembly as governor of the state. One of Georgia's more colorful politicians, Lester warbled bird calls and rode bicycles backward in parades. My favorite characterization of his politics is that, next to integration, he disliked "liberals, smoking, and drinking."

Besides t-shirts, he sold pick handles called Pickrick Drumsticks. When African Americans came to desegregate the Pickrick, Lester and his customers picked up the ax handles kept near the fireplace to make sure the interlopers didn't feel welcome. The Pickrick Drumstick became the symbol of his resistance to desegregation, and Lester would always be glad to autograph one when he was around.

Since its heyday, Underground Atlanta has been revived a couple of times in the intervening decades. After closing in the early 1980s, it has been re-opened as a shopping and tourist attraction, but it still struggles.

With one or two exceptions, what I remember are quick business trips, short family visits, or missed connections in the nation's busiest airport. I missed the 1996 Olympics; the truth is I chose to avoid them. This time I planned to see World of Coke as a tourist. Coca-Cola is the backbone of Atlanta's business community. It's reputed that Coca-Cola has created more millionaires per capita in Chattanooga than in Atlanta, but you have to remember that Atlanta has a lot more heads than Chattanooga does. Not only has Coke made lots of people rich but Coke employees have done well. They're well-paid, loyal, and rarely leave for another local job.

Normally I avoid tours, but this one seemed OK. The tour allows you to view the bottling process and see the vault where the secret formula is held. The recipe for Coke isn't patented—it's just a secret. If it were to get out, anyone could copy it. For years, the only copy of the written formula was pledged to Coke's lenders as security for the company's debt. The banks have since released the secret formula, and it now resides in a vault at the World of Coke. Ever since his sixth-grade trip, my son has sworn that the best part of the tour is the sugar rush from the Taste It room, where you can sample Coke products from all over the world. The products are separated by continent, and it's interesting to see how tastes vary continent to continent from sweet to tart. He warned me to stay away from the bitter drink called "Beverly" at the European stand. I think it's sold in Italy; if you have standard North American taste buds, stay away.

About forty-five miles past the Georgia line, I topped a hill and the Atlanta skyline spread out before me. A real city—not just a southern city but an American city. I was sure I'd find something to do.

Traveling South Georgia

South Georgia is defined as anyplace south of metropolitan Atlanta. It's about 250 miles from the center of Atlanta to the state line of Florida, and the state is about 250 miles wide. So it's a large landmass. I'd never been to south Georgia and must admit to a certain prejudice. In 1975, I remember expressing surprise that my father, a Georgia native, was not supporting Jimmy Carter, his fellow Georgian, for president. My father, a good southern Democrat, turned and intoned evenly, "Nothing good has ever come from south Georgia." I quickly replied that the Allman Brothers Band came from Macon, and it was pretty good. He allowed as how he wasn't going to discuss a hippie band no matter where they were from, and the conversation died. He voted for Gerald Ford and lost.

I envisioned south Georgia as one large peanut farm inhabited largely by rednecks driving pickup trucks with gun racks and Confederate flag decals on the back windshields. I was pleasantly surprised when I hit Macon County and then Sumter County and saw rolling green hills. There were a lot of pickup trucks, but just a normal number for rural America. I didn't notice an unusual number of Confederate flag decals either.

At the Macon-Sumter County line is a 26.5-acre rolling field, the site of Andersonville, the notorious Civil War prison. Technically, Andersonville is the name of the nearby train depot and the town surrounding it. Camp Sumter, hastily constructed a few miles from town, held the prisoners of war.

Camp Sumter during the Civil War (courtesy of the Library of Congress)

Camp Sumter today

During the early parts of the conflict, the two sides exchanged prisoners of war pursuant to the Dix-Hill Agreement which allowed the sides to swap prisoners rather than hold them captive. In 1863, Secretary of War Henry Stanton rethought the benefits of the agreement because the South had less manpower and fewer supplies. The burden of holding prisoners was marginally greater on the South, to say nothing of its greater need for soldiers. As a result of these dynamics, the North began to "slowplay" and then finally expressly refuse to exchange prisoners. Secretary Stanton stated, "To release all Rebel prisoners would ensure Sherman's defeat and would compromise our safety here. We do not propose to reinforce the Rebel army by exchanging prisoners."

This policy change was not popular in the North. In a letter to the *New York Times*, poet Walt Whitman expressed the following sentiment:

> ...the public mind is deeply excited, and most righteously so, at the starvation of the United States prisoners of war in the hands of secessionists....Whose fault is it at bottom that our men have not been exchanged?...In my opinion the anguish and death of these 10 to 15,000 American young men, with all the added and incalculable sorrow, long drawn out amid the families at home, rests mainly upon the heads of members of our own government.

Because the prisoner exchanges no longer reduced the number of Yankee prisoners, the Confederate government began looking for additional prison space. Construction began in December 1863 on Camp Sumter. Originally the camp was designed to hold 10,000 prisoners on 16.5 acres. Construction was not very far along when prisoners began arriving and by June 1864 the prison population exceeded 20,000. As the number of Yankee prisoners increased, the Confederates expanded the prison, bringing the total prison area to 26.5 acres. By August 1864, over 33,000 Yankee prisoners were held in the open air within this 26.5-acre prison compound.

As a result of the lack of planning, materials, supplies, and manpower, the Confederates could only maintain perimeter security. The Union prisoners could not maintain military order, so the inmates attacked and stole from one another. Andersonville Prison was a hellhole. Of the 45,000 inmates held there, nearly 13,000 died. Many died from starvation, malnutrition, and disease. The two most common causes of death were chronic diarrhea and scurvy, which accounted for over 7,500 deaths.

As the war wound down, conditions at Andersonville were publicized throughout the country. After the war, Henry Wirz, the commandant at Camp Sumter, was tried as a war criminal even though the United States did not try Wirz's bosses, John Breckinridge or Jefferson Davis. In the aftermath of Lincoln's assassination, the environment for the man who oversaw the deaths of 13,000 Union soldiers was not a good one. Though it was peacetime, and, unlike Breckinridge and Davis, Wirz had never served in the Union army, Wirz was convicted and sentenced to death by a Union military court. On November 10, 1865, Henry Wirz was hanged in the courtyard of the Old Capitol Prison (now the site of the United States Supreme Court). He was the only man executed for war crimes during the Civil War.

After the fall of the Confederacy, ownership of the prison camp reverted to private hands. Nature reclaimed it, and the land became a cotton farm. In 1891 the prison land was acquired for public purposes and in 1910 taken over by the federal government. During the early part of the twentieth century, states began erecting monuments to their citizens who had died on the grounds: 2,572 died from New York; 1,030 from Ohio; 1,811 from Pennsylvania. Even Tennessee, a Rebel state, lost 738 men there.

Camp Sumter is a now a National Historical Site. The original camp has been outlined with white posts and two sections of stockade have been reconstructed. A national prisoner-of-war museum is located within walking distance of the camp. The museum does not focus solely on Camp Sumter but tells the story of the half million Americans held as prisoners of war throughout American history. It attempts to provide a larger context for the Civil War prisoner-of-war story. This emphasis might have been helpful generations earlier, since Andersonville's notoriety explains in part the harsh attitudes toward the South after the war.

The Camp Sumter National Historic Site contains the graves of almost 13,000 men who died during their captivity. Now a national cemetery, it is an honored burial ground for present-day veterans and their dependents. But on a sunny July day, you can walk the quiet open fields and think of those poor souls who many years ago were captured fighting and sent to such a hellhole.

The nearby town of Andersonville, Georgia, is a small down-in-the-mouth settlement of a few hundred people. Embracing tourism—the Civil War buffs visiting Andersonville National Historic Site across the highway—Andersonville has attempted to turn back the clock to make the town look vaguely nineteenth century.

From Andersonville, it's a short stretch to Americus, Georgia. Americus was built on a hill, and legend has it that during the summer of 1864 its residents could smell the stench of Andersonville Prison. Americus is a very pretty, small town, perhaps best known as the international headquarters of Habitat for Humanity. A few miles past Americus is Plains, Georgia, hometown of the first southern president to be elected since the Civil War. (LBJ, a Texan, doesn't count. Though it seceded from the Union, Texas is western.) Plains is a small town with a one-block commercial district on one side of the highway and the Billy Carter Museum and gas station on the other side.

It was late afternoon and I still had Georgia's Little Grand Canyon to see, so I pushed west past Lumpkin, the county seat of Stewart County. I was still surprised at the rolling hills; this is pretty country. I had plenty of time to admire the countryside because I was behind a pickup truck with Alabama tags that was full of cantaloupes. With a full load of melons, the driver's top speed was forty miles an hour. There was no room to pass on the winding road.

Arriving at my destination at the far end of Stewart County, I found that there was no longer a visitors' center at Georgia's Providence Canyon State Park. A sign informed me of the various charges for using the park, now operating on an honor system.

The Little Grand Canyon isn't one big canyon but a series of sixteen canyons which grew from a bunch of smaller gullies. It's the only canyon in the United States not formed by a river. The gullies were formed 150 years ago as a result of poor farming practices. The gullies carried off the thin layer of topsoil. Once the topsoil eroded, the rains carried away the clay subsurface and created larger gullies. As the gullies got bigger, they became canyons up to 150 feet deep.

Providence Canyon in the 1930s (courtesy of the Library of Congress)

Providence Canyon today

Blaming the canyon's formation on poor agricultural practices 150 years ago doesn't entirely explain the situation. Stewart County's agricultural practices couldn't have been that much worse than those in other places— and the South isn't dotted with river-less canyons. So what happened here?

Clearly, rapid erosion turned gullies into canyons in a short period of time. Poor farming practices started the problem. Farmers didn't rotate crops; they kept planting cotton until the land played out. Once the land was abandoned, a particulate found in the subsurface of the soil caused rapid erosion. Once the topsoil eroded and rainwater hit this particular substratum, the Providence level, it reacted differently due to the kaolin deposits in the subsurface. As rainwater percolated to the Providence subsoil, it hit deposits of impermeable kaolin, a valuable natural resource most commonly used in the paper-coating industry or as filler added to plastic and rubber compounds. When rainwater hit those kaolin deposits, the water began moving sideways in a process known as pipe flow. This sideways movement of water created a phenomenon called mass wasting where the subsoil quickly sloughed away. Man's activities played a role in making the canyons, but nature did most of the work.

The canyons are not significantly larger than they were in the 1930s when Jonathan Daniels visited. Other than the growth of scrub pine, about the only change in the canyons is the addition of some automobiles. Evidently, Stewart County residents pushed or drove some cars into the canyons in the 1950s and left them. The State of Georgia considers them too much trouble to remove, so they just sit there rusting.

Happy Animals. Good Cheese.

I took the back roads leaving Providence Canyon. Just before getting back on the highway, I saw a couple of quail hot-footing it along the road. Appropriate, since I was headed to Thomasville, the next stop on the map and the epicenter of Georgia bird hunting. Fifty or so plantations around Thomasville provide some of the best quail hunting in the United States. Since the end of the Civil War, wealthy industrialists have owned large tracts of land in south Georgia for hunting—and for just getting away from bitter northern winters.

Bird hunting has become quite a gentleman's sport. For a proper hunt, you need horses, dogs, dog handlers, a mule wagon, and, of course, lots of undeveloped land. Hunters walk across a field until they "flush" a covey of quail from the underbrush. *Flush* really isn't a descriptive word because a flushed quail leaves the underbrush like Herschel Walker running through the Georgia line of scrimmage. But the small birds are even tougher to take down. Alabama and Florida hunters may disagree with the use of a University of Georgia running back in this analogy, but you get the point. If a hunter is not properly attentive, he has no chance of shooting the rapidly moving, small target. Even if properly attentive, the hunter must be a skilled shot to get one of these little scudders. Over the past fifty years, the Georgia wild quail population has declined substantially because of the loss of habitat and the proliferation of predators. My Uncle Jit, who has hunted quail all over the United States, lamented the decline of birds in Georgia and declared that the bird hunting in Texas may be just as good now.

Downtown Thomasville is doing well. The business district is mostly high-end shopping. On Broad Street, the main thoroughfare, occupied and well-maintained buildings line the main street. These buildings are not populated with rent-to-own appliance stores and cheap clothing stores that feast on poor people. The Bookshelf, an independent bookstore; Hick's, a clothing store; and the Gift Shop, which sits in a handsome 1885 Victorian building, are just a few of the shops. Name me one other town of less than 20,000 people that has two high-end outfitter stores. Stafford's and Kevin's meet the demand for hunting attire.

But I wasn't tracking quail on this hot July afternoon. I was tracking cheese.

First the backstory: My wife and I were celebrating our thirtieth wedding anniversary in New York City at the Blue Hill Restaurant, a tony restaurant in Greenwich Village. (I didn't realize just how fancy it was until a few weeks later when the news reported that President and Mrs. Obama had dined there.) Anyhow, we were in this fancy New York restaurant. I opened the menu and it listed a cheese from Thomasville, Georgia. My wife observed that one usually associates cheese-making with colder climates—not with the South—and I thought about how a south Georgia cheese maker had gotten on the menu of a fancy Greenwich Village restaurant. Then it crossed my mind that the Blue Hill restaurant wasn't more than a few blocks from Billy Reid's store; you'll remember him from Florence, Alabama. If these are strange thoughts for an anniversary dinner, remember we've been married a long time.

Sweet Grass Dairy is about five miles north of Thomasville on 140 acres that was once a cotton farm. The owners are Jeremy and Jessica Little, a couple I estimated to be in their late twenties. The Littles bought their farm a few years ago from Jessica's parents, Al and Desiree Wehner. Jessica's parents, well-known pioneers in sustainable agriculture, started Sweet Grass and two other farms in south Georgia over the past fifteen years.

To understand what Jeremy and Jessica do, one first needs to know something about sustainable agriculture. Sustainable agriculture is best described by what it is not: *sustainable* is not conventional or modern agriculture. No one criticizes modern agriculture directly because it has delivered tremendous gains in productivity and efficiency. Food production worldwide has risen during the past fifty years and the World Bank estimates that between seventy percent and ninety percent of the recent increases in food production are the result of conventional agriculture rather than greater acreage under cultivation. Because of this increased efficiency, U.S. consumers expect abundant and inexpensive food, even if it is produced by a few large business concerns using large integrated processes. Follow the bumper sticker advice and refrain from criticizing the American farmer with your mouth full.

Advocates of sustainable agriculture note that conventional farming frequently results in indirect costs involving environmental degradations and socioeconomic transfers. Sustainable agriculture minimizes the indirect effects of conventional farming. As the National Sustainable Agriculture Information Service explains:

> In recent decades, sustainable farmers and researchers around the world have responded to the extractive industrial model with ecology-based approaches, variously called natural, organic, low-input, alternative, regenerative, holistic, biodynamic, biointensive, and biological farming systems. All of them, representing thousands of farms, have contributed to our understanding of what sustainable systems are, and each of them shares a vision of "farming with nature," an agro-ecology that promotes biodiversity, recycles plant nutrients, protects soil from erosion, conserves and protects water, uses minimum tillage, and integrates crop and livestock enterprises on the farm.

For example, a conventional dairy operation raises its cows in a concrete-floored barn and triple-crops the land. The modern farmer can make up for reduced nutrients caused by the "efficient" cropping by using chemicals or fertilizer. Most dairies do not allow natural breeding cycles; instead they keep the animals tightly confined and milk them frequently. As a result, the useful life of a cow in a conventional farm is two-to-three years. But conventional dairy operations provide dairy products efficiently and cost effectively.

In contrast, with a sustainable farming operation such as the Littles' or the Wehners', the animals are allowed to roam. And these farmers rotate the crops to allow for organic methods of mineralizing the soil rather than supplementing with chemical nutrients and fertilizers. The Littles also incorporate the New Zealand–style rotational grazing method, which allows the soil, animals, and humans time for rest. With these methods, the Littles' animals live substantially longer lives than they would under conventional methods. In simple economic terms, the Littles reduce their capital expenditures at the expense of reducing output. This trade-off produces fewer products, which must be sold at a slightly higher price. However, the higher price also indicates a higher-quality product. Jessica said, "We give our animals a better life, and they give us better milk."

Happy boys in front of happy goats

Sustainable agriculture isn't the same as organic farming. Last year, the Littles used pesticides to make some of their grass grow. Also, Jessica noted that a cheese operation is not a kind place for boy goats. The guys are sold to local restaurants for veal. She noted that some people actually get upset about those sales. (City folk, I guess, who don't realize where their meat comes from.)

So how do you go from a sustainable dairy operation to a cheese-making operation? The short answer in this case is the empty-nest syndrome. On a business trip to Milan, Italy, Jessica's mother, Desireé, took a bite of gorgonzola. Since her three children had left home, she had the time and decided to learn cheese-making. First, she found and read *Cheesemaking Made Easy*. From there it was trial and error. The dogs ate the errors. But before long, Desireé became a cheese maker.

While Jessica's mom was feeding gorgonzola rejects to the family pets, Jessica and Jeremy were off living in the Atlanta suburbs and working in the food service industry. Jessica worked at an upscale Atlanta restaurant; the last thing she was contemplating was a return to Thomasville to help out in a new agricultural venture. But in 2002, that's what they did. Three years later, the Littles took over the cheese-making operation. With contacts in Atlanta, Jessica and Jeremy found it easiest to break into the Atlanta restaurant market. Sales grew by word of mouth. Now, numerous awards later, Sweet Grass Dairy cheeses are known throughout the country. In 2010, they opened a retail shop in downtown Thomasville. They also sell their products on the Internet. Despite the great recession, Sweet Grass Dairy's sales of high-end cheeses and their revenues are still growing.

Jessica laughed when I told her I had found out about Sweet Grass Dairy during a visit to New York City. She said that one of her earliest customers was Murray's Cheese Shop on Bleecker Street in Greenwich Village—only a few blocks from the Blue Hill Restaurant. Small world.

Tallahassee

I arrived in Tallahassee after a summer rainstorm. It's a pretty city, with oak trees, Spanish moss, and rolling hills. At first, I thought the lack of activity downtown was due to the weather. I found other southern state capital cities—Jackson, Montgomery, Little Rock—pretty lively compared to the capital of the Union's fifth-largest state on that July evening. Even Thomasville, Georgia, was perkier than downtown Tallahassee.

But Tallahassee was quiet because its two main industries, government and education, were on vacation. The state legislature was not in session so there was not a lot of governing to do. Little-known fact: Tallahassee is home to more than 500 local, state, and national associations (think lobbyists). It ranks third, right behind Washington DC and Chicago, Illinois, in total number of lobbyists. On a per capita basis, Tallahassee has the number-one concentration of associations anywhere in the country. There must be a lot of lawmaking going on during the rest of the year.

Tallahassee is also a big college town, home to the 40,000 students enrolled at Florida State University and the 12,000 students at Florida Agricultural and Mechanical University, both of which were on hiatus between summer school sessions. Without students, lobbyists, or legislators around, the place seemed deserted. I was the only person renting a room on the eleventh floor of the hotel that night.

One of the prettiest state capitol buildings in the country sits a few blocks away. Right behind it is one of the ugliest state capitols in the

355

country. In the early 1970s, Florida's old capitol building was outdated and outgrown, even though it had been expanded in 1902 and 1923. Though threatened with demolition, it was saved and repurposed as a museum. It's the pretty one.

The new capitol was one of the last structures designed by the prominent twentieth-century architect Edward Durell Stone, a native Arkansan who moved to New York to make his living. Stone's signature New Classicism design was intended to symbolize the growth and development of Florida. Unfortunately, the twenty-five-story "box" towers over the attractive original capitol building.

Two Florida state capitols. The ugly one is in back.

The next morning, I visited the Leon County Tourism Development Council to see what Tallahassee had to offer. I arrived in the midst of the beginning of football season. Once the Fourth of July holiday is over, most Floridians (and most southerners for that matter) begin discussing football in earnest. The first step in this process is for everyone to predict the outcome of the games of their favorite football team. Once everyone has projected their score for every game, the arguing ensues and lasts until the season is over. That year the projections for the big game of the year, Florida versus Florida State, were more about score than outcome. Even the most diehard Seminole fans conceded that the prospect of victory against the Gators was remote.

In November of 2000, Tallahassee was the center of the universe as the battle of the "hanging chads" played out—to determine whether George W. Bush or Al Gore had won the presidency. National reporters and powerful political figures got a big shock when they were informed they had to vacate their rooms during the weekend of the Florida–Florida State game. As one local commentator said, "You've got to get your priorities right. The world stops when the Florida–Florida State game is played."

There's a lot of football here. Around Tallahassee, this means the Florida State Seminoles; elsewhere in the state, it means the University of Florida Gators, and in south Florida, the University of Miami. The University of Central Florida and the University of South Florida have up-and-coming national programs. Floridians fill the rosters of these five top-level Division I programs. Florida high schools produce so much talent that many players migrate to universities in other states. But Florida does more than produce players: In the mid-1960s, University of Florida professors invented Gatorade to help the Gator football players with the dehydration caused by playing football in 100-degree temperatures.

A few miles from downtown, I encountered a road canopied by oak trees, called Miccosukee. I was traveling Miccosukee in hopes of talking with members of the Miccosukee Land Cooperative, a hippie commune from the 1970s, which still exists today. Technically, it's a co-op, not a commune. As Chuck Mitchell, a member of the co-op, noted to the *Tallahassee Magazine*:

> It's not a commune. Community must be voluntary. There are lots of communes and cult farms and ashrams, where everyone has to get up and meditate at a certain time, attend certain functions, live a certain way, do certain work. Compulsory sharing is a contradiction in terms. There's no community in a prison.

So it's a cooperative. Of the co-op's 240 acres, approximately two-thirds are private and divided in one-to-ten acre lots. The remaining land is held for common use. If you want to sell your house, the co-op has the right of first refusal. After forty years, the co-op is going strong. It has 200 residents, many of whom are out in the community, teaching as well as owning and operating businesses. One is even an elected official, a Leon County commissioner.

I dropped by unannounced and a friendly young man with long hair and a beard said he would like to talk to me about the co-op but he had an engagement. He suggested I go "talk to Cliff" and gave me directions:

> Go back on Miccosukee Road and take a left on Imaginary Road and go two or three houses, I think it's two houses, and...Well, man, there's another road, with a Spanish name, I think, goes off to the right. Cliff's house should be right there. Gotta go, man.

I followed his directions, even finding the Avenida de la Luna. (If my Spanish is correct, the English translation is Moon Avenue.) I knocked on a few doors; no one answered. Even though I didn't talk with anyone, I drove around and saw the fire station, community center, and a number of homes that sat off the road.

Returning to Miccosukee Road and the next intersection, I stopped at Omara's Produce for a sandwich and a drink. Omara's has a brick column out front with a stone pig on top to advertise the barbecue. He also had some tomatoes on display outside. Sadly no barbecue was available that day. Tomatoes and cold drinks were about all they had at Omara's. Owner Herndon Chandler allowed that business was bad because his main customers were construction workers and work had dried up. Herndon said he used to have a restaurant in Tallahassee over by the college, Florida A&M University, but it had burned down a few years ago. Since then he's tried to make a living here, but without much success. Two men drove a car into the parking lot. We both went outside, me to finish my drink and him to greet his visitors. It became clear that Herndon was more interested in what the visitors had to say. I finished my drink and moved on.

Omara's Produce

Ybor City

Central Florida sure is a crowded place. The St. Petersburg–Tampa area, which covers only a portion of the western side of central Florida, has a population equal to the population of the entire state of Arkansas and only slightly less than the population of South Carolina.

Originally a winter resort, the area boomed after World War II when air-conditioning became common. St. Pete still retains some of that resort theme because it's smaller, less dense, and has the Don CeSar Hotel on the beach. With its watchtower and pink walls, and despite the condos which now flank it, "The Don" sets the tone of this resort area of sun and sugar-white beaches on the Gulf of Mexico.

The Don CeSar has a pretty interesting history, opening in 1928 and being taken over by the federal government after Pearl Harbor, some thirteen years later. The Don served the government until 1967 as a military hospital, a convalescent center, and finally an administration center. A few years after being sold to private interests, it reopened as a luxury hotel and since that time has welcomed visitors to the Sunshine City. (St. Pete contends that it gets sun 360 days a year. It rained the day I was there.)

With its vibrant Hispanic culture, Florida differs from the rest of the South. One of my misimpressions of Florida was that its Hispanic influence was Cuban. There's no doubt the Cuban influence is strong in Florida, particularly in south Florida. But, in central Florida, the Hispanic community is variegated: Mexicans, Puerto Ricans, and Central and South Americans all contribute to the melting pot of modern Hispanic life here.

In Tampa, the melting pot includes a strong Spanish flavor. Ybor City, Tampa's Latin Quarter, was founded by Spaniards looking to relocate their cigar operations from Cuba. It was a matter of free trade. Just before the Civil War, Congress imposed high tariffs on Cuban cigars. During the war, the tariffs didn't make much difference. But once peace came, this tax policy put a crimp in the cigar industry and the owners looked for ways to get around it. The Spanish tobacco manufacturers figured that Cuban tobacco could be shipped in bulk to the United States, rolled into cigars here, and be considered "American made"— and thereby avoid the tax.

In the mid-1880s, Mr. Ybor moved his tobacco operations to a three-story brick building in what would later become known as Ybor City. Many other cigar tycoons followed so that by the turn of the century, Ybor City had become the cigar capital of the world. They came to Tampa because of its location: Tampa Bay was due north of Cuba's main shipping point and the closest point to a United States railway connection. In Tampa, the Cuban tobacco was rolled into cigars and then transported by train north to the rest of the United States.

The cigar industry was quite different from other Florida business endeavors of the time, primarily fishing or ranching. A cigar roller was an artisan producing perfect hand-rolled cigars. Rollers worked on the production system. To keep their minds occupied as they worked, the workers collectively hired a "lector" to read aloud to them during the day. The lector sat on a platform above the workers and read newspapers, novels, and magazines to the workers. Cigar rollers were well informed about current events. Victoriano Manteiga, one lector who moved on, founded a local newspaper, *La Gaceta*. Mr. Manteiga's grandson still publishes *La Gaceta* in Ybor City; it is the nation's only tri-lingual newspaper, carrying stories in English, Spanish and Italian.

Unlike other southern workers, cigar rollers created mutual aid societies by contributing five percent of their wages to the common good. Their mutual aid society provided medical care, gymnasiums, and auditoriums for the community's common benefit. The Cuban community had two social clubs, one for those with lighter skin coloring and the La Union Marti-Maceo for darker-complexioned Cubans. (Remember this is during the time of Jim Crow.)

Ybor City never really recovered from the Depression and the decreased demand for cigars. When demand recovered, hand-rolled cigars gave way to machine rolled largely because the sellers of machine-rolled cigars engaged in a "spit" campaign. They contended hand-rolled cigars were less pure because they contained human saliva, whereas machined-rolled were "spit free." During the balance of the twentieth century, when a cigar factory went out of business, no business replaced it.

Urban renewal contributed further to Ybor City's decline when it destroyed much of the historic fabric of Ybor City. Part of the urban-renewed land was used to build Interstate 4. The interstate created additional physical barriers in the neighborhood, which led to more deterioration in Ybor City. During the 1970s, Ybor City's prospects were worse than Chattanooga's. But as in Chattanooga, things improved. First, Ybor City became a music and entertainment district. Artists began using the abandoned buildings for loft spaces. Later, small businesses moved in. Today Ybor City is on the rise.

The Columbia has been a part of Ybor City's business district throughout the city's ups and downs. Founded in 1905, the Columbia has been operated by the same family. The fourth generation operates it today. It covers a full city block and advertises that it can seat 170 people in fifteen dining rooms. Patrons get dinner and a show because two forty-five-minute Spanish dance shows are performed in the evening. I got there just as the second show was wrapping up. In colorful Spanish costumes and accompanied by castanets, dancers perform the flamenco, a traditional Spanish dance, on the Columbia's hardwood floor.

The Columbia serves a trademarked salad. And they have an on-premises cigar roller who sits at a desk turning out hand-rolled cigars. After I left, I couldn't remember whether I had seen any "no smoking" signs in the Columbia—or anywhere else in Ybor City.

The Columbia Restaurant

Cracker from Kissimmee

Orlando is as far south as the Journey took me. Little Rock and Hot Springs are almost 1,000 miles away and the nation's capital is over 900 miles to the north. There's still plenty of Florida left below us. Miami is almost 300 miles farther south, and Key West is over 400 miles away. But those places are in south Florida. It's different and not truly southern. It has been that way for years, as the governor of Florida explained to Jonathan Daniels during his trip in the '30s:

> Why, North Florida and South Georgia are about the same, same folks, same ways of making a living. Florida is a Southern State sharing the fate of the South. Of course, North Florida and South Florida are different. There are a lot of Northerners in the South and they're different from the old farm and plantation folks in the North. They usually say down here that Ocala is about the dividing line.

Ocala is just north of Tampa and Orlando. South of Ocala, the American South kind of plays out. South Florida, with its northern transplants and Cuban influence, is said to be different. The same phenomenon occurs in western Louisiana and Arkansas where cowboy boots and hats herald the start of a different American region.

It's not that far from Tampa to Orlando, about eighty-five miles from downtown to downtown by way of Interstate 4—a shortened version of the trip between Birmingham and Atlanta with franchised eateries, convenience stores, and other attributes of suburban life at every exit. The difference is it's flat down here and there's not much green vegetation.

Twenty miles before the exit to downtown Orlando, the exit to Walt Disney World Resort appears. I wasn't tempted. Many years ago when my son Will was young, I decided to forgo Disney World. Any attraction that uses signs informing you how much longer the wait in line is going to be is not for me. I told my son I'd be glad to pay for him to go when he was in college if he still wanted to visit. He took me up on the deal and had a great time.

Disney World's arrival in 1971 is considered the most significant single event in Orlando's history. Locals refer to events as BD, before Disney's arrival, or AD, after Disney. Before Mickey Mouse showed up, Orlando was a small county seat, the trading center of the citrus-growing region. Disney, Universal Orlando, and SeaWorld have changed the area into a top destination for tourists.

Today, Orlando is the self-described capital of the New South. Orange-growing has given way to high tech. Orlando has the twelfth-largest cluster of technology companies and is the epicenter of modeling simulation and training: Madden NFL computer football is produced here. It's also home to America's sixth-largest university, the University of Central Florida, and Florida's newest medical school. Metropolitan Orlando, which anchors the eastern side of central Florida, has over two million people.

Like Chattanooga's Mayor Littlefield, Mayor Buddy Dyer is a cheerleader for his city. A state legislator, Dyer ran for attorney general and was defeated. This was the same election cycle when Florida governor Jeb Bush won re-election in a landslide. Newly re-installed, Governor Bush recruited the then-mayor of Orlando for a position in his administration. Dyer ran for mayor in the special election and won.

Like most politicians, he was comfortable talking policy. He spent a lot of energy revitalizing the Parramore area, the historic African-American area of town; getting the new event center relocated; and finding the funds for the medical center's infrastructure. He was also a member of a group of mayors against illegal guns, but that's not what made him famous. He's famous because he's a cracker from Kissimmee, a small town southwest of downtown Orlando. In Florida, *cracker* doesn't mean someone of Scots-Irish descent as it does in other parts of the South. It means either a cattle herder or a long-time resident—that is, someone living here before air-conditioning, mosquito repellant, or sunscreen. Mayor Dyer meets all these qualifications. He is descended from the Spanish cowboys, cowboys in Florida didn't use ropes to herd cattle but instead used a whip. They cracked the whip, and the name *crackers* stuck.

He's even more famous for the lessons he learned growing up in rural Florida. One day the mayor was jogging in his neighborhood. As he ran, he noticed something coming up on his left. It was a seventy-pound pit bull. The pit bull passed Buddy Dyer heading directly toward Dyer's neighbor who was walking her Jack Russell terrier. The pit bull grabbed the terrier in its mouth; its owner screamed in panic. Dyer jumped into action. Growing up in Kissimmee, he had owned a pit bull. "They are like a gator. They don't crush something; they take it, shake it, and break its neck," he said. The mayor jumped on the pit bull's back and grabbed its jowls. He figured he could hold onto the animal's jowls and keep him from shaking his head. He told me it felt like he held the pit bull for ten minutes—with his neighbor lady screaming the entire time. It wasn't that long. A few neighbors heard the ruckus and came to help. The team of three men tried to get the pit bull to drop the Jack Russell terrier. Dyer said that as the men fought with the dog he wondered what would happen if they were successful: Would the beast turn his attention to the guy on his back if he was forced to drop his prize? Luckily, it all turned out well for the mayor and for the Jack Russell terrier.

The next morning, the lead story throughout America was that the governor of New York, Elliot Spitzer, had resigned over his involvement with a prostitute. But not in Orlando. In Orlando the lead story was Mayor Dyer's going one-on-one with a pit bull. The phone in the mayor's office rang all day long. E-mails and phone messages came from voters saying, "I've never voted for you, but because of what you did, I'll vote for you from now on." Dyer now gives a speech to young people, the theme of which is this: "You never know when opportunity is going to present itself, and you need to be ready to seize that opportunity."

I'm sure there are plenty of big city mayors in the North who have real life skills. But I'll bet none of them would know how to save a terrier from the clutches of a pit bull.

The First Coast

Branding—creating catchy names for places—can sometimes go too far. In Florida, branding has gotten out of hand. Due east of Orlando is the Space Coast, which has famous Cape Canaveral, Kennedy Space Center, and rocket ship launchings. To the north is the two-county Fun Coast, which includes Daytona Beach. After the Fun Coast, the First Coast emerges. In the branding world, First Coast has two meanings: It establishes the area as the first place Europeans landed in America, and it recognizes the first beach coast that northerners hit when crossing into Florida.

Florida has 399 miles of Atlantic Coast and twice that amount of coast on the Gulf of Mexico. That's a lot of coastline development. After a while, all beach development starts to look the same. From the Fun Coast northward there are small beachfront homes and large condo projects facing the blue seas of the Atlantic Ocean. There are also plenty of seafood places. But if sand, sea, and humidity are not your thing, you're in the wrong place.

Driving into St. Augustine on the old road, Florida A1A brings you face to face with the area's dual personality. St. Augustine, a relatively small town of 12,000 people, constitutes the southern point of the First Coast. Founded in 1565 by the Spanish, it's the oldest European settlement in the continental United States. Sites along the road authentically represent the history of this very, very old place—the Castillo de San Marcos National Monument, for example.

St. Augustine has a long history of catering to tourists. There are also truly historic tourist attractions, like Ripley's Believe It or Not! and the St. Augustine Alligator Farm, incorporated in 1908. Floridians get their first chance to lift dollars from vacationing snowbirds at these venues. Outlet malls, miniature golf, water activities—they're all here. (But I didn't find any purveyors of fresh-dipped corn dogs as I had in Gatlinburg.)

The northern side of the First Coast is Jacksonville, Florida's largest city, with a population of 875,000. Jacksonville is also America's largest city in terms of land mass. Jacksonville consolidated with Duval County years ago, creating a municipal area of 875 square miles. Politically, merging the city and the county was a progressive move.

The city fathers haven't always been that progressive. In the early part of the twentieth century, the film industry, then located in New York City, wintered in Jacksonville. The industry found Jacksonville's mild winter climate and its beaches, buildings, and swamps great locations to shoot their silent films. In the days before tax credits, the industry developed a five-building complex on the river for film-making. One studio building of the five remains standing, and it has been converted into a museum celebrating Florida's silent film history. Ultimately, the film industry moved west to California due largely to the conservative political climate in Jacksonville.

Jacksonville is located at the mouth of the St. Johns River, one of the few rivers in America that flows northward. The St. Johns starts in central Florida and winds its way northward. It moves slowly because Florida is so flat. There is only a drop of thirty feet from the headwaters of the St. Johns to its mouth.

Jacksonville has bridge crossings that rival San Francisco's. It's hard to believe how high they build bridges these days. From the bridge in Jacksonville, you get a great view of the Port of Jacksonville, which handles twenty-one million tons of cargo each year. Crossing the St. Johns River is certainly more impressive than crossing the Mississippi River into New Orleans or at Greenville on the new bridge.

Between the two posts of the First Coast lies a good example of modern Florida. Former scrub land now has carefully manicured second homes and retirement locations. It's crowded here. Except for a few years,

Florida has increased its population every year during the past two generations. Many of the new residents came to the First Coast. One lady remarked to me, "I wonder how many more people this big sand bar can hold before it sinks."

The center of the First Coast is Ponte Vedra. Ponte Vedra is reported to be named after Pontevedra, Spain, the name of the town one of the original developers mistakenly thought was Christopher Columbus' hometown. (Not even close: Columbus hailed from Genoa, Italy.) While there is no underestimating the power of the beaches here, the bigger draw to Ponte Vedra is golf. Over thirty golf courses are located within fifteen miles of Ponte Vedra Beach.

Golf is big business in Florida. There are 1,100 golf facilities, employing more than 167,000 people. According to a study done in 2007, golf directly increased Florida's economy by $7.5 billion dollars. That sum doesn't include the indirect impact golf creates in the development of residential communities.

The modern Florida golf industry began in 1978, when the developer of the Sawgrass development offered 400 acres of land to the Professional Golfers' Association for one dollar. The PGA took the deal and built a championship golf course. The Sawgrass course is now the home of the Tournament Players Championship and the headquarters of the PGA Tour. The course has what is perhaps the most famous hole in modern American golf, the island green at No. 17. This green is surrounded by water and is the site of televised drama each year when the best players in the world step up and either hit the green or the water.

The green was not part of the original course design. When the course was constructed from the Florida swampland, the developers discovered sand, not swamp, around the proposed seventeenth green. This sand was a pleasant discovery because the sand could be used elsewhere on the course to reduce the cost of construction. One day as the course was nearing completion, the architect gave his wife a tour around the course. Since the sand had been excavated, a crater existed around the green. The architect's wife, a fine golfer in her own right, suggested that rather than refilling the hole with dirt, they fill it with water and create an island green. From that idea, the famed 17th at Sawgrass was created.

Stuck in South Georgia

Jacksonville is a major American city with tall buildings, a large university, and even an NFL football team. It also has all of the problems of a modern American city: sprawl, traffic, crime. Plus one problem that most metropolitan areas don't have—nuisance alligators. Now I'm not suggesting that nuisance alligators are a huge problem—unless you're caught in an alligator's jaws.

Florida began keeping data on alligator attacks in 1928. Their database contains 579 incidents. Since 2000, twelve people have been killed by these beasts. In 2006, alligators killed three people in a five-day period, and two more people died in 2007. Injuries and attacks on pets and farm animals are not recorded.

Once a gator grows to four feet, it poses a threat to people, pets, and livestock. Houses and golf courses have consumed wild marsh lands, and alligator-human contact has increased exponentially. Alligators have a natural fear of humans. If humans feed them, they become comfortable with humans. The problem arises, as one expert noted, because gators can't distinguish between the meal and the waiter.

Both Florida and Georgia license people to trap nuisance alligators. I located an alligator trapper who catches 80-90 of these critters a year. Jackie Carter lives outside of Folkston, Georgia, at the edge of the Okefenokee Swamp in a small community called Cypress Siding. I had always thought Okefenokee was a put-up name for a fictitious place in the *Pogo* comic strip. But the Okefenokee is real; it really sits on the eastern side of the Georgia–Florida state line. The Okefenokee is the largest swamp in North America and one of the largest in the world. One interesting fact about the Okefenokee is that the swamp actually burned in April–May 2007. The area of burning swamp was larger than the entire state of Rhode Island.

I didn't ask for directions because I planned to call when I got close to Folkston. I didn't worry when Jackie failed to answer his phone. I thought I would explore the area until he returned my call. Jackie lives just off U.S. Highway 1. Before the interstate system, Highway 1was the main route between Miami and New York City and Boston. With the interstate system complete for a couple of generations, this stretch of U.S. 1 connects local traffic between the rural areas of extreme south Georgia.

I still hadn't heard from Jackie when I turned off the highway onto the road that I thought led to his house. A few hundred yards up that road, I looked for the left turn that my printed directions said to take, but I didn't see a road. I continued about a mile farther along this paved road covered with sand. I saw a sign saying that I had just entered the Okefenokee National Wildlife Refuge. A few hundred yards later, the road ended at a small parking lot. The nearby boat dock and landing area provided access to the swamp. I wandered onto the boat dock. The water was dark and perfectly calm. Nothing moved. It was completely quiet. There were no sounds at all, no birds or other wildlife chirping. The absolute quiet concerned me. Ten to fifteen thousand alligators live in this almost 400,000-acre refuge.

It was eerie—too quiet. Out on the landing at the swamp's edge, I wondered if the area alligators hung out near the boat dock looking for a late afternoon snack. I had heard that they move pretty fast on land and I wondered whether I could make it to the car if one of those monsters came from the swamp looking for a man meal. I dismissed that thought because nothing moved in the swamp, not even the air. After a few minutes, I got bored and decided to explore the nearby pine forests while waiting for Jackie's call.

What appeared to be white sand covered the road and the recently planted pine tree field. Looking down at the road, the substance was clearly sand, but out in the field, the substance gave the appearance of a recent dusting of snow. In the sixty-degree weather, the presence of snow seemed incongruous. I've always liked fields of recently planted pine trees, and the thin layer of sand pleasantly contrasted with the green of the pine trees. I slowly drove down the sand-covered country road viewing this quiet rural scene.

Sand-covered (not snow-covered) pine tree field

I was curious about the sand's presence because the nearest beach was miles away. I pondered the sand mystery as I came to the turn that I thought took me to Jackie's house. I started down the side road. Within a couple hundred yards, my reverie ended when my car hit a sand pit and got stuck up to its axles in sand. Completely mired, I left the comfort of the car and walked to the nearest house about a quarter of a mile away. No one was home.

Truth be told, as I trudged back in the sand toward the main road on foot, I gave up on Jackie. As I struggled to keep my footing in the sand, I realized that the sun was setting and there wasn't much daylight left. I began to wonder what had possessed me to take this swamp detour anyway. I could have found a seafood or barbecue restaurant and cast about for interesting characters there. There was no reason to be all alone out in the Okefenokee Swamp.

I assessed my prospects. I looked at my cell phone. I was lucky; at Cashiers and out on the Natchez Trace Parkway, I'd been in areas so rural that they lacked cell phone coverage. But next to America's great swamp, I had at least three bars of cell coverage. I wondered if Folkston had a cab company. I then contemplated how long I should wait before calling a cab. Could it get out here before dark? Would it come out here after dark? Without a cab or Jackie's help, I could be spending an uncomfortably long night under the tall Georgia pines.

House closest to my car

Reaching the main road, I saw a man working on his house. I approached him slowly so that I didn't startle him. It's rural, and strangers don't just walk by. I explained quickly that I was coming to see Jackie

Carter and that I'd gotten stuck. He was initially distrustful and asked why I was going down that road because Jackie's house was in the other direction. I pulled my Internet-generated directions from my pocket and showed him the evidence that I had for going down the road from which I had walked. He relaxed after seeing written confirmation of my directions. He apologized for not having a four-wheel-drive truck to pull me out. He continued saying not to worry because Jackie should be back at any time. He told me it was the last day of deer season, and Jackie was out deer hunting with a friend. He assured me that Jackie or his hunting partner would have a truck which would do the job.

Almost on cue, Jackie called apologizing, saying that in the deer woods he'd had his phone on silent. I, in turn, apologized for getting stuck. I quickly added, in my defense, that I hadn't anticipated beach property this far inland. Jackie laughed and informed me that I was standing on Trail Ridge, a sand ridge that completely surrounds the swamp. He said he'd be there in a few minutes to pull me out. When he got there, he noted that Trail Ridge was particularly thick here and lots of people get stuck. He had already called his friend Rinky Dink, who had the truck which could pull me out of the sand. The neighbor, now identified as Spud, offered me a "Co-cola" to drink while we waited for Rinky Dink. In a few minutes, Jackie and Rinky Dink—about 6'8" and 350 pounds—attached a chain to my car's axle. A quick pull from Rinky Dink's big truck, popped my little car from the sand pit, no worse for wear. Within seconds, I returned to the main road and headed to Jackie's house.

Jackie is a Vietnam veteran whose family goes back six generations in this area. When he left for Vietnam, his father had a business extracting peat moss from the swamp. It was lucrative because Okefenokee peat moss was highly prized as potting soil. But during Jackie's tour of duty, the U.S. government bought the land his dad leased, made it a part of the national wildlife preserve, and moved Jackie's family's house from the swamp to the highway. When Jackie said that he grew up in the swamp, he meant it literally.

At that time, alligators were endangered because restrictions on alligator hunting were ineffective. In the early 1970s, federal laws were passed that made it a federal crime to sell the meat or skin of an alligator. After the change in federal law, alligators began making a comeback. By the end of the next decade, alligators had done so well that nuisance alligators became a problem. In 1989, the State of Georgia issued the first licenses to trap nuisance gators. Because Jackie had been around gators all his life, he applied for and became one of fourteen trappers originally licensed by the State of Georgia. These licensees field calls throughout their area once a nuisance gator is reported to the authorities.

Jackie explained that alligators are opportunistic eaters: They will eat just about anything. Jackie noted that the swamp doesn't have many snakes because the gators control them. They eat snakes, turtles, small mammals, and birds. They have also been known to take down animals as large as bears and white-tail deer. Jackie explained that gators can't chew; instead, they just chomp down on their prey. Either the victim drowns or is dismembered when the gator spins in a death roll. Generally, alligators just bite and swallow. For large animals too big to swallow, the gator pins the carcass under the water and lets the water decompose it until it's manageable to consume.

In hunting these creatures, Jackie uses a baited hook with a gallon-size plastic jug attached to the line. It's like catching a really big fish. Other times he'll use a harpoon with a line and jug attached so that he snares the gator with a rope. I asked him which method he uses most, and he said the snare method, adding, "It's the most fun." Once the gator is snared, Jackie slips a noose over the mouth and puts it behind the jaws of the gator. With the noose in place, he places rubber bands made from tire inner tubes around the animal's snout. When the mouth is bound, the remaining danger is the swishing tail. It can break a leg. The creature is then wrestled or pulled into the boat. While gators have nibbled on him some, he's never been bitten badly. A gator once sunk his boat during a battle. Luckily he was near the shore and could leap quickly out of danger.

Alligator trappers don't get paid for trapping nuisance gators; they keep the proceeds from selling the creature. Jackie doesn't get any money for the small ones which he transports and releases into the Okefenokee. Larger ones he kills and sells the skin and meat, but as Jackie notes, "In this market, a gator's hide and his meat won't pay for a man's gas." He keeps the head of the gator and boils it to remove the skin. The process also causes the gator bones to separate. As a hobby, he puts gator skulls back together. He keeps a few skulls but gives the rest of them to friends or University of Florida fans.

Jackie Carter working on a gator skull

When I asked Jackie when he might retire, I thought he would give age or injury as the reason to hang up his alligator snare. But he just said, "If the price of gasoline goes much higher, I'll be giving it up."

Savannah

After spending the day stuck in the sands of south Georgia and staying late with Jackie Carter, I arrived in Savannah very late and very hungry. I asked the desk clerk for a restaurant recommendation. She replied, "All the restaurants have closed their kitchens by now, but I bet you can find a bar down the street that will serve you something." A real expectation-lowering response. I nodded and turned to Water Street, the street along the Savannah River. It doubles as the entertainment district of Savannah, a small city of 135,000 people.

The bartender at the very first place I reached said that the kitchen was open and he'd recommend the "low-country boil." The low-country boil consisted of boiled shrimp or crawfish with potatoes and corn on the cob. It sounded a lot like the meals that the Zaunbrechers sold at their crawfish boil stand in the Cajun Prairie. I said, "Great. Gimme some of that please." The bartender followed up by asking if I wanted a "half and half," shrimp and crawfish. Even though it was a little early in the year for crawfish, I stayed with the all-crawfish boil. I hadn't seen any boiled crawfish for a long time. Peeling crawfish must be like riding a bicycle— or John Zaunbrecher Jr. taught me well. I'm sure anyone watching was impressed with how deft I was at crawfish-peeling.

Having ordered, I turned to the people next to me, self-described "tourists" from Waycross, Georgia. Waycross is on the western side of the Okefenokee Swamp directly across from Folkston and 125 miles from

Savannah. They laughed as they called themselves tourists, saying they came to the city once or twice a month to enjoy themselves.

Since I was fresh from Folkston, we swapped alligator stories. My tourist friends relayed theirs about the little four-foot alligator in their pond. Rather than call a trapper, they fished it out of the pond with a strong line on a fishing pole. Since the gator was hooked well, the husband led it toward his wife. The critter began to chase her while carrying a hook in its mouth. He said that alligator "shore was mad, but not as mad as the Missus was." His wife, "the Missus," laughed and noted that he may have had fun at the time, but she was headed to the front door of the house to get a shotgun "to shoot them both." Unfortunately it was locked, so she'd had to humor her husband until he led the beast away. She added that if she had been able to escape to the back door and get her hands on that gun, she might be in jail right now for manslaughter. They continued the story, adding that they killed the gator and called their son to come and take the tail for a barbecue. They cut off its head so they could have some fun with the skull and a University of Florida fan.

One thing that I found on the Journey was that humidity is always relative. I asked the Waycrossers about Savannah's summer humidity. In a great south Georgia drawl that knows no r's, my new friends allowed, "Its humidity ain't too bad; least ways, it ain't as bad as Waycross." (I realize that there are no r's in that quote—just pronounce slowly the name of their home state without using the r and you'll get the idea of how they spoke.) Another person, who'd lived mostly in Charleston, chimed in, noting that Savannah's humidity was beastly and much worse than Charleston's because Savannah is so far inland, a solid sixteen miles from the Atlantic Ocean.

As we said good-bye, the folks from Waycross assured me that I would enjoy Savannah because the to-go cup was invented here. Later, in a local Savannah bookstore, a book tote reflected the same sentiment:

IN ATLANTA
They ask what you do for a living
IN CHARLESTON
They ask who your grandmother was
IN MACON
They ask what church you go to

BUT IN SAVANNAH
THEY ASK WHAT YOU WANT TO DRINK

Savannah was established in 1733. Some say it was a utopian experiment through which England sent "white trash"—they called them paupers—to the New World, perhaps to see if they could change their ways and become successful there. Others contend that the English positioned the poor people there as fodder for the defense of Charleston. By establishing Savannah, the British created a southern point of first defense against the anticipated invasion of the Spanish from Florida.

James Oglethorpe brought thirty-five families and a town plan. It was America's first planned community. Oglethorpe laid out the town on a grid with a "square" for each ward in the city. These squares initially were intended to be used as common space for military drilling and exercises. The original city had four squares, which ultimately grew to twenty-one. Nineteen of the twenty-one squares still remain—as little pocket parks.

Trustees ran the eighteenth-century utopian community. They imposed specific restrictions:

No slaves
No Roman Catholics
    (Remember the Spanish to the south were the enemy)
No strong drink
    (beer was OK), and, finally,
No lawyers
    ("Free from that scourge and pest of mankind called lawyers")

One by one these restrictions fell. Liquor was made legal in 1742, and after England and Spain settled their regional disputes in 1748, Catholics were accepted. The need for slaves to produce cotton caused slavery to be allowed in 1750, and, finally, lawyers were permitted in 1755.

Most of the twentieth century was not particularly good to Savannah. Savannah's economy could be described as moribund. It was a sleepy southern city. With few new industrial or business interests looking to locate there, Savannah's squares and historic buildings were not destroyed. As a result, downtown Savannah's historic building stock compares favorably today to that of any city in the United States.

John Berendt's *Midnight in the Garden of Good and Evil*, a non-fiction work about the murder of a respected antiques dealer in Savannah, was on the *New York Times* bestseller list for 216 weeks after its release in 1994. A movie by Clint Eastwood followed in 1997. The book and movie brought lots of tourists to Savannah. Residents of Savannah now describe events as "pre-book" and "post-book."

Another reason for Savannah's rebirth is the growth of Savannah College of Art and Design. Founded in 1969, SCAD now has over 9,000 students. In 1979, SCAD renovated its first building in Savannah and now occupies about seventy historic buildings throughout downtown. With college students out on the streets at all times of the day and night, Savannah has the feel of a larger city. The art and design students give Savannah a bohemian vibe not generally seen in small southern cities.

Broughton Street has the most vibrant small-town commercial district I've seen since Thomasville. At the center of this retail activity is the flagship store of the Savannah Bee Company. Like Sweet Grass Dairy in Thomasville, the Savannah Bee Company is owned by an entrepreneur who's developing a business doing what he thinks is important.

The Savannah Bee Company is the brainchild of Ted Dennard. The son of a low-country lawyer from nearby Brunswick, Georgia, Ted has been around bees most of his life. He saw honey for the first time as a tiny child when Roy Hightower, an elderly local man, asked Ted's father if he could put some hives on Dennard land. That childhood episode began a lifelong love of honey. Ted said, "I remember as a real little boy, three maybe four, swirling a honey comb around and seeing the different colors in the honey and being amazed that these bees could do such a thing." Roy advised young Ted, "Son, I have to warn you that these bees sort of become a way of life." Roy was right. Ted's beekeeping career began with Roy's bees; he kept them until he left for college.

Ted wanted to travel the world before starting college, but his parents persuaded him to delay his travels long enough to finish two years of college at the University of the South at Sewanee. There he met a retired minister near campus who raised bees. The minister rented Ted a small cabin. Having a bee outlet made school more tolerable. Ted's landlord advised him, "If you set your mind right and study these bees, you can see the hand of God in all that they do."

The bees kept Ted in college beyond the two-year stint he'd promised his parents he'd do. After graduation, Ted taught beekeeping for two years in the Peace Corps. Returning to Savannah after the Peace Corps, he put hives near a stand of Tupelo trees on the nearby Ogeechee River. Ted's bees fanned through the river valley and produced a rare varietal honey called Tupelo honey. Within a few years, he started selling his honey to a store in Savannah. The honey was so good that other local stores soon called.

In 2002, he printed a price list and took his honey to market in Atlanta. The trip was successful, and Ted received a number of orders. After the positive reception in Atlanta, he decided making honey would be his full-time job. When he told his brother of his grand venture, his brother said that Ted was nuts and predicted that he would soon be bankrupt. Despite this less-than-encouraging response from his sibling, Ted forged ahead with his new venture.

Ted developed a simple business plan. The first step is educating consumers. He believes that American honey is where the wine industry was fifty years ago. Fifty years ago, most people didn't drink wine and those who did either were not aware of the distinctions in wines or didn't appreciate those distinctions. Back then most restaurants either didn't carry wine or didn't carry any good wines. Today, that's all changed. American wine consumers now appreciate distinctions among wines, and the domestic wine market has expanded as a result of that appreciation. Ted would like to do the same with honey. Specifically, Ted wants to educate American consumers about artisanal honeys. He believes that once they appreciate the differences of really fine honeys, the market will grow.

So here's a short introduction to honey. The first kind is the "multi-floral" honey. This is the cheap stuff found on the grocer's shelf. The second type is "varietal," honey which has a specific source or flower. The third type is "artisanal." The beekeeper, generally a small producer, keeps tight control over his hives, setting them in specific places. An artisanal honey requires literally following the blooms of a specific flower and harvesting the honey during certain times to produce a higher-quality product.

Ted presents his Tupelo honey in a beautiful bottle with the following label:

Tupelo
(Nyssa ogecha)
Tupelo honey tastes buttery and melts on your tongue. It never crystallizes. Harvested for a few days each April in Southern Georgia, it is one of the rarest and most valuable honeys in the world.

Ted Dennard with his honey

Ted is a honey man. A connoisseur, he touts Sourwood honey. But he was quick to say that a good Sourwood is hard to find. He's not satisfied with the Sourwood honey that he currently offers and is looking for another source. He's also an international honey man, having recently begun buying great honeys from Italy.

The Savannah Bee Company offers other bee-related products: Beeswax Hand and Nail Salve, lip balms, and a throat spray which contains propolis, a resin that bees produce to seal the honeycomb. It is thought to have certain beneficial effects on humans. Ted said he uses the throat spray and believes that it has helped him ward off colds. He gave me a couple of bottles to sample, along with a bottle of his Tupelo honey.

As a small business owner, Ted's days are filled with hustling new markets, overseeing production, learning accounting standards, and trying to find financing for a growing company which now has twenty-eight full-time employees. Despite his schedule, he still makes time to work his bees because he contends that bee-keepers live longer. He said, "Working the bees is the best part of the day. Once you are comfortable with bees, you can concentrate on them. It is Zen-like. You lose track of how long you are in there. Too little of my day is spent with the bees."

Georgilina

The free magazines set out on most hotel room desks are a perk of modern travel. Savannah's River Inn featured the current issue of the *Savannah Magazine,* which was celebrating twenty years of publication. The magazine had invited its readers to submit "20 Big Ideas for Our Future." Big Idea #3 caught my eye: "Erase the South Carolina/Georgia state line and think in bioregional rather than political terms."

This idea makes sense geographically speaking because the eastern states of the South striate north to south. On the east coast, the coastal plains first appear, then the hill country, and as you travel farther west, the mountains rise. The political lines ignore these geographic distinctions as they run east and west cutting across geographic bands. Regardless of the arbitrary political boundaries, people in the banded geographic areas have more in common, and more common economic opportunities, with one another than with other areas of their own states. The low country is a good example. This coastal region starts just north of Jacksonville, Florida, and extends at least to Myrtle Beach, South Carolina. Two states and a small part of two others include the low country, but the low country is distinctly different from the rest of their respective states. People simply do things a little differently in the low country.

Take dancing, for example. A friend who has spent time in the low country related the following story. Early in his business career, he was a young banker for a large multi-national bank. One night my friend entertained the head of the international unit from London, England. As they made small talk, the Englishman inquired how the young man had met his wife. The low-country boy divulged that they'd met while shagging. The boy continued the story by saying that he was a pretty good shagger. One night this girl he'd known casually asked him to shag. He noticed that the Englishman swallowed and almost choked as he heard the story, but the young man continued, saying, "Oh yeah, she's good at shagging. I think that first night we shagged four hours."

The young man couldn't figure out why he was getting such a strange response from this Englishman for recounting an innocent story. The older gentleman said something to the effect that he was glad they had something in common that they could do together. My friend replied that yes, it was great, but that they hadn't had much time to shag recently. He then offered to call his wife and they all could go shagging together that night. The Englishman asked my friend exactly what shagging meant in America. My friend explained that the shag was a local swing dance which had originated on the beaches near Myrtle Beach. They shared a good laugh when the older man told him what shagging means to an Englishman.

Shagging is a low-country phenomenon. It was honored by the South Carolina legislature in 1984 as the state dance of South Carolina. Outside of the low country, shagging is little known, even though it has been exported to other parts of the country by low-country refugees. Shag descended from the jitterbug, the Charleston, and a little known dance called the Big Apple. The Big Apple was an African-American group dance. Later the frantic pace of those dances slowed and took the tempo of rhythm and blues.

Though it's considered a beach dance, this Carolina swing dance has elements of both east coast and west coast swing. Sometimes, it's called "beach swing." Shag requires a great deal of footwork. It's often said the shag is danced from the waist down—and that shaggers can hold their beer or cigarettes while dancing.

Shag music is pretty familiar. It's rhythm and blues—soul with a few disco songs mixed in. Songs like "Under the Boardwalk," and most songs by Barry White, are staple items on the shag playlist. There were a few strange songs, such as William Bell's "Easy Coming Out, Hard Going In." One song, "Wake up Mommy; Daddy's Drinking Whiskey Again," seemed out of place with these mostly over-fifty white people who were turning, spinning, and pivoting to the music. Shag music historically has a bi-racial origin. Both whites and blacks shagged in the low country, though during the days of segregation not at the same places.

Since I had gone zydeco dancing in Cajun country, I thought I'd give this shagging a good once over. The Savannah Shag Club meets every

Wednesday at Doubles, a night club in Savannah near the bypass. On Friday nights, they dance at the local American Legion. My contact for the Savannah Shag Club was Gayle Spilliards. Gayle has been a member since 1993 and has been an officer or director for many years. She introduced me to other members, explaining that the club had functioned for over twenty-five years and presently had 136 dues-paying members.

The more active club members travel on weekends to shag events throughout the low country. The weekend before, members of the club had visited the Hilton Head Shag Society. Gayle and her friends were making plans for the spring Society of Stranders—SOS—held annually in Myrtle Beach. This is the biggest shag event of the year. Shaggers descend on the Grand Strand at Myrtle Beach for ten days of dancing. Virtually all of the best dancing and dancers hit the Grand Strand shag clubs during SOS.

As I watched the dancers, I noticed that there were some protocols: No one declined a dance invitation, and no one offered instruction to a dance partner. In her running commentary of the dancers, Gayle told me that some women dancers were covering for their partners' ineptitude. Some women wore shoes with lights. In the darkened room, these foot lights twinkled and magnified the dancer's quick foot movements. As the night progressed, the members had a drink or talked with one another, but for the most part, they danced. When the music stopped, few people left the dance floor. Partners changed, and people started dancing to the next song.

I left thinking of Mr. Eighty-Six in Opelousas and wondering how he would do here.

Coastalitis

In *A Southerner Discovers the South*, Jonathan Daniels relates a conversation with a Savannah doctor who described the residents of the low country as "the most ignorant, pitiful, and poverty-stricken whites in Georgia....Many of them are scrawny humans hardly fit for oppression...[One] boy, sent to Savannah, had malaria, hookworm, pellagra and from malnutrition his thighbone had pierced his pelvis." "Coastalitis," the doctor continued, "is a terrible disease."

Coastalitis, as it was known is the 1930s, is gone now. Modern diets and improved healthcare have taken care of it. The term *coastilitis* can now have a new definition. Coastilitis describes the change in America's coastline. There are close to 300 barrier islands off the Atlantic and Gulf coasts of America. Some are mere sandbars; others are relatively large tracts of land containing thousands of acres. Together they form perhaps the most elaborate chain of barrier islands in the world. From New England to Florida, these islands have important functions: providing fishing areas, screening the mainland from big storms, and maintaining estuarial systems. Today, barrier islands provide land for leisure and retirement housing. Handsome entrances to new subdivisions dot the highway from Savannah to Charleston. The closer to the coast, the closer together these developments become. Housing not only has overtaken the mainland's coastline but also most of the barrier islands which lie just off the coast.

A few of Charleston's suburbs are highly developed barrier islands: James Island, Daniel Island, Sullivan's Island, and Isle of Palms. Each day, islanders leave their ocean-side retreats and cross bridges to work in Charleston or North Charleston. The commuters constitute a significant portion of the 644,000 residents in the greater Charleston area.

Developing barrier islands for recreation is nothing new. One island, Jekyll Island, was owned and operated as a resort for the offspring of the Gilded Age robber barons from the late nineteenth century until World War II. These rich Yankees wintered at Jekyll and were known to the locals simply as "the millionaires." But the pace of developing these islands has quickened during the past generation. Tybee, Hilton Head, Edisto, and Kiawah are just some of the familiar names of the more developed barrier islands, but there are plenty of others. Not only have more of these islands become developed, but many islands have changed from rural to urban due to the density of the development. Some barrier islands suffer rows of fast-food restaurants and rush-hour traffic congestion.

Morris Island is a very small island that has no housing or commuter traffic. The only building on the island is a lighthouse. The east side of Morris Island looks out on the Atlantic Ocean. The west side of the island peers toward the big houses lining the coast of James Island. The north side looks across Fort Sumter to Fort Moultrie and Sullivan's Island. The big houses on the developed barrier islands contrast dramatically with the barrenness of the sand and scrub of tiny Morris Island.

Morris Island was almost lost to development. In 2004, a developer bought the island to create twenty building lots on Morris Island's sixty-two acres. It was to be a very exclusive housing project for the wealthy. When public opposition arose, another developer, the Ginn Company, purchased Morris Island for $6.8 million and gave the Trust for Public Land, a non-profit private land conservation organization, an option to purchase the island for $4.5 million. When the group couldn't raise that much money, the Ginn Company reduced the option price. In 2008, the Trust for Public Land purchased Morris Island for $3 million from the Ginn Company. When asked why his company would take such a loss to protect a developable piece of property, Bobby Ginn noted the importance of Morris Island. He added that his company had a number of developments in the Charleston area and then said simply, "We're not a parasite of what's here."

Morris Island is historic. It's the actual location where the Civil War hostilities commenced. Here on January 9, 1861, cadets from the Citadel fired on *The Star of the West* as the ship attempted to come into Charleston's harbor. This was some three months before Rebel artillery started shelling Fort Sumter. Later, the 54th Massachusetts Volunteers, the first African-American unit recruited in the North, attacked Battery Wagner on Morris Island. The attack made famous in the movie *Glory* was a key battle in the Civil War:

> "Fort Wagner was the key to Morris Island, and Morris Island was the key to Fort Sumter. Once the North captured it, they could place batteries there and destroy Fort Sumter, which controlled access to the harbor," says Stephen R. Wise, director of the Parris Island Marine Corps Museum and author of *Gate of Hell: Campaign for Charleston Harbor 1863*.

Morris Island fell. Once it was in Union hands, the Federals began their assault on Fort Sumter and Charleston. In January 1864, some 1,500 shells were fired into Charleston from Union positions on Morris Island. The story of the Immortal 600 began with this shelling. In June, the Confederate commander informed the Yankees that he had placed fifty Union officers including five generals in "commodious quarters in a part of the city occupied by non-combatants." If the Yankees wanted to continue shelling civilian areas of Charleston, they might hit some of their own.

In retaliation, the Union general ordered 600 inmates from the Fort Delaware POW camp be delivered to him. He built an open-air stockade on the northern edge of Morris Island between the Yankees' positions and the Confederate artillery at Fort Sumter. He placed the inmates from Fort Delaware in these stockades, where the POWs became human breastworks defending the Yankees' position. The POWs arrived on September 7 and lived in the open-air stockade on starvation rations until they were moved to Fort Pulaski at Savannah, Georgia, on October 21. They spent the balance of a miserable winter near Savannah before being returned to Fort Delaware. My great-great-grandfather was one of the poor POWs on Morris Island, and I wanted to visit the place.

There is no scheduled service to Morris Island, so I contacted Captain J. Howard Weil to transport me to Morris Island on his boat. It's about a twenty-minute trip from the shore to the island. Landing on the northern side of the western shore is best. It's sheltered somewhat from the ocean currents and has a flat sand area where we could beach the boat.

Captain Weil, my ride to Morris Island

It was a mild January day, but the locals were still talking about the weather of a few weeks before when the temperature had plummeted to an almost unbelievable low of twenty-two degrees. That day, the weatherman forecast a day-time high in the low sixties. We left Charleston harbor at 9:00 a.m. The morning air was brisk.

We landed without a problem, beaching the boat so that we didn't even get our feet wet hopping onto the island. The island is only a few miles long and not very wide. Our plan was to visit the only building on the island, a lighthouse located on the other side. Before leaving the beach, we came upon a sign listing activities prohibited on the island. Captain Weil said the city had posted the sign after a big Fourth of July party.

Welcome to Morris Island

This Historically and Environmentally Significant Park is Open From Dawn to Dusk
*****
In Respect to All Park Users, The Following Activities are Prohibited:
Littering & Vandalism
Use of Alcoholic Beverages and Drugs
Use of Metal Detectors and/or Digging
Failure to Remove Animal Waste
Motorized Vehicles
Unleashed Animals
Fireworks and Weapons
Golfing
Profanity
Camping

I studied the sign and wondered who had compiled the inappropriate activities listed on the sign. Golf is prohibited and, right after that, profanity. Had the July 4th celebrants played golf, and golfing caused the profanity? Or does the list reflect a bureaucrat's views on the sport? Looking down the beach, I asked the captain if any other sports were prohibited on the island. He didn't think so. I followed up by asking if beach bowling was big around here. If not, how does a bowling ball get on a beach? Did the current bring it? If a person brought a bowling ball, did they bring pins? If so, where are the pins? The unexplained beached bowling ball bothered me.

Leaving the bowling ball and the beach, we explored the island. Captain Weil explained that the actual sites of Battery Wagner and the POW stockades are probably under water now. Jetties built a century ago changed the harbor current, and the changed current eroded the north side of the island which faces Fort Sumter. Even today the Fort doesn't seem very far away, especially if you had artillery.

Beach bowling ball

Exploring Morris Island wasn't easy. Wearing a long-sleeved shirt and long pants is advisable even in the summer months because the vegetation is prickly. Near the water line, the island's grasses were sharp, and prickly pears climbed up my socks. The air was dry, the wind constant, and the view of the Atlantic Ocean magnificent. But after thirty minutes of fighting the sharp grasses, we gave up the idea of walking the entire length of the island. It's a narrow island so we simply crossed to the harbor side through the stand of trees running through the center, or high ground, of the island. From there, we walked back to the boat.

Giving up on the island walk within a half mile of starting because of the inhospitable nature of the island gave me pause. In the closing months of 1864, my ancestor had been forced to camp here on starvation rations between two warring armies. I was here voluntarily.

Ft. Sumter from Morris Island

Morris Island stockade during the Civil War (courtesy of the Library of Congress)

Carolina Gold

Charleston would be a great place to end my ten-state Journey of the South. Confident and bustling, Charleston seems to be the dynamic city of the modern South. No doubt the arrival of the Boeing plant has given Charleston a boomtown atmosphere. Boeing's decision to build its new Boeing 787 aircraft in North Charleston required a 600,000-square-foot factory and created an estimated 3,800 jobs for the area. This is no small thing.

Charleston has echoes of a lot of places I had seen. Billy Reid from Florence, Alabama, has a shop on King Street. He has a lot of competition: High-end men's stores such as Ben Silver, Grady Ervin & Company, Berlins for Men, and M. Dumas and Sons are located within a few blocks of Billy's store. He's the new guy here, while Ben, Grady, the Berlins, and the Dumases have been on King Street for years. But I'm sure Billy's holding his own.

The downtown area often is called the Peninsula. Downtown Charleston is the strip of land between the Ashley and Cooper Rivers. It ends where those two rivers meet. Charleston's an old port town, and the port hints of Mobile and New Orleans, especially New Orleans' Garden District. But no one would confuse Charleston with New Orleans. Too many people have told me stories about the time they lived in Charleston and were asked about their families. Those connections still weigh in Charleston, especially if you trace your lineage to one who fought against the Yankee invaders. Your grand-mother's identity still matters here.

The old South vibe from the fine houses south of Broad also brings back memories of that fine lunch with Buzz Harper in Natchez. And remember the vibrancy of Greenville, South Carolina's downtown? Charleston's peninsula has got that in spades. Walking down King Street or its tributaries after dark is not frightening because so many other people are around. The students from the College of Charleston give a walk around Charleston the same funky flavor that the Savannah College of Art and Design gives Charleston's little brother, Savannah's Broughton Street.

And there's the food. Charleston prides itself on food. Locals win James Beard awards each year. In early March they hold a highly regarded Food and Wine Festival. If you are a foodie, Charleston's a great destination.

In Charleston, the term *Creole*, last seen in Louisiana, reappears in Mt. Pleasant, a Charleston suburb, where a Gullah restaurant offers a dish of Gullah Rice. In Opelousas this dish would be called jambalaya.

But I have to say that I don't get the emphasis on shrimp and grits. Every place offers shrimp and grits and wants to tell you that theirs is the best. I don't like grits—never have. And I feel strongly that putting a boiled crustacean on grits is a waste. A minority view perhaps, but I feel strongly about it. Grits are coarsely ground corn which has been cooked with a hot liquid. In Charleston, they add hot milk to milled corn for their grits. They're generally served as a side dish for breakfast, but many places offer shrimp and grits at lunch or dinner.

Here's my advice, gleaned from decades of experience: When someone touts their grits, tell them you don't like grits. They'll invariably agree that grits by themselves aren't very good, but then they'll say, "You should try them with cheese. I'm sure you'll like my cheese grits." Sometimes you hear that grits with red eye gravy, butter, or ham are good. Don't believe it. Adding substances is simply a subterfuge to hide the taste because GRITS JUST DON'T TASTE GOOD.

Charleston can lay claim to something much better—"Carolina gold" rice. Carolina gold is a heritage strand of rice which hearkens back to the old days when South Carolina was the center of rice culture. It's amazing the stuff is still around since the last commercial Carolina gold operation ceased about a hundred years ago. Fifty years ago, Carolina gold rice was almost extinct. In 1985, a Savannah doctor received a sample of the old seed from the USDA gene bank. From that initial shipment, Carolina gold rice has rebounded. It's a long-grain rice with sweet and tender grains and exceptional taste. It's more vibrant than a bowl of white rice. It's healthier too, since many nutrients are lost in processing white rice. Most restaurants using Carolina gold rice note that fact on their menu, so why don't they serve shrimp and gold?

Eating a bowl of Carolina gold with red beans brings memories of the duck festival in Stuttgart or the Cajun Prairie near Opelousas. Rice is hard to beat, especially with shrimp. So pardon me if I can't understand laying shrimp on grits. Moreover, using Carolina gold rice in a serving of hoppin' John or limpin' Susan lets the dish stand on its own—almost like a chicken or shrimp perlou. And getting to eat those dishes is another reason to end the Journey here.

Flatland to Fall Line

Jonathan Daniels didn't end his Journey of years ago in Charleston. He made the terminus Columbia, the last city Sherman destroyed during the Civil War.

The drive from Charleston to Columbia takes about two hours. Leaving the low country, it's a trip across the coastal plain of South Carolina into an area known as the midlands, the start of South Carolina's hill country. In the colonial days of rice and indigo, the coastal plain was South Carolina's wealth, but no longer. This area is poor and looks remarkably like the Mississippi Delta: small towns, based almost entirely on agriculture, which for the last half century, have slowly dried up.

On the way to Columbia, I took a detour to Darlington. A buddy of mine who does good works in Rwanda told me he'd introduce me to a guy from South Carolina he'd met in Africa. In fact, the "guy" had been governor of South Carolina in a previous life. My friend said he'd make a phone call and put us together.

South Carolina politics have always seemed a little unusual to me. A t-shirt slogan I saw in a Chattanooga restaurant sums it up: "South Carolina—Fighting Northern Aggression since 1861." South Carolina's politicians historically have seemed extremely combative: John C. Calhoun and his southern fire-eaters; Wade Hampton and his paramilitary outfit, the redshirts; "Cotton Ed" Smith, who got his nickname by saying in 1908, "Cotton is king and white is supreme." And finally Strom Thurmond, the Dixiecrat, who split from the Democratic Party rather than integrate. Today's South Carolina politicians may be a little less bellicose than their predecessors, but they're still a pretty feisty bunch.

Initially, I wasn't optimistic about the meeting because I had been unsuccessful in getting interviews with "important political figures" such as the junior senator from Virginia, Jim Webb, or the governors of Mississippi and Louisiana. Modern-day politicians have websites and voice mail. It is virtually impossible to talk to a human being in the modern political office unless you precede the call with a campaign contribution or have a contributor call for you.

My friend played phone tag with his friend David Beasley. Once he made contact, David assured him that he'd talk with me. "Just call him," he said. My friend relayed the message just as I arrived in Columbia. So I called him.

David Beasley

He said he was pretty tied up that afternoon, but he could meet me the next day. I explained that I was scheduled to meet the South Carolina attorney general the next day. After a pause, he said that he would make himself available for an hour if I could get to Darlington that afternoon. I asked how far Darlington was from Columbia. "About an hour," he replied. I asked if he was available in an hour. He said, "Make it two hours," and I said, "I'm on my way."

One hour with David morphed into three. He told me he had begun his political career as a Democrat with election as a twenty-one-year-old college student to the South Carolina House of Representatives. Then he became the youngest majority leader in the country in 1987. A few years later, he became a Republican, and soon after ran for governor. He was a one-term governor, which means that something bad happened during that term. Some have said that the video poker industry targeted him for defeat after he tried to ban it. Others have said it was the flap over removing the Confederate flag from over the state house, for which he received a John F. Kennedy Profile in Courage Award.

Whatever the reason, he found himself an ex-governor at the age of forty-one, returning to his home in Society Hill, South Carolina, a village outside of Darlington. He returned to the business world for a while. Now he spends much of his time trying to increase understanding among Christians, Jews, and Arabs with his Center for Global Strategies. David talked at length about bringing foreigners, particularly Arabs, to Darlington. In David's view, foreigners can learn about America by attending a barbecue and driving four-wheelers in rural Darlington, South Carolina. They have fun and leave with a better impression of America than they would have received attending a conference in Washington, New York, or Los Angeles.

He also talked about changes in NASCAR. Darlington has one of the most venerated NASCAR tracks. As a local dignitary, David saw the NASCAR crews up close for a long time. In the old days, drivers social-ized with locals and were considered regular people. He shared a story of a famous driver who left a barbecue to drive to an old country store outside of Darlington. The good ole boy went to see one of his truest fans, giving an autographed hat to the owner's son, who was "a little slow." David said it's hard to describe the young man's face when he saw his hero entering that little general store, coming specifically to see him. Unscripted little things like that probably don't happen much on the modern NASCAR circuit.

As I left Darlington, after three hours with David, I reflected on the politicians I had seen (and not seen) on the trip. The ones I met were open, optimistic, and straightforward. I wondered if tomorrow would be different when I met the attorney general of South Carolina, Henry McMaster. Henry was in the midst of a four-way race for the Republican nomination for governor. In this overwhelmingly Republican state, the nomination is tantamount to election. I had no doubt that a politician in the middle of a gubernatorial election would be full on—the center of the universe, rushed, but controlled—full of sound bites—and, more important, wouldn't have time for stories like David's. I didn't expect to find any of the openness that I received from the ex-pol in Darlington. Was I ever wrong!

The next morning I walked through downtown Columbia to the campaign headquarters of McMaster for Governor a few minutes before my 9 a.m. meeting. Columbia is very much like the other southern capitals. It's a smaller version of Tallahassee and Baton Rouge because, like those two cities, Columbia is home to both the state capital and the state's largest university, the University of South Carolina. Plenty of automobile traffic on the streets and little foot traffic on the sidewalks, just like the other capital cities.

As I expected, he was delayed; I assumed because he was at a fundraising breakfast. Wrong again. He'd been at a staff meeting. He started many campaign days with a staff meeting at the AG's office; despite the pressures of the campaign, he still worked his day job. I was ushered to his small conference room at about 9:30. I overheard his campaign aide tell him that he had a bunch of calls he *absolutely* had to make before lunch. I thought, *Great, my 15-20 minutes are getting cut already.* And wondered what I would do in Columbia with the rest of the morning.

I was not prepared for the next ninety minutes. First, let me say that Henry's accent is a dead ringer for my Uncle Bill's. My Uncle Bill used to say, "It's a liite, briite niiight in nawth Jawja." Henry had the same, absolutely perfect southern drawl. I mean the slow cadence, the lack of r's, the whole package. He referred to the "Coupa rivah" and later mentioned that a woman was a real "doll baybee." At times, I quit thinking about what he was saying and just enjoyed how he said it.

Henry McMaster

Since he had been on the campaign trail, I asked if he knew my friend Lester Galloway or had ever visited Blythe Shoals, South Carolina. He laughed and said that no, he hadn't, but he had been to "Possum King and Sugar Tit."

We talked about South Carolina's latest fight against northern aggression—the Supreme Court case he'd filed against the State of North Carolina for taking water from the Catawba River. I questioned why he hadn't made the oral argument before the Supreme Court. Most lawyers who have that once-in-a-lifetime chance would not pass it to another lawyer. Henry leaned back and smiled. He explained that he really wanted to argue the case, but the preparation would have required too much of his time to do a good job. With all of his other obligations, he concluded that it was too important a case for him to take the argument just to satisfy his ego.

After half an hour or so, a campaign aide lurked outside the conference room. Obviously, we'd gone past the time allotted for the interview. Henry brushed past him walking out of the room to look for a South Carolina map. He needed the map to show me where the Catawba (known as the Wateree in South Carolina) had nearly dried up in the recent drought. He used the map to emphasize why action had to be taken: His people were hurting. As he was making the broader point of the river's importance to the state, the aide finally came into the conference room to take a more active role in moving the campaign along.

I remembered what Mike Beebe, governor of Arkansas, had said about Arkansas politicians—that they needed to be personable to get elected. I suspect that the same can be said for South Carolina.

Epilogue: June 2013

Reviewing the manuscript brings back many great memories of touring the South. But I'm reminded that nothing stays the same. Some changes, like those to Mr. Jefferson's University, Kings Mountain, and Andersonville, are slow and imperceptible. Some changes are dramatic. The Gulf Coast has endured another environmental disaster. Tornados have swept up across Mississippi and Alabama, inflicting significant damage. And in 2011 there was a great flood, but this time the Mississippi River levees held and the flood damage was not material.

Other changes are more organic. It's worth noting that the Cherokee's gambling enterprises in western North Carolina are going great—with 2,300 employees, western North Carolina's largest employer. The casino has been so successful the tribe is contemplating opening a second one in Murphy, nearer Atlanta and the Georgia state line.

Mayor Littlefield's term as Chattanooga's mayor ended recently. He proposed and implemented, by a narrow margin, a tax increase. This action sparked outrage in some quarters who then sought to have him recalled. The recall movement was unsuccessful but his critics followed him through the end of his term.

In Nashville, Third Sunday is no more. In the summer of 2012, after 112 straight months of potluck dinners, Doak Turner's house sold and he moved to another part of town. Struggling songwriters and musicians have one place fewer to meet and network. Last time I was in Nashville,

I dropped into Ellendale's, a restaurant near the airport, and took in Tom Shinness' show. I was reminded how talented a musician he is.

Other updates to note: Buz Harper died in Natchez on February 17, 2011, at the age of 74 after a brief battle with cancer. In May of that year, the ferry boat between St. Francisville and New Roads terminated service. Now the road to the old ferry ends at a boat launch, so if you're not familiar with the area or are relying on a GPS system, you could drive right into the Mississippi River.

The Great Southern golf course is still holding on. In fact, it's more than holding on. A new clubhouse is under construction, but the Board reports a "biblical level" infestation of mole crickets. In June 2013, they celebrated 105 years of operation.

As I travel through central Alabama, I still try to locate a Milo's hamburger stand. There was some litigation with Milo's Tea Company. Evidently, the hamburger stands started selling tea that was not Milo's Tea in their Milo's cups. In March of 2013, the two entities settled their dispute and Milo's tea once again fills Milo's tea cups.

Things are still going gangbusters at Sweet Grass Dairy. They've moved the store that was once on the highway to downtown Thomasville. They've also refined their operations to cows—no more happy goats.

My son, Will, graduated from UT and moved to Charleston to take a job with the Boeing Company, helping to build the new airplanes. They announced a further expansion which will add an additional 2,000 jobs to their North Charleston plant.

Henry McMaster lost his bid to become governor of South Carolina and, after his term as attorney general ended, returned to the private practice of law in Columbia. Before then, however, he settled the dispute with North Carolina without having to get a decision from the Supreme Court on the merits. The settlement lays out a process for assessing any future water transfers and sets standards for reducing water use during droughts.

I'm sure that I've missed some changes somewhere on this 4,600-mile Journey. A good excuse to go back and do it all again.

Notes on Sources

Like so many other things in my life, this project was never really planned. It just sort of spread into my life like Johnson grass. As I explained in the Introduction, I read an old book, became intrigued with the map contained in the old book, and then set out to see the places on the map. It was only after I began traveling that I began any formal research or "scholarship." (The term seems presumptuous because I was only trying to understand what I was seeing.) From there I kept reading. I don't consider or intend this work to be journalism, history, or scholarship. I've recounted my experiences on the road; to these direct experiences, I've added such additional material as I felt was necessary to complete the picture.

I have refrained from footnotes or endnotes tying down the source of each "fact" outside my direct experience. But that doesn't mean I don't owe people for their contributions. I borrow from Peter Applebome, who writes in the opening of his wonderful book *Dixie Rising*:

> But if this is largely a work of journalism, it is informed throughout by the history, scholarship and journalism of others. It seems a little pretentious and contrary to the spirit of the book to end with formal footnotes or endnotes....It would be churlish and misleading not to acknowledge the enormous debt I have to others, both in the specifics of this book and what I've learned from them over the years. As a result, I've chosen to acknowledge my sources below in a form that I hope will allow me to credit those whose work helped inform and shape my own reporting and writing.

I researched for two reasons. The first reason was to discover interesting events or to meet interesting people when I came to these places. This research required significant traipsing though the World Wide Web. The second reason for research was to provide context for what I saw. For example, Cannon Mills and Kannapolis or Loray Mills and Ella May Wiggins might have little meaning without some background or history. Similarly, Copperhill, Hillhouse, the sunken lands of Arkansas, and the Little Grand Canyon in Georgia are interesting to see, but more interesting with a little background information. I've listed the major sources in the bibliography to acknowledge those whose efforts made mine easier and also to help those readers who want additional information. If there is a source I have overlooked, I apologize. Any error is entirely mine and is completely unintentional.

Early in my Internet research, I came across this thing called Wikipedia. It proved to be an invaluable resource for things great and small. As Mr. Applebome put it, it would be "churlish and misleading" to limit them to a few footnotes. (I assume Wikipedia is a "them" and not an "it." Maybe I ought to look it up in Wikipedia.) I know that it can't be beat when you need to know the number of steps in a zydeco dance, the amount of outmigration from Greenville, Mississippi, in the first decade of the twenty-first century, or any other of a number of facts.

Most of the book arises directly from my experiences on a ten-state, eighty-two-city Journey. I've reported the significant experiences, or should I say the most memorable ones? I know this: Every traveler relies on the kindness of strangers. Some of the people I met made the Journey a little easier. Others made it a little brighter. From the people who are paid minimum wage to help, such as motel clerks and waitresses, to people upon whom you impose to ask directions, to those with whom you intersect for a few moments on your way, countless people made a journey memorable. These people provide the atmosphere, the tone for much of the story I tell.

An example: In Raleigh, North Carolina, I peered into the front window of a barbershop. The barbershop's clientele was largely, if not entirely, African American. Attached to the window was a chart of thirty or so of the haircuts offered. There was a picture of each haircut, with a caption underneath. I became so engrossed in the various styles offered that I failed to notice the proprietor had sidled up beside me.

He said with a smile, "For ten bucks, I'll give you a Mohawk. Or how about a High Fade? I'll give you a cut that your friends won't believe."

I said, "I'd do it for my friends, but my wife back in Little Rock might not understand me coming home with a High Fade."

Hearing I was from Little Rock, he proceeded to quiz me about Bill Clinton, Nolan Richardson (the Arkansas basketball coach who had been fired), and race relations in my part of the South. He seemed genuinely interested in my little corner of the world. I discovered he was an NC State basketball fan when one of his friends/customers, a former fan of the Duke Blue Devils, interjected himself into the conversation. The barber's friend said that the last time Duke won the national championship, he went to the campus that night to join in the celebration. But the campus was closed to outsiders, and he couldn't join the celebration. He declared that he thought the closing was racist—that they meant to keep him and other local blacks from the celebration on the mostly white campus. The barber gently poked fun at his buddy. He said that Duke closed its campus to keep out outsiders, both white and black. It wasn't racist, he explained, not wanting any poor people around. He said, "Rich people don't really see color when they try to keep the poor at bay." Before he could continue, he got called away by a co-worker. But first he shook my hand and said that next time I was in Raleigh, his offer of "a High Fade for ten bucks" would still be good.

The barber obviously didn't cut many white people's hair, but he was not above teasing a balding, middle-aged passerby. Conversations like this happened in all ten states. I didn't try to discover these people's names or anything else about them. I took the conversations as they were intended: strangers just being friendly to another stranger. These people deserve credit and my thanks.

Sources

Books

Applebome, Peter. *Dixie Rising*. New York: Harcourt, Brace & Co., 1997.

Arnold, Dean W. *Old Money, New South: The Spirit of Chattanooga*. Chattanooga: Chattanooga Historical Foundation, 2006.

Ashmore, Harry S. *Epitaph for Dixie*. New York: W.W. Norton & Company, 1958.

Blackmon, Douglas A. *Slavery by Another Name*. New York: Doubleday, 2008.

Blount, Roy, Jr. *Crackers*. Athens: University of Georgia Press, 1998.

Bolsterli, Margaret Jones. *During Wind and Rain: The Jones Family Farm in the Arkansas Delta, 1848-2006*. Fayetteville: University of Arkansas Press, 2008.

Bordewich, Fergus M. *Bound for Canaan*. New York: Harper Collins, 2005.

Bragg, Rick. *All Over But the Shoutin'*. New York: Pantheon Books, 1997.

Calhoun, Sim C., and David G. Sansing. *Natchez: An Illustrated History*. Natchez: Plantation Publishing Co., 1992.

Carter, Hodding, and Carl H. Pforzheimer. *Southern Legacy*. Baton Rouge: Louisiana State University Press, 1950.

Carter, Jimmy. *An Hour Before Daylight: Memories of a Rural Childhood*. New York: Simon & Schuster, 2001.

Cash, W. J. *The Mind of the South*. New York: Alfred A. Knopf, Inc., 1941.

Cobb, James C. *Away Down South: A History of Southern Identity*. New York: Oxford University Press, 2005.

Crawford, Alan Pell. *Twilight at Monticello: The Final Years of Thomas Jefferson*. New York: Random House, 2008.

Crutchfield, James A. *It Happened in Georgia*. 2nd ed. Guilford: The Globe Pequot Press, 2002.

Cunningham, Ray. *Southern Talk: A Disappearing Language*. Asheville: Bright Mountain Books, 1993.

Curtis, Christopher Paul. *The Watsons Go to Birmingham, 1963*. New York: Yearling, 1995.

Dabney, Joseph Earl. *Mountain Spirits: A Chronicle of Corn Whiskey from King James' Ulster Plantation to America's Appalachians and the Moonshine Life*. Asheville: Bright Mountain Books, 1974.

Dameron, J. David. *King's Mountain: The Defeat of the Loyalists, October 7, 1780*. Cambridge: De Capo Press, 2003.

Daniels, Jonathan. *A Southerner Discovers the South*. New York: Macmillan, 1938.

———. *Tar Heels: A Portrait of North Carolina*. New York: Macmillan, 1938.

Davis, Allison, Burleigh B. Gardner, and Mary R. Gardner. *Deep South: A Social Anthropological Study of Caste and Class*. Chicago: University of Chicago Press, 1941.

Dinsmore, John Walker. *The Scotch-Irish in America*. Chicago: Winona Publishing Co., 1906.

Egerton, John. *Speak Now Against the Day: The Generation Before the Civil Rights Movement in the South*. New York: Knopf, 1994.

Epps, Garrett. *The Shad Treatment*. Charlottesville: University of Virginia Press, 1997.

Erskine, Jim and Susan. *The Southerner's Instruction Book*. Gretna: Pelican Publishing, 1994.

Faragher, Scott. *Chattanooga: Best of the Lookout City*. Lookout Mountain: Milton Publishing, 2001.

Faris, John T. *Seeing the Sunny South*. Philadelphia, London: J. B. Lippincott Co., 1921.

Fisher, David Hacker. *Albion's Seed: Four British Folkways in America*. New York: Oxford University Press, 1989.

Gannon, Michael. *Florida: A Short History*. Rev. ed. Gainesville: University Press of Florida, 2003.

Gatewood, Willard, and Jeannie M. Whayne. *The Arkansas Delta: Land of Paradox*. Fayetteville: University of Arkansas Press, 1993.

Gibbs, Chad. *God & Football: Faith & Fanaticism in the SEC*. Grand Rapids: Zondervan, 2010.

Greenspan, Anders. *Creating Colonial Williamsburg*. 2nd ed. Chapel Hill: University of North Carolina Press, 2009.

Hare, Julianne. *Tallahassee: A Capital City History*. Charleston: Arcadia Publishing, 2002, 2005.

Harrell, Virginia Calohan. *Vicksburg and the River*. Vicksburg: Harrell Publications, 1986, 2004.

Helferich, Gerard. *High Cotton: Four Seasons in the Mississippi Delta*. New York: Counterpoint, 2007.

Hemphill, Paul. *Lovesick Blues: The Life of Hank Williams*. New York: Penguin Group, 2006.

Hendrickson, Paul. *Sons of Mississippi: A Story of Race and Its Legacy*. New York: Alfred A. Knopf, 2003.

Hill, Jimmy, and Billy Warren. *A Walk Down Walnut*. Florence: Lambert Book House, 2005.

Hines, Barbara, and Preston Russell. *Savannah: A History of Her People Since 1733*. Savannah: Frederic C. Beil, 1992.

Hirschman, Elizabeth C. *Melungeons: The Last Lost Tribe in America*. Macon: Mercer University Press, 2005.

Horwitz, Tony. *Confederates in the Attic*. New York: Random House, 1998.

Huffman, Alan. *Sultana: Surviving Civil War, Prison, and the Worst Maritime Disaster in American History*. New York: Harper Collins, 2009.

Jenkins, Sally, and John Stauffer. *The State of Jones: The Small Southern County that Seceded from the Confederacy*. New York: Anchor Books, 2010.

Joslyn, Mauriel Phillips. *Captives Immortal*. Shippensburg: White Mane Publishing Co., 1996.

Link, Albert N. *A Generosity of Spirit: The Early History of the Research Triangle Park*: Research Triangle Foundation of North Carolina, 1995.

McGill, Ralph. *The South and the Southerner*. Boston: Little, Brown & Co., 1959.

McKay, John. *It Happened in Atlanta*. Guilford: Morris Book Publishing, 2011.

McIlhenny, E. A. *The Alligator's Life History*. Lawrence: Society for the Study of Amphibians and Reptiles, 1976, 1987.

McWhinney, Grady. *Cracker Culture: Celtic Ways in the Old South*. Tuscaloosa: University of Alabama Press, 1988.

Mendoza, Alexander. *Confederate Struggle for Command*. College Station: Texas A&M University Press, 2008.

Meyer, Duane Gilbert. *The Highland Scots of North Carolina*. Chapel Hill: University of North Carolina Press, 1957.

Naipaul, V. S. *A Turn in the South*. New York: Knopf/Random House, 1989.

Nickell, Joe. *The Kentucky Mint Julep*. Lexington: University of Kentucky Press, 2003.

O'Briant, Don. *Backroads Buffet and Country Cafes*. 2nd ed. Winston-Salem: John F. Blair, 1999.

Percy, William Alexander. *Lanterns on the Levee*. Baton Rouge: Louisiana State University Press, 2002.

Pillsbury, Richard, and Charles Reagan Wilson. *Geography*. 2nd ed. Chapel Hill: University of North Carolina Press, 2006.

Poland, Tom, and Phil Sawyer. *Save the Last Dance For Me*. Columbia: University of South Carolina Press, 2012.

Pomerantz, Gary. *Where Peachtree Meets Sweet Auburn*. New York: Penguin Books, 1996, 2009.

Price, William S., Jr. *The Bill of Rights and North Carolina*. Madison: Madison House Publications, 1991.

Reed, Dale Volberg, and John Shelton Reed. *1001 Things Everyone Should Know About the South*. New York: Broadway Books, 1996, 2002.

Reed, Julia. *The House on First Street: My New Orleans Story*. New York: Harper Collins, 2008.

Salecker, Gene Eric. *Disaster on the Mississippi*. Annapolis: Naval Institute Press, 1996.

Salmond, John A. *Gastonia, 1929: The Story of the Loray Mill Strike*. Chapel Hill: University of North Carolina Press, 1995.

Salter, Charles E. *The Georgia Rambler*. Charleston: History Press, 2011.

Sancton, Thomas. *Song for My Fathers: A New Orleans Story in Black and White*. New York: Other Press, 2010.

Segars, J. H. *Andersonville: The Southern Perspective*. Gretna: Pelican Publishing, 2001.

Seymour, Digby Gordon. *Divided Loyalties*. 3rd ed. Knoxville: The East Tennessee Historical Society, 2002.

Smith, Mack Allen. *Honky-Tonk Addict*. Birmingham: Colonial Press, Inc., 1996.

Stevenson, Mark Allen. *Tennessee Valley Authority in Vintage Postcards*. Charleston: Arcadia Publishing, 2005.

Taylor, Joe Gray. *Eating, Drinking & Visiting in the South*. Baton Rouge: Louisiana State University Press, 1982.

Taylor, Michael W. *Tar Heels: How North Carolina Got Their Nickname*. Raleigh: North Carolina Office of Archives & History, 1999.

Thompson, James C., II. *The Birth of Virginia's Aristocracy*. Alexandria: Common Wealth Books, 2010.

Travis, Clay. *Dixieland Delight: A Football Season on the Road in the Southeastern Conference*. New York: Harper Entertainment, 2007.

Vann, Barry. *Rediscovering the South's Celtic Heritage*. Johnson City: Overmountain Press, 2004.

Weary, Dolphus, and William Hendricks. *I Ain't Comin' Back*. Wheaton: Tyndale House Publishers, 1997.

Webb, James H. *Born Fighting: How the Scots-Irish Shaped America*. New York: Broadway Books, 2004.

Whayne, Jeanie. *Delta Empire: Lee Wilson and the Transformation of Agriculture in the New South*. Baton Rouge: Louisiana State University Press, 2011.

Wilder, Roy, Jr. *You All Spoken Here*. Raleigh: Gourd Hollow Press, 1977.

Other Sources by Chapter

The Third Battle of Manassas

"Disney (B): The Third Battle of Bull Run." Harvard Business School. Publication No. 9-898-019. (September 27, 2000).

Nolin, Elizabeth M. "Historic American Engineering Record." Arlington Memorial Bridge. HAER No. DC-7. (1988).

Pollard, Trip. "A New Generation of Boondoggles." *Bacon's Rebellion* (November 28, 2005). Online at www.baconsrebellion.com/Issues05/11-28/Pollard.php.

"The Proposed Manassas National Battlefield Park Bypass (Battlefield Bypass)." *Prince William Conservation Alliance*. Online at www.pwconserve.org/issues/transportation/Battlefield%20Bypass/index.html.

"Washington's First Traffic Jam: Some Things Never Change." *Washington Post*, June 5, 2002.

Zenzen, Joan M. "Producing the Pasts of a National Park." *Perspectives on History* (February 2000). Online at www.historians.org/perspectives/issues/2000/0002/0002pub1.cfm.

Polo Place

"Colonial Parkway," National Park Service. Online at http://www.nps.gov/colo/parkway.htm.

Crews, Ed. "Tavern Music." *CW Journal* (Winter 2003–04).

"Ideological Origins of the Williamsburg Restoration." American Studies at the University of Virginia. Online at http://xroads.virginia.edu/~UG99/hall/AMSTUD.html.

"Organized Foxhunting?" *Foxhunt Virginia*. Online at www.foxhuntva.com/web/index.php?option=com_content&task=view&id=18.

Rozelle, Ritchie. "Horse, Humans and Long Hammers." *Southern States*. Online at http://southernstates.com/articles/eq/features/fall2009_polouva.aspx.

"Welcome to Roseland Polo." Original Roseland document.

What's a Cavalier?

"Becoming Virginians." *Virginia Historical Society*. Online at www.vahistorical.org/sva2003/virginians.htm.

"Grand Opening of Expanded Virginia Museum of Fine Arts." Museum Publicity, May 2, 2010. Online at http://museumpublicity.com/2010/05/02/grand-opening-of-expanded-virginia-museum-of-fine-arts/.

"Memorial Building." United Daughters of the Confederacy. Online at http://www.hqudc.org/facilities/index.html.

"Neat Stuff Inside." Virginia Historical Society brochure, printed 2009.

"Serving Virginia, Looking Out to the World: The Development of the Virginia Museum of Fine Arts." Online at http://www.vmfa.mediaroom.st.va.us/history.html.

What's a Tar Heel?

"Old North State and Tar Heel State." *Thomas' Legion: The 69th North Carolina Regiment.* Online at http://www.thomaslegion.net/nc.html.

Powell, William S. "What's in a Name?: Why We're All Called Tar Heels." *Tar Heel Magazine* (March 1982). Online at http://alumni.unc.edu/article.aspx?sid=3516.

"What's a Tar Heel?" University of North Carolina at Chapel Hill. Online at http://www.unc.edu/about/history-and-traditions/whats-a-tar-heel/.

The Research Triangle

Weddle, Rick L. "Summary of Remarks and Supporting Data Panel I: North Carolina's Changing Economy." Presented to Hearing on China's Impact on the North Carolina Economy: Winners and Losers. University of North Carolina at Chapel Hill, September 6, 2007.

Weddle, Rick L., Elizabeth Rooks, and Tina Valdecanas. "Research Triangle Park: Evolution and Renaissance." Presented to 2006 IASP World Conference, June 2006.

Trains, Furniture, and Krispy Kreme

Arai, Juliette. "Krispy Kreme Doughnut Corporation Records, ca. 1937–1997." National Museum of American History. Online at http://amhistory.si.edu/archives/d7594.htm.

"High Point Museums NC," High Point Museum. Online at http://www.highpointmuseum.org/HPfurniturecompanies.htm.

O'Sullivan, Kate. "Kremed! The Rise and Fall of Krispy Kreme is a Cautionary Tale of Ambition, Greed, and Inexperience." *CFO Magazine* (June 1, 2005).

Patterson, Donald W. "A Billion Dollar Boon: 100 Years of High Point Furniture Market." *Greensboro News-Record*, April 25, 2009.

Towel Town No More

"$700 Million Biotech Campus Envisioned for Kannapolis," North Carolina Biotechnology Center. Online at http://www.ncbiotech.org/news_and_events/industry_news/700_million_biotech_campus.html.

Fisher, Hugh. "Fieldcrest-Cannon Reunion Draws Hundreds." *Kannapolis Citizen*, May 28, 2008.

Ford, Emily. "From Textiles to DNA: First Pillowtex Employee to Land A Job at N.C. Research Campus Now A Lab Technician." *Kannapolis Citizen*, April 23, 2009.

———. "N.C. Research Campus Changes Landscape." *Kannapolis Citizen*, February 24, 2009.

———. "No End to N.C. Research Campus Hurdles." *Salisbury Post*, February 27, 2010.

Lester, Debbie. "The Dale Trail Revisited." *Bella Online–The Voice of Women*. Online at http://www.bellaonline.com/articles/art2624.asp.

"Pillowtex: Five Years Later—The History and Culture of Kannapolis." *Independent Tribune*. Online at http://independenttribune.net/index.php/pillowtex/article/part_1.

Sister City

Campbell, Malcolm. "Catawba River Rising." *Charlotte Magazine*. Online at www.charlottemagazine.com/core/pagetools.php?pageid=12192.

"Catawba River Interbasin Transfer Controversy Resolved." *Lincoln Tribune*, January 20, 2010.

Copeland, Larry. "Drought Eases, Water Wars Persist." *USA Today*, March 18, 2008.

Marks, John. "Drought Improves to Stage 2." *Lake Wylie Pilot*, January 14, 2009.

———. "Experts: 'Drought Plan Worked.'" *Lake Wylie Pilot*, April 15, 2009.

———. "IBT Water Wars Settled in Compromise." *Lake Wylie Pilot*, January 27, 2010.

North Carolina Department of Environment and Natural Resources. *No Drought in North Carolina for First Time in Two Years*. Press release, May 14, 2009.

They Glue Lug Nuts on Wheels

Berkowitz, Bonnie. "Fast-Paced Action in NASCAR Pits." *Washington Post*, May 12, 2008.

Bernstein, Viv. "On Pit Row, It's First and Tire Change." *New York Times*, August 15, 2006.

Dawalt, Larry. "Success Measured in Seconds for Heath Cherry." *Gaston Gazette*, October 19, 2006.

Fish, Mike. "In the Pits." *CNN Sports Illustrated*, May 7, 2001.

"History of NASCAR." NASCAR. Online at http://www.nascar.com/news/features/history/.

Kruse, Michael. "After the Crash." *Charlotte Magazine* (May 2009).

LeMasters, Ron, Jr. "Post-Race Prize Money: Who Gets What." NASCAR. Online at http://nascar.printthis.clickability.com/pt/cpt?action=cpt&title=NASCAR.com.

Wolfe, Tom. "The Last American Hero is Junior Johnson. Yes!" *Esquire* (March 1965).

Ella May's Ghost

Barrett, Michael. "Developers Buy More Time for Restoring Loray Mill." *Gaston Gazette*, February 3, 2009.

———. "Loray Mill Developers Still Fighting to Clear Financial Hurdles." *Gaston Gazette*, November 20, 2009.

"Ella May Wiggins." University of North Carolina Library. Online at http://sites.unc.edu/storyforms/gastonia/ella.html.

Graham, Nicholas. "June 1929—Strike at Loray Mill." University of North Carolina Library, North Carolina Collection, June 2004. Online at http://www.lib.unc.edu/ncc/ref/nchistory/jun2004/index.html.

Jackson, Daniel. "Loray Mill Project Close Again, but Also Facing a Lawsuit." *Gaston Gazette*, June 9, 2009.

Mock, Gary N. "Gaston County, North Carolina." *Textile Industry History*. Online at http://www.textilehistory.org/GastonCountyNC.html.

Murray, Jonathan. "Textile Strike of 1934." North Carolina History Project. Online at http://www.northcarolinahistory.org/encyclopedia/284/entry.

"Preserve America Community: Gastonia, North Carolina." *Preserve America*. Online at http://www.preserveamerica.gov/gastoniaNC.html.

Turbyfill, Dianne. "Loray Mill Rocks Out!" *Gaston Gazette*, February 9, 2010.

Weisbord, Vera Buch. "Gastonia, 1929 Strike at the Loray Mill." *Southern Exposure* (Winter 1974).

America's First Civil War Battle

"A Walk in the Woods." *Overmountain Victory National Historic Trail* (2005): 1–8.

Hub-Bub in the Hub City

Applebome, Peter. "Arts in America: The Semi-Pros Thrive on Homemade CD's and Prizes." *New York Times*, May 27, 1999.

Brown, Ben. "Singularly Spartanburg." South Carolina: People and Places. *Southern Living*, 26–27.

"Hub City Beginnings." *Hub City*. Online at http://hubcity.org/press/about/.

Lane, John. Comment on Larry McGehee, "Cornbread & Sushi at Wofford." *Southern Seen* (December 30, 2006). Online at http://kudzutelegraph.com/node/149.

Lang, Jameelah. "Hub-Bub Writer-in-Residence Shares Her Experiences." *Herald-Journal* (March 21, 2010).

Sharbaugh, Patrick. "Unscripted: Hub-bub Hullabaloo." *Charleston City Paper*, November 9, 2005.

Downtown New South

"Greenville Textile Heritage Designs." Zazzle. Online at http://www.zazzle.com/india38.

Henry, Bryan. "Model for Montgomery: Revitalizing Downtown 3/3." *WSFA 12 News*, November 9, 2009.

The Mountains

"Brevard North Carolina Officially Named 'White Squirrel Capital of the World.'" Press release. PRWeb, May 10, 2005. Online at www.prweb.com/releases/2005/05/prweb238329.htm.

"Caesar's Head State Park." South Carolina State Parks. Online at http://www.south-carolinaparks.com.

"December 1804: The Walton War." University of North Carolina Library. Online at http://www.lib.unc.edu/ncc/ref/nchistory/dec2006/index.html.

"History of the White Squirrel." Brevard North Carolina. Online at
http://www.brevandnc.org/historyws.php.

"History of the White Squirrel: White Squirrels-Brevard." White Squirrels. Online at
www.whitesquirrels.com/cart/index.php?main_page=page&id=2&chapter=0.

Jackson, Dot. "History: The Last Resort." *The Magazine of Greenville* (July 2009).

"Lions and Tigers and...White Squirrels?" White Squirrel Institute. Online at
http://www.whitesquirrelinstitute.whitesquirrelfestival.com/whitesquirrels.htm.

"The Walton War." Chattooga Conservancy. Online at
www.chatoogariver.org/index.php?req=walton&quart=W2005.

Cashiers

"High Hampton Inn—A Historic North Carolina Inn." High Hampton Inn & Country
Club. Online at http://www.highhamptoninn.com/history.aspx.

Letter from Jonathan Daniels to Josephine Daniels. Jonathan Daniels Papers.
Collection Number 03466. Southern Historical Collection, University of North
Carolina at Chapel Hill.

Franklin

"Franklin & Nantahala North Carolina Visitor & Relocation Guide." Franklin Area
Chamber of Commerce (2009).

The Smoky Mountains

"Cherokee Indians: Eastern Cherokee Indians." Cherokee-Indians. Online at
http://www.cherokee-indians.com/history-eastern-cherokee-indian.

"Harrah's Cherokee Casino & Hotel in North Carolina Breaks Ground on New 532-Room
Guest Tower." Harrah's Cherokee Casino & Hotel. Press release, July 10, 2009.

Walton, Marsha. "The Business of Gambling." CNN, July 6, 2005. Online at
http://www.cnn.com/2005/US/07/06/cnn25.top25.gambling/.

Norris, the Planned Community

"From the New Deal to a New Century." Tennessee Valley Authority. Online at
http://www.tva.gov/abouttva/history.htm.

"Teaching American History—Norris Historic District." Middle Tennessee State
University. Online at http://frank.mtsu.edu.

Hard-bitten Land

Cochran, Kim. "The Copper Basin." Georgia Mineral Society. Online at http://www.gamineral.org/copperbasin.htm.

Dixon, Chris. "Up From the Mines in Tennessee." *New York Times*, December 14, 2007.

"Ocoee Whitewater." Tennessee Valley Authority. Online at www.tva.gov/river/recreation/wwc.htm.

"Polk County." Blue Ridge Smoky Mtn. Highlander. Online at http://www.theblueridgehighlander.com/polk_county_tennessee/index.html.

Chattanooga Rebound

"Chattanooga Coca-Cola History." Chattanooga Coca-Cola Bottling Co. United, Inc. Online at http://chattanoogacocacola.com/.

Naylor, Kenneth. "About Face: How Social Capital Changed Chattanooga." Next American City n/k/a New City. Online at http://www.americancity.org.

"The Road to Chattanooga," Volkswagen Group of America. Online at http://www.volkswagengroupamerica.com.

Alabama Wholesale

"Alabama Tornado Database." National Weather Service Archives—Birmingham, AL. Online at http://www.srh.noaa.gov/bmx/?n=tornadodb_main.

"Sustainable Life—Sustainable Style." Alabama Chanin. Online at http://www.alabamachanin.com.

Driving the Natchez Trace Parkway

Gardner, Malcolm. Excerpt from *The Natchez Trace–An Historical Parkway*, National Park Service—The Regional Review, April 1939. Online at http://www.cr.nps.gov/history/online_books/regional_review/vol2-4d.htm.

"Natchez Trace Parkway Arches are Complete." History.com. Online at http://www.history.com/this-day-in-history/natchez-trace-parkway-arches-are-complete.

Nashville Hootenanny

"The Guitartown Project," Gibson Guitar Corporation. Online at www.gibson.com/GuitarTownWebsite/.

"The Steel Guitar—A Short History." *Thanks for the Music—Country Music News.* Online at http://thanksforthemusic.com/history/old/steelguitar.html.

What's a Julep?

Cohen, David. *God Shakes Creation.* Hampton & Brothers: 1935.

Day Trip to Arkansas

"Dyess (Mississippi County)." Encyclopedia of Arkansas History & Culture. Online at http://www.encyclopediaofarkansas.net/encyclopedia/entry-detail.aspx?search=1&entryID=2397.

"Historic Earthquakes: New Madrid Earthquakes 1811–1812," U.S. Geological Survey, April 1974. Online at http://earthquake.usgs.gov/earthquakes/states/events/1811_overview.php.

"Southern Tenant Farmers' Union." Encyclopedia of Arkansas History & Culture. Online at http://www.encyclopediaofarkansas.net/encyclopedia/entry-detail.aspx?entryID=35.

State of Arkansas v. Hatchie Coon Hunting & Fishing Club, Inc. 372 Ark. 547, 279 S.W.3d 56 (2008).

The Delta in Mississippi

Montgomery, Haley. "A Delta Story: Sherard Plantation." Resources for Health and Economic Renewal in the Mississippi River Delta. Online at http://deltadirections.org/delta_region/.

Moser, Christopher. "County School Board Votes to Close Sherard." *Clarksville Press Register*, January 15, 2010.

Smith, Fred. "Cooperative Farming in Mississippi." *Mississippi History Now* (November 2004). Online at http://mshistorynow.mdah.state.ms.us/articles/219/cooperative-farming-in-mississippi.

Cosmopolitan Helena

"Five Pillars." KIPP: The Knowledge is Power Program. Online at http://www.kipp.org/our-approach/five-pillars.

Lambe, Will. "Small Towns: Big Ideas." *Case Studies in Small Town Community Economic Development.* N.C. Rural Economic Development Center (December 2008).

Nelson, Rex. "KIPP Graduation Day." *Arkansas Democrat-Gazette*, May 21, 2010.

Sides, Hampton. "Anyone For a Dip?" *Live Bravely Outside* (October 1, 2007). Online at http://outsideonline.com/.

"Quapaws—River Rat." Quapaw Canoe Company. Online at http://www.island63.com/quapaws-river-rat.cfm.

"What is Crowley's Ridge?" Southeast Missouri State University—Regional History. Online at http://www2.semo.edu/regionalhist/FAQ_ridge.html.

Duck Gumbo

Capooth, Wayne. "Stuttgart: Where Mallard is King." *Delta Waterfowl Magazine*. Online at http://www.deltawaterfowl.org.

Water, Water Everywhere

"In Hot Water." Hot Springs National Park Arkansas, 1980.

"Plato, Texas County, MO is the 2010 Center of America." United States Census Bureau. Online at http://www.census.gov.

Nitta Yuma

"Delta and Pine Land Company." Funding Universe—Company Histories. Online at http://www.fundinguniverse.com/company-histories/delta-and-pine-land-company-history/.

Ewing, Earl, Jr. "A History of the Delta and Pine Land Company." Washington County Historical Society, January 28, 1979. Online at http://web.tecinfo.com/~wchip-man/washco_hist/history_of_the_dpl_company.htm.

Gaul, Gilbert M., and Dan Morgan. "A Slow Demise in the Delta." *Washington Post*, June 20, 2007.

McKinney, Wanda. "Why There Are So Many Great Mississippi Writers." *Southern Living* (June 20, 2008).

"Nitta Yuma." Alan Huffman Blog, March 25, 2011. Online at http://www.alanhuff-man.blogspot.com/2011/03/nitta-yuma.html.

A Coffee Shop in Vicksburg

Gerald, Paul. "Good and Old." *Memphis Flyer* (May 4, 1998).

"How the Attic Came to Be." The Attic Gallery—Vicksburg, Mississippi. Online at http://atticgallery.homestead.com/atticstory~ns4.html.

"Lesley K. Silver." The Attic Gallery—Vicksburg, Mississippi. Online at http://attic-gallery.homestead.com/silver.html.

Mississippi Praying

"Jerry Mitchell's Entry and Biography." *Clarion Ledger*. Online at http://www.clarion-ledger.com/apps/pbcs.dll/article.

Mitchell, Jerry. "The Preacher and the Klansman." *Clarion Ledger*, March 24, 1998.

Ricchiardi, Sherry. "Out of the Past." *American Journalism Review* (April/May 2005).

"*Switchfoot Email," Lollapalooza 2010, 'Sabotage' Switchfoot Style, and More!*" Online at http://wereawakening.blogspot.com/2010/04.

Not a Soul in Sight

Elliott, Jack D., Jr. "Paving the Trace." *Journal of Mississippi History* (Fall 2007).

Janiskee, Bob. "Park History: Exploring the National Parkways." National Parks Traveler. Online at http://www.nationalparkstraveler.com.

The Rose Lady Comes to Camellia

Dardick, Karen L. "Camellia Crusaders." *Garden & Gun Magazine* (December 2008/January 2009).

———. "A Magnolia State of Mind." *Los Angeles Times*, February 11, 2007.

Gaudet, Mary Jane. "Join Master Gardeners at Festival." *Natchez Democrat*, September 16, 2008.

Grayson, Walt. "Look Around MS: Symphony of Gardens." *WLBT* 3 (April 25, 2008). Online at http://www.wlbt.com/global/story.asp?s=8228263&ClientType=Printable.

Stallcup, Katie. "National Geographic Includes Natchez." *Natchez Democrat*, October 7, 2007.

The Salon at Ravennaside

"Characters of Natchez, MS: Buzz Harper." Tanner C. Latham Blog, April 5, 2008. Online at http://tanfansunite.blogspot.com/2008/04/characters-of-natchez-ms-buzz-harper.html.

Latham, Tanner C. "The Allure of Natchez." *Southern Living* (March 2009).

"Nicholas Cage Buys House in New Orleans' French Quarter for $3,450,000." Berg Properties. Online at http://www.bergproperties.com/.

McDonald's Comes to St. Francisville

"CDF Opposes Big Box Retail." West Feliciana Parish Community Foundation. Online at http://www.stfrancisville.org/index.php?option=com_content&task=view&id=7&Itemid=2.

Clark, Steve. "Expecting to Fly." *Greater Baton Rouge Business Report*. Online at http://businessreport.com/article/20081215/BUSINESSREPORT0101/312169974.

Davis, Susan G. *The Felicianas*. Folk Life in the Florida Parishes. Online at http://www.louisianafolklife.org/LT/Virtual_Books/Fla_Parishes/book_florida_feliciana.html.

Crossing the River by Ferryboat

Butler, Anne. "Farewell to the St. Francisville Ferry." Felicianas—East and West Feliciana Parishes. Online at http://www.where2guide.com?Articles/jan07/jan07.html.

"The Louisiana Ferry Experience," Yahoo GeoCities. Online at http://www.geocities.com/t_2m/Louisiana_Ferry.html?200915.

Perry, Ernie. "Economic Dimensions of Ferry Operations in Missouri, Kentucky and Tennessee: The Dorena-Hickman Ferry." Prepared for the Missouri Department of Transportation Organizational Results, August 2008.

Baton Rouge, Huey Long, and the Movie Industry

Alford, Jeremy. "Huey Long & Castro Carazo." *Country Roads Magazine*. Online at http://www.countryroadsmagazine.com/index.php?option=com.

"Cast and Crew Information." Film Baton Rouge. Online at http://filmbatonrouge.com/.

"Film Tax Credit Program has 'Negative' Impact for State, Says Audit." WWLTV, April 29, 2013. Online at http://www.wwltv.com/news.

Goundry, Nick. "Battle: Los Angeles Doubles Louisiana for California." The Location Guide. Online at http://www.thelocationguide.com/blog/2010/10/battle-los-angeles-doubles-louisiana-for-california/.

"Huey Long: The Man, His Mission and Legacy," Huey Long. Online at http://www.hueylong.com.

"Louisiana State Capitol History," Allsands.com—Grains of Knowledge. Online at http://www.allsands.com/history/places/louisianastate_sxb_gn.htm.

Perilloux, Gary. "Film Industry Seeing La. 'Action!'" *Advocate* (January 3, 2010).

Wall, Richard. "The Rebellious Spirit of Huey Long." Lew Rockwell.com (December 13, 2003). Online at www.lewrockwell.com/wall/wall19.html.

"What Is the Benefit Called?" Film Baton Rouge. Online at http://www.filmbaton-rouge.com/content/inccentives/.

Wilkes, Donald E. "Who Killed the Kingfish?" *The Athens Observer*, September 12, 1985.

On to Opelousas

"City of Eunice, Louisiana, Courir de Mardi Gras 2008." City of Eunice, Louisiana. Online at http://www.eunice-la.com/mardigras08sch.html.

Clarke, Rod. "Cajun Rejuvenation on a Louisiana 'Prairie.'" *Boston Globe*, May 14, 2006.

Johnson, William. "Costumes Abound at Eunice Courir." *Daily World*, February 21, 2007.

Kimmel, Fred. "Louisiana's Cajun Prairie: An Endangered Ecosystem." *Louisiana Conservationist Magazine* (Summer 2008).

"Our Heritage." Zydeco Cajun Prairie Scenic Byway. Online at http://zydecocajunbyway.com/index1.html.

What's a Coon Ass?

David, Dana. "Le Voisinage: Evolution of Community in Cajun Country." *1999 Louisiana Folklife Festival Booklet*. Online at http://www.louisianafolklife.org.

Roach, Calvin. "Living Legends." The Acadian Museum. Online at http://www.acadianmuseum.com/legends.php?viewID=38.

Zydeco Dancing

"Acadian, Cajun or Creole? There is a Difference!" Landry Stuff.com. Online at http://www.landrystuff.com/creole.htm.

Broussard, John, and Ben Sandmel. "Zydeco Music: Questions and Answers," Louisiana—Culture, Recreation and Tourism. Online at http://www.crt.state.la.us/tourism/lamusic/zydecoq&a.htm.

Lavergne, Gary M. "The Grand Derangement: Cajuns Settle Louisiana." Lives of Quiet Desperation. Online at http://www.garylavergne.com/derangement.htm.

"What is Cajun & Zydeco Dance & Music." Rochester Cajun Zydeco Network. Online at http://rochesterzydeco.com/cajunzydeco.html.

Boudin, Sugar Cane Farming, and More Crawfish

Albert, Derek. "2008 Cane Harvest in the Books." *Teche News*, January 6, 2009.

Jurenas, Remy. "Background on Sugar Policy Issues." Congressional Research Service Report for Congress, updated July 26, 2007.

————. "Sugar Policy and the 2008 Farm Bill." Congressional Research Service Report for Congress, January 29, 2009.

"The Louisiana Sugar Industry." Brochure distributed by American Sugar Cane League.

"Pending Sugar Import Decision Holds Serious Ramifications." *Louisiana Farm & Ranch*, May 2009.

Schneider, Keith. "Thousands of Sugar Workers Reap Bitter Harvest." *New York Times*, June 3, 1988.

The Road to New Orleans

Bernard, Shane K. "Edward Avery McIlhenny & the Origin of Bird City." In *Tabasco: An Illustrated History*. Oxford: University Press of Mississippi, 2007.

"Welcome to Avery Island: Home of Tabasco." McIlhenny Company Brand Products— Tabasco. Online at http://www.tabasco.com/tabasco_history/avery_island.cfm.

Once the Levees Break

Bowser, Betty Ann. "Will New Levees Protect New Orleans From the Next Hurricane?" PBS Newshour—The Rundown, A Blog of News and Insight, August 26, 2010. Online at http://www.pbs.org/newshour/rundown/2010/08/.

Broach, Drew. "Aaron Broussard Sent to Prison for Less than 4 Years, Less than Expected." *Times-Picayune*, February 25, 2013.

Hammer, David. "Greg Meffert, Former City Tech Chief, Pleads Guilty in Kickback Scheme." *Times-Picayune*, November 2, 2010. Online at http://www.nola.com/politics/index.ssf/2010/11/.

Johnson, Kevin. "More Cops Charged in Post-Katrina Bridge Shootings." *USA Today*, July 13, 2010.

"The New Orleans Jazz & Heritage Festival." New Orleans Jazz & Heritage Festival. Online at http://www.nojazzfest.com/info/faq/.

Plyer, Allison. "Facts for Features: Hurricane Katrina Recovery." Greater New Orleans—Community Data Center. Online at http://www.gnocdc.org/Factsforfeatures/HurricaneKatrinaRecovery/.

Rich, Nathaniel. "Jungleland." *New York Times*, March 21, 2012.

Russell, Gordon. "Ray Nagin Indictment: First New Orleans Mayor to Face Corruption Charges." *Times-Picayune*, January 18, 2013. Online at http://www.nola.com/crime/index.ssf/2013/01/.

Sayre, Alan. "Five New Orleans Police Officers Indicted in Post-Katrina Shooting, Burning." *Huffington Post*, June 11, 2010.

Mississippi Gulf Coast

Chan, Sewell. "Portrait of Mississippi Victims: Safety of Home Was a Mirage." *New York Times*, September 27, 2005.

"Charles Gray: 'The Rolls-Royce Guy.'" *Sun Herald*, June 19, 2009.

"Deal in the Works for Great Southern Golf Club," *WLOX 13*, June 2, 2008. Online at http://www.wlox.com/Global/story.asp?S=8413856.

"Hurricane Katrina: 1 Year Later." *NCSHPO News* (October 2006).

Partain, John. "The Great Southern Golf Club." *Sun Herald*. Online at http://www.sunherald.com/images/beforeafter/greatsoutherngolf.html.

"Preservation." Hancock County Historical Society. Online at http://hancockcounty-historicalsociety.com/preservation/preservation.htm.

Mobile

"A Brief History." Wintzell's Oyster House. Online at http://wintzellsoysterhouse.com/.

Hank, Biscuits, and Green Roofs

"2008 RSA Annual Report." *The Retirement Systems of Alabama*, 2008.

Addy, Samuel, and Ahmed Ijaz. *Economic Impacts of RSA-Owned Investments on Alabama*. Prepared for the Retirement Systems of Alabama, December 2008.

Ferrari, Valerie. "Hank Williams' Alabama Grave." Yahoo Voices, October 25, 2006. Online at http://www.associatedcontent.com/article/.

Hubbard, Russell. "Bronner Proposes RSA Buy Jeffco Sewer System." *Birmingham News*, July 24, 2008.

Rawls, Phillip. "Across Alabama State Pension Fund Develops Upscale Hotels to Make this Southern State a Destination." *Herald Tribune*, January 21, 2007.

"The Robert Trent Jones Golf Trail in Alabama." *Executive Golfer* (February 2012).

Sharp, Shane. "Along the Robert Trent Golf Trail: Roger Rulewich Speaks Out." Golf Now.com—Gulf Coast Golf. Online at http://www.travelgolf.com/departments/editorials/trent-jones-trail.htm.

Forty Miles to Tuskegee

"Dyann Robinson." Tuskegee Repertory Theatre. Online at http://tuskegeerep.com/artisticdirector.html.

"Tuskegee Airmen National Historic Site (Alabama)." *WAAY TV 31—First News*. Online at http://www.waaytv.com/Global/story.asp?S=5957203.

Fender Bender in Birmingham

Cose, Ellis. "A Reckoning in Birmingham." *Newsweek* (June 3, 2002).

Dunn, Jim. "Benchmarks." *Business Alabama* (August 2004).

Gaines, Charles. "The Big Heart of Birmingham." *Garden & Gun Magazine* (June/July 2009).

"Pain Over Birmingham Church Bombings Lingers." *USA Today*, September 14, 2003.

Underwood, Madison. "Marking a Milestone: The Birmingham Pledge Turns 10." *Birmingham Weekly* (April 13, 2008).

Wickham, DeWayne, and Tukufu Zuberi, eds. "Kerner Plus 40 Report." Institute for Advanced Journalism Studies. Online at http://www.ifajs.org/events/spring08/Kerner40/Report.pdf .

Iced or Hot? Sweet or Un?

Baltazar, Amanda. "Tea from Another Time." *UpClose* (August 2010).

Brooks, Staci Brown. "Milo's Tea Brews Big Plan for its Plant, Distribution." *Birmingham News*, February 24, 2004.

Edge, John T. "Sweet Tea: A Southern Icon." *Atlanta Journal Constitution*, September 20, 2007.

Guckeen, Amy. "Newcomers Welcome with Southern Hospitality." United States Army, March 12, 2010. Online at http://www.army.mil/article/35820/Newcomers_Welcomed_With_Southern_Hospitality/.

Mackay, Steven. "It's Teatime (Milo's Style) in Bessemer." *Birmingham Business Journal*, December 9, 2002.

Milazzo, Don. "Sauce is Still Boss, but Milo's Tea Takes Off." *Birmingham Business Journal*, 1999.

"Milo's Famous Tea History: Early Years (1946–1989)." Milo's Famous Tea. Online at http://www.milostea.com/history/.

Milo's Tea. "Milo's Tea Customer Are Thirsting for More." Press release, July 11, 2008.

"The Ready-to-Drink Iced Tea Explosion." The Free Library. Online at http://www.thefreelibrary.com/.

Savitry, Aninditta. "The US Ready-to-Drink Tea Market: Trends and Competea-tion." All Business—Your Small Business Advantage. Online at http://www.allbusiness.com/.

"Tea and Ready-to-Drink Tea in the U.S." Packaged Facts, November 1, 2007. Online at http://www.packagedfacts.com/Tea-RTD-1282368/.

Traveling South Georgia

"Andersonville Civil War Prison Historical Background." U.S. National Park Service. Online at http://www.nps.gov/history/seac/histback.htm.

"Andersonville Prison," *New Georgia Encyclopedia*. Online at http://www.georgiaency-clopedia/org/nge/Articl.Jsp?id=h-789.

Burger, Nash K. "Was Andersonville's Wirz Really Guilty?" *The National Observer*, November 8, 1965.

Sutter, Paul S. "Georgia's Little Grand Canyon—Environmental History." *Oxford Journals—Environmental History*. Online at http://www.findarticles.com/p/arti-cles/mi/_qa3854/is_200610/ai_n17196546.

Happy Animals. Good Cheese.

Earles, Richard. "Sustainable Agriculture: An Introduction." ATTRA, The National Center for Appropriate Technology, 2005.

Fletcher, Janet. "Splendor in Sweet Grass' Green Hill." *San Francisco Chronicle*, December 12, 2008.

Reese, Krista. "Sweetgrass Dairy: The Taste of Success." *Georgia Magazine* (June 2008).

"This is Quail Country." *Garden & Gun Magazine* (March/April 2008).

Tallahassee

Dehart, Jason. "Recalling the Recount." *Tallahassee Magazine* (November/December 2009).

———. "Treading Water." *Tallahassee Magazine* (May/June 2008).

"Foraging the Forgotten Coast." *Garden & Gun Magazine* (January/February 2008).

Hodges, Dave. "Association Leaders Mark 50 Years." *Tallahassee Democrat*, July 5, 2009.

Menzel, Margie. "Miccosukee Mindset: Back to the Land." *Tallahassee Magazine* (March/April 2009).

Roberts, Diane. "Classy Tallahassee." *St. Petersburg Times*, May 27, 2001.

Ybor City

"Black Genesis—Tampa." Soul America—Black Cultural Travel Made Easy. Online at http://www.soulofamerica.com.

"Columbia": Gem of Spanish Restaurants. Restaurant Menu.

"Don Vicente de Ybor Historic Inn." The Don Vicente de Ybor Historic Inn. Online at http://donvicenteinn.com/history1.

Huse, Amy. "Tampa Roast: The Story of Naviera, the Oldest Coffee Mill in America's Most Caffeinated City." *Tampa Bay's Cigar City Magazine* (May/June 2009).

"Reading 1: The History of Ybor City." U.S. National Park Service. Online at http://www.nps.gov/history/NR/.

Simanoff, Dave, and Mary Shedden. "Ybor City's Waking Up." *The Tampa Tribune*, March 26, 2006.

Cracker from Kissimmee

Caldwell, Roger. "Can Orlando's Blueprint Deliver on its Promises?" *The Pine Hills News*, September 16, 2008.

Haner, Noelle C. "Biz Community Steps Up Interest in Parramore." *Orlando Business Journal* (June 24, 2005).

"Orlando Mayor Rescues Terrier from Pit Bull Attack." CBS 4, March 11, 2008. Online at http://miami.cbslocal.com/watercooler/Orlando.pit.bull.2.674527.html.

The First Coast

"Jacksonville." Coast Paradise. Online at http://www.coastparadise.com/homes/florida/.

"Relocation Information." St. Johns County Chamber of Commerce. Online at http://pontevedrachamber.org/relocation/index.cfm.

Rubin, Karen. "In St. Augustine, City of 'Oldests,' Experience History, Nature Anew." *Travel Writers' Magazine*. Online at http://www.travelwritersmagazine.com/.

Thrasher, Paula Crouch. "The First Coast Has Been Heart of Florida Since Day 1." *Orlando Sentinel*, August 5, 2001.

Stuck in South Georgia

"Alligator Catches Whitetail Deer." Southeastern Outdoors, August 23, 2004. Online at http://www/southeasternoutdoors.com/wildlife/reptiles/article/alligator-eats-deer.html.

Johnson, David. "Date Idea: Hunting for Gators?" *The Times-Union*, August 27, 2006.

Minor, Elliot. "Georgia's First-Ever Gator Hunt Bags 64." *Athens Banner-Herald*, October 18, 2003.

"Statewide Nuisance Alligator Program." Florida Fish and Wildlife Conservation Commission. Online at http://myfwc.com/WILDLIFEHABITATS/Alligator_nuisance.htm.

Stripling, Michelle. "Georgia's Gators: The Modern Dinosaurs." Sherpa Guides. Online at http://www.sherpaguides.com/georgia/.

Walker, Tracie. "Alligator Trappers in Florida." Yahoo Voices. Online at http://www.associatedcontent.com/.

Savannah

"About Us." Savannah Shag Club. Online at http://savannahshagclub.com/About_Us.html.

Barnes, Allison. "Savannah Bee Company." *Healthy Living* (July 2009).

Carr, Annabelle. "Sultry Savannah." *Garden & Gun Magazine* (February/March 2009).

"Savannah Bee: Our Story," Savannah Bee Company. Online at http://savannahbee.com/our_story.

"Savannah City Plan." *The New Georgia Encyclopedia*. Online at http://www.georgiaencyclopedia.org/nge/Article.

Coastalitis

Davis, Bill. "Developing the Past." *Charleston City Paper*, February 8, 2006. Online at http://www.charlestoncitypaper.com/charleston/feature.

"Morris Island Now Protected." The Trust for Public Land. Online at http://tpl.org/tier3_cd.cfm?.

Carolina Gold

Borns, Patricia. "South Carolina's Delta Gold." *Boston Globe*, July 26, 2009.

"Carolina Gold." John Martin Taylor Blog: Hoppin' John's. Online at http://hoppin-johns.net/carolinagold.aspx.

"The Charleston Accent." *Charleston Magazine* (January 2010).

Florio, Donna. "All You Need to Know About Rice." *Southern Living*. Online at http://www.southernliving.com/food/entertaining/grains-gold-00400000005941/.

Rauzi, Robin. "Slow Dance with Charleston, South Carolina." *Los Angeles Times*, July 30, 2006.

Smith, Nick. "Best Place to Shake Your Thirst on Homegrown Leaves." *Charleston City Paper*, March 4, 2009.

Songs from the Journey

"Drive South"
John Hiatt
The Best of John Hiatt
1998

"The Black Rats of London"
Bruce Hornsby & The
Noisemakers
Levitate
2009

"Tobacco Road"
Southern Culture on the Skids
Countrypolitan Favorites
2007

"Mill Mother's Lament"
Pete Seeger
American Industrial Ballads
1957

"Four Wal-Marts"
Baker Maultsby
Bingo=Sin
1998

"TVA"
Drive-By Truckers
*Fine Print: A Collection of
Oddities and Rarities, 2003–2008*
2009

"Dixie Chicken"
Little Feat
Dixie Chicken
1973

"Fatback & Egg on Bun"
Baker Maultsby
Bingo=Sin
1998

"Will the Circle Be Unbroken"
The Nitty Gritty Dirt Band
Will the Circle Be Unbroken
1972

"Uncle Frank" [Alternate Track]
Drive-By Truckers
*Fine Print: A Collection of
Oddities and Rarities, 2003–2008*
2009

"Tennessee Plates"
John Hiatt & The Guilty Dogs
Hiatt Comes Alive at Budokan
1994

"Old Man River"
William Warfield
Show Boat
1966

"Five Feet High and Rising"
Johnny Cash
The Essential Johnny Cash
1959

"Last Two Dollars"
Johnnie Taylor
Good Love
1996

"Molly Man"
Moses Mason (Red Hot Old
Man Mose)
*Alabama: Black Secular &
Religious Music (1927–1934)*
1928

"Crossroads"
Dion
Bronx in Blue
2006

"The Sound (John M. Perkins'
Blues)"
Switchfoot
Hello Hurricane
2009

"Riding with the King"
T. K. Hulin
Larger than Life
2007

"Light Up Mississippi"
Thriving Ivory
Through Yourself and Back Again
2009

"Telephone Road"
Steve Earle/The Fairfield Four
El Corazón
1997

"Stay In or Stay Out/Pass the
Dutchie"
Chris Ardoin and Double
Clutchin'
Turn the Page
1998

"Zydeco Land"
T-Broussard & The Zydeco
Steppers
Super T
2008

"South of I-10"
Sonny Landreth
South of I-10
1995

"Get Up Get Down"
T. K. Hulin
Larger than Life
2007

"Dance Back from the Grave"
Marc Cohn
Join the Parade
2007

"Hundred and Ten in the Saddle"
John Fogerty
Blue Moon Swamp
1997

"Southern Gul"
Erykah Badu
Erykah Badu
1999

"Rebels"
Drive-By Truckers
Fine Print: A Collection of
Oddities and Rarities, 2003–2008
2009

"Nightshift"
The Commodores
Nightshift
2010

"None of Us Are Free"
Solomon Burke with the Blind
Boys of Alabama
Don't Give Up on Me
2002

"Honky Tonkin'"
Hank Williams
Gold
1947

"Homeland"
John Hiatt
The Open Road
2010

"Oh Atlanta"
Little Feat
Feats Don't Fail Me Now
1974

"Georgia"
Ludacris
Ludacris Presents: Disturbing tha
Peace
2005

"Chicken Fried"
Zac Brown Band
The Foundation
2005

"The Southern Thing"
Drive-By Truckers
Southern Rock Opera
2001

"Johnny Dollar"
Bradford and Bell
Carolina Soul
1980

"In the Low Country"
Bruce Hornsby & The
Noisemakers
Levitate
2009

"Pee Dee Man"
Baker Maultsby
Bingo=Sin
1998

"Minutes to Memories"
John Mellencamp
Scarecrow
1985

Index

About the Author

Photo © 2013 Cindy Momchilov/Camera Work, Inc.

Mark Nichols was born in Knoxville, Tennessee. He graduated from Hanover College in Indiana in 1974 with a BA in economics. Mr. Nichols received his law degree from the University of Arkansas in Fayetteville in 1977. After working for Arkansas governor David Pryor, he returned to school and earned an LLM in corporate law from New York University in the spring of 1980. He practiced law in Little Rock from that time until 2011.

Mr. Nichols' wife, Cheri, is a historic preservationist, and the Nichols family has been involved in the rehabilitation of several historic buildings in Little Rock's Quapaw Quarter, including their own Victorian home. Mr. and Mrs. Nichols have one son, Will, who resides in Charleston, South Carolina.

CPSIA information can be obtained at www.ICGtesting.com
Printed in the USA
LVOW12s0550220114

370318LV00004B/9/P